www.wadsworth.com

www.wadsworth.com is the World Wide Web site for Wadsworth and is your direct source to dozens of online resources.

At www.wadsworth.com you can find out about supplements, demonstration software, and student resources. You can also send email to many of our authors and preview new publications and exciting new technologies.

www.wadsworth.com
Changing the way the world learns®

Light on the Path

A Christian Perspective on College Success

JOHN A. BECK

MARMY A. CLASON

THOMSON
WADSWORTH

Australia · Canada · Mexico · Singapore · Spain · United Kingdom · United States

THOMSON

WADSWORTH

Light on the Path: A Christian Perspective on College Success
John A. Beck / Marmy A. Clason

Publisher: Carolyn Merrill
Project Manager, Editorial Production:
    Kate Hedgpeth
Technology Project Manager: Joe Gallagher
Manufacturing Manager: Marcia Locke
Permissions Editor: Bob Kauser
Project Manager/Copyeditor: Sharon Grant

Photo Manager: Sheri Blaney
Cover Designer: Brittney Singletary
Compositor/Text Designer: Publishers' Design
    and Production Services, Inc.
Printer: Webcom
Cover Art: © Dale Wilson / Masterfile

Printed in Canada
1 2 3 4 5 6 7   09 08 07 06 05

For more information about our products, contact us at:
Thomson Learning Academic Resource Center
1-800-423-0563
For permission to use material from this text or product,
submit a request online at **http://www.thomsonrights.com**.
Any additional questions about permissions can be
submitted by email to **thomsonrights@thomson.com**.

Library of Congress Control Number: 2004118213

ISBN 0-534-27244-4

Thomson Higher Education
25 Thomson Place
Boston, MA 02210-1202
USA

Asia (including India)
Thomson Learning
5 Shenton Way
#01-01 UIC Building
Singapore 068808

Australia/New Zealand
Thomson Learning Australia
102 Dodds Street
Southbank, Victoria 3006
Australia

Canada
Thomson Nelson
1120 Birchmount Road
Toronto, Ontario M1K 5G4
Canada

UK/Europe/Middle East/Africa
Thomson Learning
High Holborn House
50–51 Bedford Road
London WC1R 4LR
United Kingdom

Latin America
Thomson Learning
Seneca, 53
Colonia Polanco
11560 Mexico
D.F. Mexico

Spain (including Portugal)
Thomson Paraninfo
Calle Magallanes, 25
28015 Madrid, Spain

Dedicated to the success of
Aaron, Peter, Jonathan, Jared, Jacob, and Hannah.

Dedicated to the happiness of
Bernie, Barb, Tom, Steve, Annette, Jim, and Sue,
who know that endurance is the basis of success.

Surely goodness and love will follow me
all the days of my life,
And I will dwell in the house of the LORD forever.

(Psalm 23:6)

Contents

9 *Saying It Just Right: Writing and Speaking Successfully*   *155*

10 *Making the Tough Decisions: The Role of Christian Values*

11 *Seeking and Maintaining Healthy Relationships* — *191*

Preface

Your word is a lamp to my feet and a light for my path.

(Psalm 119:105)

Collège students, who are starting down the pathway of college life, get well-meaning advice from a variety of people including family members, friends, and campus professionals. This textbook presumes that those same students will also benefit from the advice, direction, and encouragement offered to them in God's Word. Its authors are persuaded by the Apostle Paul's declaration: "For everything that was written in the past was written to teach us, so that through endurance and the encouragement of the Scriptures we might have hope." (Rom 15:4) The Bible portrays itself as a "light" that can dispel the shadows of confusion and the darkness of doubt falling upon the path of life. The authors take that claim seriously, affirming with the inspired poet, "Your word is a lamp for my feet and a light for my path." (Psalm 119:105) Consequently, this first-year orientation textbook proposes to add the Bible's beacon of light to the traditional direction and encouragement offered first-year college students.

We know that the new students arriving on a Christian campus come in all shapes and sizes. Some students have just graduated from high school, while others are returning to college after a time in the work world. Some students have family members who had previously attended college, while others may be the first in their family to go. Some students who matriculate at a Christian school are Christians, while others are not. No matter in what category you find yourself, you can be sure that you will face a variety of challenges as you enter college. Those challenges can threaten both your sense of well being and your ability to be successful. That is why we believe that students who are making this transition deserve spiritual, emotional, and intellectual support from the institution as they make the transition. And we believe that such support and encouragement can be delivered most effectively within a semester-long orientation course. This book is designed to function in just such a class.

Of course, it is possible to orient new students to college life in such a class without using the Bible. Most first-year orientation textbooks propose to do just that. But from the perspective of many Christian schools, the absence of the Bible's voice comes with a steep price. First of all, it means that the contribution of the Bible on traditional first-year topics like time management, motivation, and stress management is unclaimed. Consider the story of Mary and Martha. When these women display different priorities in their time management plans, Jesus himself speaks about a plan of action designed to establish priorities and reduce stress (Luke 10:38–42). Within the pages of this book, those contributions of the Bible to first-year success will be brought to the reader.

Secondly, the secular textbook also leaves topics important to the Christian school unaddressed. How does the Bible fit into the life of the well-educated person? How does the voice of the Bible shape the conversations we have in history classes, science classes, and art classes? What do we do when the voice of the Bible and the voice of science come into conflict? By contrast to other textbooks, this one will honor those questions and others like them, exploring ways in which the Bible makes a contribution to higher education.

Thirdly, because of differing world views, the presentation of certain topics in the secular textbook may place that book's position in direct contradiction to the ethical and moral position of the school. For example, the approach to alcohol, sexuality, and relationships advocated in other textbooks may find itself in direct violation of the school's code of ethical conduct. This book will honor the Bible as a source of moral planning.

And finally, many first-year textbooks give very little attention to the spiritual development that the Christian college or university sees as critical to the development of its students. By contrast, this book will encourage the use of Bible reading, spiritual reflection, prayer, and worship as part of the process that leads to greater happiness and success during college.

While it is possible for Christian colleges and universities to employ a secular textbook for its first-year orientation courses, it is more desirable to have a book that finds itself in greater harmony with the needs of the school. That is why we present a first-year orientation textbook that addresses the unique needs of evangelical Christian schools of higher learning. Each chapter will offer the reader the following features: biblical contributions, meaningful exercises, Internet sources, a spiritual reflection journal, and the encouragement to pray. The heart of each chapter will present the attitudes and behaviors that will lead to greater success and happiness as a college student. This summary will include not only the material traditionally found in first-year textbooks but also biblical illustration and references where appropriate. By design, the message of the Bible will shine through the pages of this book and onto the path being walked by the student entering college.

Ideas that are not reviewed and practiced are quickly forgotten. That is why each chapter will include exercises that may be used both inside and outside of class. These exercises will provide opportunities for further reflection on the chapter topic and opportunities to practice new learning habits that will foster success.

Times of change are also times for spiritual growth. Consequently, each chapter will also offer opportunities for Bible reading, spiritual reflection, and prayer. In connection with the chapter topic, the spiritual formation of our readers will be encouraged by offering biblical texts that may be used for personal meditation. That meditation will lead to insights that may be kept in the spiritual reflection journal. And since prayer has traditionally been a source of empowerment for Christians, each chapter will include the encouragement to be in prayer during the college week. The close of each chapter will contain a suggested prayer list that may be used as a starting point for this time in prayer.

Because Christian schools find themselves rooted in various denominations and belief systems, this book will be cautious not to preach from just one pulpit. We wish to be respectful of the fact that the schools wishing to adopt such a textbook espouse a variety of beliefs that use the Bible as their foundation. Given that reality, this book takes a more biblical than doctrinal approach. The authors have identified biblical texts that they believe make a contribution to the topic of each chapter. Those texts are presented to the reader with a minimum of interpretive suggestion so that the interpretation of those texts can occur within the classroom.

In the end, the authors are convinced that happiness and success are very attainable for the students reading this book. We know that each of you, no matter what your background, will be able to design a personal success plan from the pages ahead that includes direction and encouragement offered in the Bible. We will be praying for you and look forward to hearing of the ways that the Lord has blessed you during this time of transition.

This manuscript has passed through the hands of many reviewers whose comments and suggestions have clearly improved the final product. The authors wish to thank the following individuals for their meaningful contributions.

Tonya Holman, Greenville College
Charles Mattis, Abilene Christian University
Janice Heerspink, Calvin College
Jeff Gundy, Bluffton College

John Yeats, Messiah College
Mary Todd, Concordia University
Maria Avalos, Texas Lutheran University
Amy Janzen, Oklahoma Christian University
Brian McKinney, Quachita Baptist University
Barbara Sherman, Liberty University
David Marley, Vanguard University
Pamela Johnston, Texas Lutheran University
Leslie Bailey, St. Martin's College
Rosalind Alderman, St. Mary's College

Putting Light on the Path

Your word is a lamp to my feet and a light for my path.

Psalm 119:105

- What challenges will I face in my first year of college?
- How can God's Word and this course help me this semester?
- How can I set effective goals for myself?
- What can I do when I am not feeling motivated?

CONGRATULATIONS! YOU ARE NOW a college student. Whether you are the first in your family to come to college or the fifth, whether you have just finished high school or are an adult returning to school many years after high school graduation, your letter of acceptance is a wonderful achievement and distinguishes you as a person of great intellectual promise. Your choice to pursue a more advanced education places you among many of the great leaders in history and among the renowned leaders in the Bible. Moses pursued advanced learning in the Egyptian royal court as a member of the royal family (Acts 7:22). Solomon pursued advanced learning and became a distinguished author of proverbs and songs as well as a famous instructor who taught about the animal and plant kingdoms (1 Kgs 4:29–34). Daniel left home and pursued his education in the royal household of Babylon (Dan 1). Paul left his home and traveled to Jerusalem to seek higher education from the best Rabbinic scholars of his day (Acts 22:3). And Jesus himself followed the trail of higher education as he sat among the leading teachers of the Temple in Jerusalem listening carefully to what they had to say and pursuing them with questions (Luke 2:46). The God who created us with the ability to think clearly honors the practice of maturing our minds. For centuries, great leaders like those above have done just that by stepping through the doorway of higher education that lies immediately ahead of you.

Advantages of a College Education

You are not alone in your quest. According to the National Center for Education Statistics, more and more hopeful first-year students are stepping onto college campuses each year. A little more than a century ago, only about 2% of Americans continued on after high school to earn a college degree. Today nearly 75% of high school graduates are accepted as first-year students. So what is the attraction? Your walk across the stage to receive your college diploma will create advantages for you in a variety of ways. Historically, college graduates know themselves better, have a stronger sense of well being, and have the ability to compete for careers open only to college graduates. They are more effective thinkers and more confident about themselves. College graduates have more mobility in their careers, have the potential to earn up to a million dollars more in income during their lives, and are uniquely poised to make meaningful changes that will positively shape their society and the church in which they become leaders.

Challenges for First-Year Students

But to acquire all of those benefits of a college graduate, you must first successfully negotiate the transition between your former life and your college life. No two first-year students will have exactly the same experience. But you can be sure that your life this year will be different from your life last year. Change can be exciting but it will also introduce challenges into your life.

If you were in high school last year, you will find that college is a very different experience. Here you will enjoy more freedom and more free time to manage. College classes meet less frequently, but are more difficult. In those classes, you will complete more reading and produce more writing than you did in a high school class. And while every college class will cover more material, you will be tested less frequently. This means each exam will count more towards the final grade and measure your ability with significantly more information than a high school exam.

Suggestions for Adult Students

*I*F HIGH SCHOOL GRADUATION is a very distant memory for you, you may feel overwhelmed by your return to school life. While you may feel disadvantaged by your time away from classes, books, and term papers, you have gained very valuable experience during that time that will help you negotiate the waters ahead. Consider implementing the following suggestions offered by older college students who found happiness and success in their return to school.

Maintain a strong relationship with your family.

Become involved in campus activities beyond the classroom.

Ask for help when you need it.

See your life experience as a real advantage you have over younger students.

Be ready to give up some activities and free time you had enjoyed.

Plan your finances carefully.

If today marks a return to college after years in the workplace, you too will experience changes. You may sense a loss of freedom as college claims time that you had otherwise dedicated to family or recreation. As you look around the classroom at the younger faces that surround you, you may feel anxiety about returning to a school setting after years away from textbooks and term papers. And time away from work may create financial stresses that press upon both you and those who live in your home.

Everyone coming to college will be working through the process of making new friends and editing old relationships. All that change can cause the deep and dark feelings of displacement anxiety. Your appetite may be off, your sleep patterns unsatisfying, and your stress levels off the chart. It is no wonder that as many as 40% of those who begin college as a first-year student never walk across the stage to receive their college diploma. Success is simply not a given that should be taken for granted.

Guidance from This Book and God's Word

But here is the good news. You can be one of those who is successful as a college student if you take this transition in your life seriously and develop a plan that will lead to success. The book you are holding in your hands is designed to help you do just that. It is different from most other college success books because it takes into account the advice and encouragement offered in God's Word. You undoubtedly have received well-meaning advice from family and friends that is a product of their experience. Here the authors will provide you with advice and encouragement developed over years of working with first-year students while adding insights they have gained directly from the Bible. As Moses, Solomon, Daniel, Paul, and Jesus pursued higher learning in their own contexts, they did so with an awareness that God's Word can make a critical contribution to that learning process. That is why this book has the title, *Light on the Path*. It reflects the view of the inspired poet who wrote, "Your word is a lamp to my feet and a light for my path." (Ps 119:105)

This illumination will take place in a variety of areas that contribute to the success and happiness of your first year in college. Here are some of the topics discussed in the chapters ahead. It has been argued that higher education and belief in the Bible are incompatible. In the next chapter, we will assert that just the opposite is the case. Not only does the Christian faith support you in your transition to college life, it will also enhance your understanding of the world in which you live. Chapter Three will discuss the critical issue of time management. Time is a great gift from God, and no skill as a college student may be as critical to your success as the ability to manage your time efficiently. The authors believe that everyone who reads this book is a unique creation of God and that everyone will have their own distinctive ways of learning. The fourth chapter invites you to explore your personal learning style and discover ways in which you might become a more effective learner by taking advantage of the unique person you are. While your former education had focused more on facts and data, your new learning experience will focus more on developing effective thinking. Chapter Five will help you define what effective thinking is and discuss ways in which you can use your college experience to develop yourself as an effective thinker. Since there are certain fundamental skills that you will use each semester in college, subsequent chapters will address a wide variety of study skills: taking notes, reading textbooks, taking exams, writing college papers, and giving presentations. This textbook will help you evaluate the present status of your study skills and help you discover ways to improve these fundamental skills so that you may become a more efficient and successful college student. We also acknowledge that your success as a college student is more than just intellectual development and study skills. It also means taking care of your physical health and your relationships. Chapters Eleven and Twelve make a point of pursuing your habits in these critical arenas of life. The final chapter will help you look forward to the vocation you have chosen and help you think or rethink about the major you wish to pursue. Believe it or not, there are things you can be doing right now that will help you acquire an entry-level position in your chosen field or acceptance into the graduate school you have chosen.

In each of these areas, your success as a college student will be enhanced through the advice and direction that God offers you in his Word. We will challenge you to reflect on that divine advice while we challenge you to grow in your relationship with the Lord. Every chapter will invite you to read the Bible and reflect on its message in a spiritual reflection journal. We will also encourage you to open your heart to the Lord in prayer, starting with the prayer suggestion lists that accompany each chapter.

Because we do not know the exact plans that God has for you in your life, we cannot promise that you will be successful in your current quest. But we can assure you that by listening carefully to the advice offered in this book and through the Bible, you will come to a place of greater peace and happiness with your life. "For everything that was written in the past was written to teach us, so that through endurance and the encouragement of the Scriptures we might have hope." (Rom 15:4)

A Word of Encouragement

There will be days ahead when you feel like you will not make it. Take heart; the first days of your college life will be different from those that lie ahead. As you grow more accustomed to your new environment and routine, things will naturally get better. There was a time in David's life when he was feeling some of the anxiety and uncertainty you are feeling right now. Samuel, the prophet, had anointed him as the new king of Israel and the Lord had given him a great victory over the giant, Goliath. But following those momentous events, he was driven from the royal court and pursued by King Saul who was dead set on ending David's life. At just this time of uncertainty, the author of 1 Samuel has this to say about David, "In everything he did he had great success, because the LORD was with him." (1 Sam 18:14) Read that passage again, write it down, and put it in a place where you will see it regularly for the next week. God's Word reveals a reality that David was not feeling at that moment in time. Realize that God is present with you at this moment ready to support your success as you take the next steps in your life.

Plan to Succeed

As comforting as the presence of God is in our lives, the Bible does not advocate complacency. Success is no accident and should not be left to chance. The old axiom is true. Failing to plan can amount to planning to fail. While it is important to honor the power and will of God in our lives, it is also prudent to consider the Parable of the Talents (Matthew 25:14–30). God expects us to think ahead and to use the abilities he has given us wisely. While we do not control everything that will happen in our lives or everything that will happen to us in life, it is critical to take ownership of our future to the degree that this is possible. In regard to your success as a first-year college student, that means developing a success plan for yourself. We would suggest that this plan address the four areas that contribute the most to your success: spiritual health, academic habits, physical health, and the well being of your relationships.

SPIRITUAL HEALTH

We have placed spiritual health first because we believe that it has the most to offer you during this time of transition. Give careful attention to the time you set aside for reading your Bible and speaking to God in prayer. Successful people in the Bible are closely associated with both of those habits. As Joshua was beginning a new chapter in his life as the leader of Israel, God gave him this invitation: "Do not let this Book of the Law depart from your mouth; meditate on it day and night, so that you may be careful to do everything written in it. Then you will be prosperous and successful." (Josh 1:8) The Bible holds up the young man, Samuel, as a model who humbly called out to the Lord, "Speak, for your servant is listening." (1 Sam 3:10) And it celebrates the passion of the Berean Christians, "Now the Bereans were of more noble character than the Thessalonians, for they received the message with great eagerness and examined the Scriptures every day to see if what Paul said was true." (Acts 17:11) Through the reading of your Bible, the Lord wants you to enjoy both a more successful time on this earth (Prov 9:1–6) and a certain eternity. "These are written that you may believe that Jesus is the Christ, the Son of God, and that by believing you may have life in his name." (John 20:31)

Your spiritual well being will be enhanced not only by your time spent with God's Word but also by your time spent in prayer. Successful living is closely linked to speaking with God as well as listening to him. The unnamed servant of Abraham was sent to find a wife for Isaac. Read Genesis 24 and see how closely the success of his important mission was linked to prayer. It is living testimony to the fact that a believer's prayer is powerful and effective. (Jas 5:16) And it is a living example of the invitation Jesus extends, "Ask and it will be given to you; seek and you will find; knock and the door will be opened to you." (Matt 7:7) Your day as a college student will be filled with more demands on your time than you can imagine. Time spent in reading your Bible and time spent in prayer can easily take a backseat to the pressing demands of your schedule. Now is the time to design a weekly habit that sets aside time for both.

ACADEMIC HABITS

Your success plan also needs to take stock of your academic habits. Certainly you have been successful in your previous academic work or you would not be reading this book as a new college student. But many new students make a mistake in two fundamental areas. They fail to go to class and they fail to do their assignments. The power of those two habits is much greater than their simple appearance suggests. Go to class and do your assignments. Once you have committed yourself to these two fundamentals of academic growth, strive to keep an open mind as you pursue your education. If you are accustomed to thinking of school as the place where you are merely given the answers to the questions someone else has asked, be ready to find that college is more about designing your own questions and entertaining the value of various answers. Do not be frightened by ambiguity. Let the tension of the questions drive you to think beyond the old borders that blocked broader thinking so that you can see and explore life in new and refreshing ways. And on the way, be prepared to sharpen your reading, writing, and exam preparation skills. Most college students find that their old study habits and attitudes will not yield them the same results as they did in high school. Be ready to edit not only how you think but how you work as well.

PHYSICAL HEALTH

Your plan for success will also take into account the way in which you manage your physical health. While a college education works to transform your mind, your mind cannot live successfully or work effectively in a body that is in disrepair. Check your eating habits, your sleeping habits, and your exercise habits to see if you are providing a good home for your mind. Where you find a need for improvement, let your first-year success plan reflect the changes necessary to keep you thriving physically.

RELATIONSHIPS

Finally, let your success plan take into account the various levels of relationships that surround you. In the story of creation, God announced that it was not good for Adam to be alone (Gen 2:18). The same is true for you. In coming to college, you may have placed some distance between yourself and those people who have been very important to you. It will be critical for you to find new relationships on campus with students in your residence hall, on your athletic team, or in the campus organizations you elect to join. You will also have to make decisions about your former relationships. Which relationships will you maintain and which will receive a diminishing amount of your time and attention? How will you maintain the relationships you wish to keep while seeing those people less frequently?

As you can see, there is plenty to do. Since success is no accident, today is an excellent day for you to make goals related to the four areas mentioned above. What can you begin to do today that will enhance your spiritual health, your academic health, your physical health, and the well being of your relationships?

Get Started with Some Daily Goals

*I*F SETTING GOALS IS NEW to you, it will be helpful for you to experiment with some daily goals. This will allow you to get a feel for the process as well as some early satisfaction as those goals are accomplished. Identify three things that you will commit to doing every day for the next two weeks. Write them down, post them in a prominent place, and act on them. You will find great satisfaction in accomplishing even basic things like:

Exercising for 20 minutes each day

Eating at least one serving of fruit and one serving of vegetables each day

Watching only two hours of TV per day

Saying out loud two positive things that happened today

Effective Goal Setting

If you believe that you will become a more successful student by creating a success plan, then you are ready to think about how to set goals that are effective. Passion and activity are wonderful, but undirected passion and activity may be more harmful than doing nothing at all. In this portion of the chapter, we invite you to think about a series of steps that will help harness your energy and direct it more effectively. That process has four steps: writing out intention statements, turning intention statements into goal statements, developing an action plan around each goal statement, and implementing the action plan.

WRITE INTENTION STATEMENTS

The first step in the process of effective goal setting invites you to think freely about both the long-term dreams and the short-term wishes you hold at the moment. Take a packet of self-sticking notes, turn off the distractions in your life, and free your mind to explore the future. On each slip of paper, begin a sentence with, "I intend to . . . ," and then complete the sentence with whatever comes to mind. Express your wishes and passions freely. Perhaps you will come up with notes like the following.

"I intend to read my Bible."

"I intend to go to every class unless I am ill."

"I intend to get my bike fixed this week."

"I intend to become an accountant."

"I intend to introduce myself to one new person every week this month."

Note that these intention statements can range far and wide across the various dimensions of your life.

Once you have finished with this process, paste those notes either on the desk or the wall in front of you. Now begin to play with the position of those notes. Group them according to topics, rank them in importance, or organize them by level of difficulty. In brainstorming about your intentions, you have made an important step towards success. For the mere act of reflecting and writing down your intentions places you among those who are more likely to accomplish what they desire in life.

TURN YOUR INTENTION STATEMENTS INTO GOAL STATEMENTS

While writing down your intentions is helpful, they are just the raw materials you will use in creating goal statements. Goals are more than wishes, and this is the time to separate one from the other. This step will force you to identify the intention statements that are most important to you and sharpen your thinking on them. Select several intention statements that you wish to act upon and get ready to turn them into goal statements. Well-written goal statements have five characteristics. You can recall them by memorizing the acronym, SMART.

"S" stands for specific. Transform your intention statement into a goal statement by making it more clear and specific. For example, the intention statement, "I intend to read my Bible," becomes more clear and specific when it is reworded in this way: *"I will read my Bible every day during my lunch hour."* Be sure to avoid using words such as "try," "think," "hope," or "should" when composing your goal statements. They are less powerful and communicate less commitment to your plan.

"M" stands for measured. When possible, it is helpful to assign measurable values to your intention statement. This allows you to measure your progress towards the goal's achievement more precisely. For example, "I will read *five chapters* of my Bible every day during my lunch hour."

"A" stands for accepted. Others may support your intentions, but you are the one who needs to own the goal. Make sure that your goal springs from the very core of your passions and desires. Then announce that passion by changing the statement from the hopeful "I intend to . . . ," to the more powerful, "I will . . . ." "*I will* read five chapters of my Bible every day during my lunch hour *because I want to hear God speaking to me every day.*"

"R" stands for realistic. Accomplishing a goal typically means making a change in old habits and attitudes. But the change cannot be so great that it threatens your relationships, your physical well being, or your mental health. Reach high, but do so in a responsible way. This may mean editing your goal to reflect the realities of your life. Perhaps reading five chapters of your Bible every day during the lunch break is unrealistic. So the goal statement changes to this. "I will read my Bible *for thirty minutes* every day during my lunch hour because I want to hear God speaking to me every day."

"T" stands for timed. Each goal you set can have a built-in time limit. When the time limit expires, you will have the chance to inspect your progress towards accomplishment of the goal. At the end of the time period you designate, you can confirm the accomplishment of your goal or consider editing the goal to make its accomplishment more likely in the next period of time you set. "I will read my Bible for thirty minutes every day during my lunch hour *during the month of September* because I want to hear God speaking to me every day."

DEVELOP AN ACTION PLAN

Even well-written goals may not be accomplished unless they are part of a carefully designed action plan. An action plan identifies the specific tasks or steps you will take to accomplish the goal. The formation of this plan demands that you take into account challenges that will arise in acting on the goal and ways in which those challenges may be defeated.

For example, consider the goal statement we formulated above. "I will read my Bible for thirty minutes every day during my lunch hour during the month of September because I want to hear God speaking to me every day." As you consider this goal, you recall that you had previously made a commitment like this to yourself but had failed to follow through and you are concerned that your old habits will get in the way. This challenge may be met in a number of ways. Perhaps you could find an accountability partner with whom you could share this goal. Or you could create a chart for yourself on which you mark the days on which you honor the goal in your daily schedule.

Once you have brainstormed the possible challenges and possible solutions, you are ready to write down your action plan in connection with that goal. It may look something like this.

My Action Plan

Goal: "I will read my Bible for thirty minutes every day during my lunch hour during the month of September because I want to hear God speaking to me every day."

To accomplish this goal I will:

Find an accountability partner with whom to read my Bible

Make a chart for the month of September on which I note the days I accomplish this goal

---

IMPLEMENT THE ACTION PLAN

Writing out your goal and associated action plan puts you on the road to accomplishment. All that is left is implementing the plan. Consider posting the goal and action plan in a prominent place, either on your bedroom door or bathroom mirror so that you are reminded of it every day.

Remember to remain flexible. Goals are designed to be guides, not brutal task masters. There will be days or weeks when circumstances of life do not permit you to take the steps you had planned to take. That does not mean that your goal is bad or that you are a failure. It just means that life is neither regular nor perfect. A prudent amount of flexibility will actually help you accomplish your goals more regularly and make the process much more rewarding.

And Then There Is Motivation

Did we just say the magic word? Have your present circumstances left you feeling less than excited about moving forward with your college life? Then it is time to consider motivation. This connects nicely with the notion of setting goals because there is a necessary, even circular relationship between accomplishing goals and motivation. Motivation is the inner drive that moves us to act on the goals we set as well as the catalyst for making goals in the first place.

But what if you do not feel motivated? The first step is to realize that in saying that you are unmotivated, you are not describing the way you were created but your attitude towards a particular responsibility or task. We have heard students express their lack of motivation for attending classes that meet before 10:00 in the morning, but have seen the same students spring out of bed well before daylight to begin a spring break vacation. Motivation is an attitude towards a specific task or responsibility.

If you are feeling unmotivated about college, determine the source of that attitude. Perhaps you feel put off by the behaviors closely associated with college life: attending class, reading, writing, and speaking. But realize that each of those behaviors has an intimate connection with your future professional life. It begins with responsible attendance. It goes without saying that your

Criticism and the Motivation Crash

YOU WILL DEFINITELY EXPERIENCE criticism as a college student. Criticism will include but not be limited to things like grades on your exams, comments on your papers, and an instructor's critiques of answers you give during class discussion. Such criticism is designed to help you become a more effective thinker and communicator; but if it is internalized so that you feel it as a personal attack, criticism can crash your motivation. While it is important for you to experience all the constructive criticism offered for your improvement, it is also important that you keep that criticism in its place. A lower grade on an exam is not a sign that you are a bad person who will not succeed in college, but a signal that you need to rethink your approach to exam preparation for that class. The real danger to you is not in being criticized but in ignoring its value to you. Let the criticism you experience in college come in but not in so far that it crashes your motivation.

employer will expect you to show up every day and be on time for work. You are practicing that behavior when you are regular and punctual in your class attendance. College professors will ask you to write and will evaluate your writing skills. It is likely that your future career will require you to write reports and memos that are both clear and free of grammatical errors. College professors will ask you to read and be ready to evaluate what you have read. In the same way, your future employer will be asking you to read and evaluate reports as well as follow written instructions. Listening and speaking are also skills that you will apply in your future vocation, whether it be listening to presentations at meetings or giving oral reports. College gives you the chance to practice and hone these fundamental work skills.

Perhaps your lack of motivation lies elsewhere. Maybe you are feeling unmotivated about attending college in general or are feeling little passion for completing a paper for your composition class. Why am I doing this anyway? First of all, honor the question. It is very difficult for anyone to pursue a goal, particularly one as challenging as college graduation, without stopping to reflect on what it is that motivates him or her to achieve that goal. As human beings, we are motivated to engage in a task by a complex set of stimulants. Here is a short list of what may motivate us.

Sense of pride

Need for money

Desire for accomplishment

Religious or moral conviction

Desire for power

Need for respect

Fear of failure

Fear of disappointing others

Fear of personal pain

Sense of loyalty

Spirit of adventure

Prestige

Both the authors of this book enjoy scuba diving. What motivated us to pursue this form of recreation despite the risks and personal cost? The answer is found in the following illustration. At the center lies the topic and streaming from it lie the factors that motivated us.

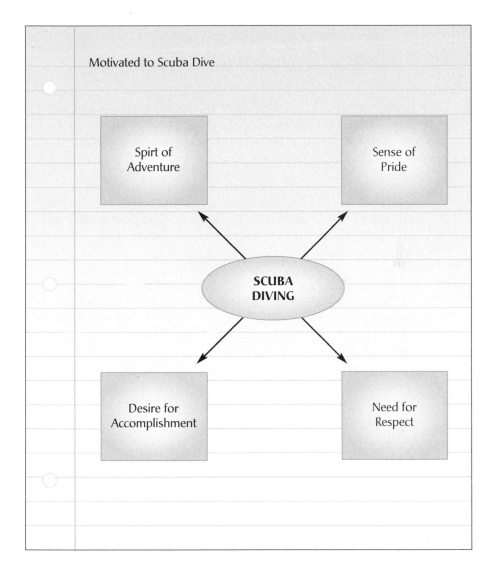

Motivated to Scuba Dive

Spirt of Adventure

Sense of Pride

SCUBA DIVING

Desire for Accomplishment

Need for Respect

Your decision to attend college and your letter of acceptance have started you down an exciting and prosperous path. This class, this book, and your Bible will combine to put light on the path you are walking. They will both encourage you during your transition and direct your steps to greater success. Now is the time to plan for success by setting goals and acting upon them. And now is the time to check your motivation, remembering that motivation is an attitude. When you are feeling unmotivated you can explore the cause of that attitude and work to repair it.

Still Feeling Unmotivated?

*A*RE YOU STILL FEELING unmotivated? The following questions address the things that can quickly rob you of your passion for a task. Answer the following questions honestly to learn more about where your motivation challenges may lie.

1. Can you focus? If you lack motivation or are having trouble completing important tasks, it may be because you are having trouble keeping your focus due to external distractions. For example, noise from your roommates or children may prevent you from attending to your task.

2. Are you able? Completion of a goal assumes that you have the ability to perform certain tasks. If you lack information or the ability to perform the task, it can rob you of your motivation. For example, if you lack the ability to conduct effective library research, you may become very unmotivated to complete a term paper.

3. Are you satisfied? To remain motivated for a task you must have the expectation that you will feel satisfaction upon its completion. For example, you are unlikely to feel motivated to complete a major course of study if it is your parents, and not you, who will feel satisfied when you graduate.

Exercises for Success

First-Year Student Fears

Below you will find some of the most common concerns expressed by students entering college and space to add concerns of your own that are not listed. Place a check by all of those that apply to you at this moment, adding to the list as necessary. Then identify the five fears that are the strongest within you.

_____   I will not have enough money to do all the things I want to do.

_____   I will not be able to manage my time for study, sleep, etc.

_____   I will have difficulty making new friends.

_____   I will have trouble relating to my parents.

_____   I will get depressed and this will affect my grades.

_____   I will get poor grades.

_____   I will feel that I do not belong.

_____   I will disappoint my parents and family with the grades I get.

_____   I will have trouble getting along with my roommate.

_____   I will get lost on campus.

_____   I will have difficulty finding a major that I really like.

_____   I will sleep when I should be in class or doing homework.

_____   I will become homesick.

_____   I will not be able to develop proper study habits.

_____   I will have trouble understanding the professors.

_____   I will be viewed by others as an inferior person.

_____   I will cheat in class to get good grades.

_____   I will have to work too much.

_____   I will not find anyone who will help me here.

_____

_____

_____

When you have completed the exercise on your own, compare your results with your roommates and classmates. You may be surprised to learn that the feelings of other first-year students are very similar to your own.

Success and Survival Plan

If you were hiking in the Rocky Mountains during the late fall and had become lost, survival experts note that your ability to survive would depend on your willingness and ability to complete three basic tasks: stay hydrated, stay warm, and stay put.

More than a few hapless hikers have put themselves at great risk by not following these basic rules. This illustration makes it clear that survival and success is an intentional process.

The same could be said of your first year in college. Now is the time to plan a strategy that will allow for success and survival in the four areas discussed above. Take out a blank sheet of paper and divide it into four areas, labeling them spiritual strategy, academic strategy, health strategy, and relationship strategy. Set aside some quiet time and brainstorm what you would like to do in each of these four areas during the next two months to improve your chances for success. After you have collected five or more ideas in each area of the page, pick two items from each category that you will try for the next two months. This is the beginning of your success and survival plan.

Goal Setting and Implementation

This chapter has described a method for setting and implementing effective goals. Now it is time for you to give the method a trial run.

Step One Write down your intention statements. Take a packet of self-sticking notes and complete the sentence, "I intend to . . . ." Write down as many intentions as you can in ten minutes. Then spend another fifteen minutes editing and organizing those notes on the desk top or the wall in front of you.

Step Two Turn your intentions into goal statements. Intention statements become goal statements when you change the words "I intend to" to "I will." Take three of the intention statements and edit them according to the SMART criteria discussed earlier in this chapter.

Step Three Develop an action plan. On a blank sheet of paper, write each edited goal statement and brainstorm all the challenges that might stand in the way of your accomplishing that goal. Then identify resources and strategies you could put into play in order to accomplish the goal noted on the top of the page. Your time in this part of the process may lead you to edit the goal slightly. Write the edited goal at the top of another piece of blank paper. Then in two or three sentences describe the action plan you will follow in completing the stated goal.

Implement Your Action Plan You will not know if you like it until you have tried it. Select at least one of the goals and its associated action plan you developed and pursue the goal for the time you have designated. In time, you may elect to edit the process described above. Until then, stick with this outline and you will find that you are charting a course towards successful accomplishment of those things that are important to you.

Picture Your Motivation

Select one of the goals on which you worked above and think carefully about what it is that would motivate you to complete it. Consult the list of possible motivating factors listed earlier in the chapter, but do not hesitate to add to that list in your quest to find what will motivate you to pursue your goal. Take a piece of blank paper and draw an oval in the middle of the page. Place the goal in the oval and then surround that shape with arrows that point to the factors that will motivate you to act.

Spiritual Reflection Journal

You are experiencing a significant amount of change in your life, and with that change comes worry. Take a few moments now to write about the things that concern you most deeply as you make this new beginning. After you have written your concerns down, read Psalm 46 and Matthew 6:25–34. Describe the ways in which these two Bible passages speak to your worries and concerns.

Time in Prayer

In your personal time in prayer or in connection with others in your class, take time to pray for the following people and needs.

- Family members back home who are supporting you

- Members of your class who are feeling homesick

- The instructors of your classes

- Your ability to design an effective success strategy

- A good night's rest

On the Net

The Internet can be a helpful resource for you as you look for ideas to make yourself a happier and more successful student. Visit the College Success page offered by Thomson Wadsworth for web links that will help you grow further on this topic. Go to *www.success.wadsworth.com* and click on Resource Web Links.

Turning the Light on Higher Education

The fear of the LORD is the beginning of knowledge.

Proverbs 1:7

- What role does college play in our culture?
- What makes the Christian college unique?
- How can I best design my academic course of study?
- How can I most effectively use my academic advisor?

*T*HE FIRST FEW DAYS and weeks of college life may leave you feeling overwhelmed. There is so much that is new and different that you may be asking when things will feel normal again. Two things will help: more practice and more knowledge. The first time you rode your bike, you did not do it as well as you do it now. The first time you wrote a high school term paper, you did not write as well as you do now. Practice may not make you perfect, but it goes a long way toward improving your skills and your comfort with any given task. The same is true of going to college. Your first semester will be very different from the other semesters because you are doing everything for the first time. There will be your first college test, your first college roommate, and your first time registering for classes. With practice, each of those "firsts" will become easier, even second nature.

Apart from time and practice, there is another way of easing the challenges that attend the first year of college. The more you know about a new experience, the less threatening it will be to you. This chapter is going to shed light on the unique type of education that is offered on a Christian college campus. We believe that the more you know about higher education, its philosophy, its purpose, its general design, and the design of your academic program, the more comfortable you will be as a college student. This chapter will discuss the general purposes of higher education within American culture. It will describe the philosophical foundations that are used within Christian higher education to determine both what is studied and how your school defines what is true and cherished. This chapter will then help you become acquainted with the general structure of an academic program so that you might better understand the road that lies ahead and be able to answer questions like the following: What courses should I take next semester? And how can I most effectively use the academic advisor assigned to me?

The Purpose of Higher Education

As you join the ranks of college students this fall, you are entering an institution that has been around for centuries. Over the years, literally millions of men and women have preceded you, leaving home for college with exactly the same intentions you have. They hoped that the time and money invested in a college education would pay off by leading to a career of their choosing. It is what people did centuries ago to get the best jobs and it is what people do today to position themselves for the most prestigious and most lucrative careers.

But some things have changed about college. Within Europe during the Middle Ages, only men who were of high social standing attended college. These elite members of society were immersed in a very structured course of study, pursuing the liberal arts. They took classes in logic, rhetoric, geometry, and music in order to hone their thinking skills and to refine their communication skills in preparation for advanced class work leading to careers in law, medicine, and theology. In the Middle Ages, the purpose of the university was to educate a few privileged men for the elite jobs of that time.

When higher education came to America, it looked very much like the liberal arts colleges of Europe. But American culture quickly began to modify that model of education. The gender barrier was slowly but surely removed. In 1849, Elizabeth Blackwell became the first woman to receive a medical degree, making her the first female doctor in American history.

Change occurred not only in the student body but also in the curriculum. By the late 1800s, the German universities were encouraging their faculty to pursue more specialized and advanced research. This idea found a warm welcome in America, where independent thinking was championed as a virtue. This shift in the academy led to a shift in the curriculum, producing a more Americanized and more specialized form of education. Faculty began to teach classes associated with their research specialty and slowly the liberal arts curriculum, that carefully dictated a prescribed set of classes, gave way to an education that had more and more elective classes from which students could design their own course of study.

Another significant change occurred in the late 1800s and early 1900s with a shift away from the Christian heritage that had nurtured the formation of higher education in America. The rise of rationalism during the Enlightenment meant that Christian belief was increasingly subjected to the test of "reasonability." Reason rather than biblical revelation became the hallmark for determining truth. Colleges that once boldly proclaimed that the "fear of the Lord" was the beginning of wisdom now saw "reasonability" as the key criterion in determining truthfulness. Consequently, colleges began to drop their requirement that faculty members be Christian and Christian components of the curriculum like compulsory chapel attendance were slowly eliminated.

During the twentieth century, even more changes impacted American higher education. At the behest of industry giants who offered the universities considerable financial support, the American university began to wrestle more and more with the balance between offering a liberal arts education and a vocational education. Liberal arts courses were designed to foster the general thinking ability of college students with courses in history, literature, and science. By contrast, vocational courses were more focused on particular careers and designed to introduce students to the practical knowledge they would need to begin their professional lives.

This tug-of-war between liberal education and vocational specialization continues on college campuses today as higher education attempts to strike a balance between liberal education and vocational education. Schools work to develop thinking skills and cultural awareness by requiring students to complete at least some liberal arts courses that investigate topics fundamental to the formation and preservation of our culture. In this way, they seek to produce well-educated men and women who have a broader base of knowledge as well as people well versed in the art of learning. At the same time, schools seek to be vocational by preparing students as professionals in a variety of career arenas through focused coursework in majors and minors.

Finally, there is one more important dimension to the college experience that is critical to its role in American culture. College students are taught to question and critique what they study, not merely accept what they hear. They will learn historical details, but also learn to question and critique the way history has been recorded and interpreted. They will learn scientific theory, but also learn to question and critique that theory and its application. Through this type of critical thinking, college graduates will step into society not just as participants but as leaders who will edit the status quo. Yes, college will prepare you for a career. But it will also make you a key player in our world, making changes that will enhance both your profession and your society.

World View and Higher Education

As your college experience is preparing you to think more effectively and function more efficiently in your chosen career, it is making subtle but critical decisions both about what to teach and how to put a value on what is taught. Here the Christian college is unique in its approach to higher education. In order to appreciate that uniqueness, we need to discuss the wide array of philosophical foundations that may be used to create those value judgments.

As the university left behind its Christian heritage during the Enlightenment, it began a search for a coherent system of belief that would help answer the critical question in life. That question is the same one that Pilate asked Jesus during his trial, "What is truth?" (John 18:38) Since the 1700s, scholars have been searching for a replacement for the Bible. And while this quest has had some negative implications for Christianity, it has also produced a rich fabric of world views that has benefited the student at the Christian college. In this portion of the chapter, we will survey the most prominent Western world view systems articulated in the history of philosophy and demonstrate how they may be integrated into the Christian world view to function as the foundation for your college education.

RATIONALISM

During the 1700s, science was advancing at a dramatic pace. It appeared that the reasoning ability of the human mind was limitless and could provide the key to defining what society should properly regard as true and cherished. This heightened regard for rational thinking gave birth to the Enlightenment, which further pushed the frontiers of science while elevating reason above all other paths to truth. This had a great impact on Christianity and the Christian university, for now even the Bible itself was suspect in what it said unless it passed the test of reasonability. This world view more than any other has shaped the thinking and methods of the secular university.

ROMANTICISM

In the late 1700s and early 1800s, the general dominance of rationalism began to erode and Romanticism rose as a challenger. The romantics argued that the cold mechanics of reason alone were insufficient to define what is true and cherished. Truth seeking needed to take into account evidence from feelings and intuition. Thus the Romantic Movement argued that beauty and those things that create beauty were just as valuable as the objects and ideas deemed rational. It was feeling, not merely thinking, that makes humans appreciate the wonder that fills their world.

EMPIRICISM AND PRAGMATISM

Another competitor to Enlightenment rationalism was the empiricism that grew up in Great Britain. John Locke argued that truth is a product of experience achieved through careful experimentation and observation. This view is closely linked to American pragmatism as it grew up in the 1870s. Pragmatism argued that the pursuit of knowledge must be practical; consequently, it measured truthfulness and value by the effectiveness of function. Something was regarded as true and cherished if it worked. Combined, the notions of empiricism and pragmatism have shaped and supported the scientific method that remains the basis of scientific inquiry to this day.

EXISTENTIALISM

During the twentieth century, the horror of two world wars led philosophers to question the hope of finding one universal system that could effectively define what is true and cherished. While some orderly patterns within our world may tempt us to look for one universal way of defining what is true and cherished, existentialism argues that life is much too complex to be explained by any one operating principle. Thus the existential world view abandons the quest for universal truth and instead views truth as relative to each individual. This leads to the conclusion that what is true for one person is not necessarily binding and true for another person. Truth is not spelled with a capital "T" nor is it best described in the singular. Rather there are many "truths" that are defined by the experience of various thinkers. The postmodern world in which we live is heavily influenced by this existential world view. And consequently the university has become very pluralistic in its pursuit of truth, uncritically accepting many different world view approaches and honoring many different conclusions, even those that appear to formally contradict one another.

The Christian World View and Higher Education

What is the Christian thinker to do in this swirling bath of natural philosophy? Christians have three options that they may follow: separate completely from secular world views, fully integrate biblical teaching with the secular world views, or integrate but then discriminate between what is valuable and what is not valuable in the secular world views. First, Christian thinkers may attempt to separate from the philosophical conversation completely. The church father, Tertullian, seems to propose this idea as early as the third century AD when he considered the role of Greek philosophy in the life of the church. He said, "What is there in common between Athens and Jerusalem? What is there in common between the academy and the church?"[1]

Centuries later during the Enlightenment, the rise of rationalism as the leading world view in the university pushed the Bible and its contribution to higher education off to the margins under the premise that most of what was said there could not be proved. Thus within higher education, the contribution of the Bible was removed from the pursuit of higher thinking and

---

[1] Tertullian, *De praescriptione haereticorum*, 7.

relegated to the private lives of those who wished to study it. This separation of the Bible and higher learning has become the status quo in almost all higher education settings. Carried to its ultimate conclusion, this would limit Christian schools to the study of the Bible and make them what one secular school president called them, "gated communities," closed to the new ideas and directions revealed by natural thinking.

By contrast, it is very possible for Christians to integrate natural philosophy and the product of such thinking into their approach to learning. You may find the thought initially disturbing. But we must acknowledge that the Bible simply does not answer every question that we might ask. The biblical poet acknowledges that fear of the Lord is the *beginning* of knowledge (Prov 1:7), but this same author does not argue that it is the sum total of all knowledge. Thus we are left to explore the world using natural philosophy to discover and appreciate the truth that lies hidden within creation itself. The Bible affirms this integration when it tells us that we may even learn things about God by exploring the world around us. "The heavens declare the glory of God; the skies proclaim the work of his hands." (Ps 19:1) Christian schools then are not "gated communities," but schools whose libraries are filled with the best thinking of the ages. Natural philosophy permeates the hallways and classrooms of the Christian school. The principles of rationalism are employed every time a thesis is demonstrated in a term paper. Appropriate use of the scientific method will earn an "A" on lab reports. Romanticism and existentialism operate in the literature class where each student is asked to report on the beauty and meaning they personally find in a Shakespearean sonnet.

But in the same laboratories and classrooms that honor the voice of rationalism and Romanticism, the voice of the Bible is also a welcome visitor and its contribution to higher education is honored. Rather than accepting the Enlightenment premise that reason is the only pathway leading to truth, the Christian school acknowledges that revelation from God found in the Bible is also truth (John 17:17, 2 Tim 3:16–17, and 2 Peter 1:21). While Christian colleges and secular colleges ask and seek to answer the same academic questions, the Christian school uses the Bible as a resource in pursuing answers to those questions. This integration is certainly helpful when addressing questions of a more spiritual nature. For example, what are the angels and what role do they play in my life? But the Bible is also a critical contributor to other conversations about the human experience. What is the origin of life on this earth? Where can I find the key to life's meaning? Certainly the various natural world views have a contribution to make in answering such questions, but their answers are not always satisfying. One biblical author attempted to find meaning in life by artificially removing the divine from the equation. In frustration, he reported, "Everything was meaningless, a chasing after the wind; nothing was gained under the sun." (Eccl 2:11)

By contrast, the pursuit of truth that includes divine revelation is rewarded with insights and comfort that natural philosophy cannot provide. When Peter came to understand the power of Jesus' message, he acknowledged that Jesus is the sole source of information on certain, critical topics, exclaiming, "Lord, to whom shall we go? You have the words of eternal life." (John 6:68) Consequently, the Bible becomes a textbook in the Christian college. It is defined as a source of truth, placed next to the other textbooks on the college student's shelf, and regularly consulted to ascertain its contribution to the matter under investigation.

But there is one more dimension to the Christian pursuit of truth that builds on this respect for the Bible as a source of truth. Every world view must have a way of discriminating between competing claims for truth. If rationally derived truth stands in conflict with truth revealed in the Bible, one's world view must have a way to resolve that tension. In this regard, not all Christians have taken the same approach. But many evangelical Christians have validated the Bible as the most powerful source of truth.

While absolutely necessary to the pursuit of higher education, natural philosophy and the product of its thinking may be tainted by imperfection. The Bible teaches that human beings were created to think perfectly with wills and minds created in the image of God (Gen 1:27). But the fall into sin ruined this gift and immediately the evidence of impoverished thinking became evident. Adam and Eve "hid" from an all-powerful and all-knowing God (Gen 3:10). Their act of poor thinking is only the first of many recorded in the Bible giving evidence that even those who believe in God have lost the ability to think perfectly. That means that every conclusion that is a product of natural philosophy is subject to error. That is why the poet of Proverbs cautions, "Trust in the LORD with all your heart and lean not on your own understanding." (Prov 3:5)

Planning Your Academic Program

Successful college students are those who not only understand the larger idea of the Christian university, but also know how to efficiently and effectively plan their academic program. If your high school experience has led you to believe that someone else will pick your classes and register you for the next term, you will need to change your perspective. That responsibility belongs to you. In this section of the chapter, we will talk about the outline of your academic program and how you may more effectively plan your course of study. We will talk about how to investigate the requirements of that academic program, design a plan for completing your course work, and give you tips on using your academic advisor.

I Don't Have a Major!

*I*F YOU HAVE NOT decided on a major or have great reservations about the major you have selected, all this talk about knowing your academic program and registering for classes may be somewhat upsetting. Perhaps you have even asked whether or not you should be in college if you do not know what career you want to pursue. We want to assure you that even if you are undecided, college is the right place to be because here you have a better chance of surveying all the potential career paths that lie before you. Furthermore, the career services office on your campus can assist you in defining the kinds of work you might like to do and specific careers that are associated with your interests. Nearly half of all college students change their major at least once during their time in college. See yourself as one step ahead of them since you are going to do some career exploration before they know they need it. While you are coming to greater clarity, speak to your advisor about a strategy for registering for classes. You still can move forward with your college plans even if you have not declared a major.

THE OUTLINE OF AN ACADEMIC PROGRAM

Graduation may seem very far away, but this is the time for you to become familiar with your academic program so that you arrive at your graduation day in the most efficient way possible. A bit later in this chapter, we will talk about the academic advisor who is assigned to assist you with program planning and registration. This person can be of great help to you. But in the end, you must know your own academic program better than anyone else. It is your time and money that will be at risk if this planning is done poorly, so make it your business to know the requirements of your program intimately.

The best place to discover the outline of the academic program on your campus is the college catalog that is published every year by your school. That catalog may be available to you in either paper or electronic format. In either case, it is critical for you to gain access to a copy of the catalog published the same year you began to attend college. Consider this catalog a binding contract between you and your school. In it, the school promises to give you a degree when you have successfully completed the program described in that catalog. From time to time, the requirements of your major may change. In that case, you typically have the right to either upgrade to the new requirements or stay with the plan they had promised you when you matriculated.

In that catalog, you will find the outline for your academic program. It may consist of four or more parts that define different categories of classes you will need to complete. A typical college program will consist of a set of general education classes (sometimes called the core classes), courses associated with your major, courses associated with your minor, and courses that are free electives.

The general education core is that part of higher education still rooted in the liberal arts college tradition. It is that part of the educational experience that all graduates from your college will have in common no matter what their major course of study may be. The size and content of the general education core is set by your school's faculty and generally includes courses in writing, literature, speech, religion, art, music, science, and philosophy. These courses have two functions. First of all, they are designed to deepen your understanding of topics on which all well-educated people are conversant. Secondly, since most of these courses will be taken before you do course work in your major and minor, they are designed to improve your thinking and communication skills. By practicing and improving those skills in these initial classes, you will be able to perform more effectively in your major and minor course work.

Apart from this general education core, you will also be taking focused course work in a major. The major is a collection of courses that is designed to give you more specialized and advanced knowledge in one area. Among the college majors offered on your campus you will find programs of study in subjects such as accounting, communication, nursing, and education. Within your college catalog, you will find both a list of majors offered by your school as well as a list of courses that must be completed in order to graduate with that major. The catalog also contains a brief description of each course offered by the college, including a note about any prerequisite courses you must complete before registering for the course you are considering.

Aside from a major, most college students will also complete a minor. The minor will require fewer classes than the major. But like the major, it gives college students the opportunity to develop more advanced and specialized knowledge in another area. Typically, the minor will complement the major course of study and enhance it in some way. For example, an interior design major may elect to minor in business since she plans to open her own interior design store. Just like the major, the catalog will provide you with both a list of the minors available on your campus and the course work associated with them.

Your school has established a minimum number of credits that you must earn before you will be considered for graduation. It is possible that you will acquire all those academic credits necessary to graduate by just completing the general education core, your major, and minor. But many college students will also have room left in their college program for elective courses. Elective courses are just what their name suggests. They are courses that you are free to choose from across the spectrum of courses offered by your school. You may elect to take courses that further support your major or you may complete several classes in areas not formally associated with your major but of personal interest to you. Here is the place to take the class in cross-country skiing, the course in Near Eastern archaeology, or the course in women's studies that has always intrigued you.

REGISTERING FOR YOUR CLASSES

Once you have the big picture of what your academic program requires, you are ready to think about registering for your classes. In this portion of the chapter, we will present a plan for completing your registration. This plan will be more generic and you will need to modify it to suit your own situation. But we believe that having a plan to follow in registering for classes will help you avoid mistakes that could cost you time and money. First of all, make sure that you have a file folder that is dedicated exclusively to holding items related to planning your academic program. That includes items such as advanced placement credits, an updatable worksheet that indicates what courses you have completed and what courses you still need to complete, grade reports of those completed courses, and any letters of waiver you might receive. Meticulous record keeping will not only keep you better organized but will also provide you with the necessary evidence if one of your accomplishments is disputed at the time of your graduation.

When it is time for you to register for your courses, take that file folder in hand. In particular, you will need to get or make a worksheet that summarizes your academic program, a list of courses offered in the next term, a blank weekly calendar on which you can work out your schedule, and a registration form. The first step in the process of registering for next term is to make sure you have updated your academic program worksheet so that you are aware of what required courses you have already completed. Be sure to take into account the course work you are doing in the current semester, plus any transfer or advanced placement credits you have earned. The next step is to make a list of courses that you potentially could take in the coming term. Be sure to keep in mind special requirements of your major, courses that may require prerequisites, and course rotation (since not every course is offered each term).

Set aside that list of potential courses for a few minutes and put the blank weekly calendar in front of you. On that calendar, block out those times during the week when your weekly schedule will not allow you to be in class. This may include time previously claimed by work, family, an athletic team, or a social organization. After this step has been completed, you are ready to blend the list of courses you need to take, the course schedule for next term, and your weekly schedule to determine what classes to take. Through trial and error you will find the right combination of classes that fits both your schedule and your program needs.

If you become frustrated with the process, do not give up. The sooner you register for your classes the better. As the current term comes to a close, more and more of the seats in any given class will be filled by other students. And typically there is a limit as to how many people are permitted to register for a given class. If you get your name in too late, you may be able to put your name on a waiting list, but this is no guarantee that you will find your way to a seat in that room next term. Register early and save yourself the grief of having to weave around closed classes as you prepare your schedule.

Should I Be Working While Going to School?

THE ANSWER TO THAT question depends on how much you are planning to work. A college student who is taking fifteen or more credit hours already has a full-time job. If you add the hours you spend in class to the hours set aside for doing homework, you will easily fill a forty-hour week. If you plan to work another full-time job, you are taking on a workload that very few people can carry. It is certainly possible, even desirable, for you to have a part-time job. How much you can work at a part-time job will depend somewhat on your academic ability and your ability to successfully juggle a busy schedule. But if you are going to truly succeed in college and enjoy life as a college student with all the benefits it offers, limit the amount of time you spend in your part-time job to fifteen hours per week.

ACADEMIC POLICIES

The academic catalog of your school will also contain the institution's academic policies. These general policies impact every student on campus, no matter what major he or she may be taking, and include items such as additional graduation requirements (like community service projects or portfolios), final exam waiver policies, and the minimum grade point average required to be a student in good standing. While these policies many not directly affect your program planning for any one term, they are important policies that will impact your

Academic Probation and GPA

*A*T MOST COLLEGES, you will be required to maintain a minimum grade point average (GPA) to continue as a full-time student. Check your college catalog to determine the minimum GPA required to be a student in good standing and the policies that govern students who find themselves on academic probation. Remember that attending college is not a right but a privilege extended to those who can successfully accomplish the work. Be aware of your GPA and have an academic plan that keeps you as a student in good standing.

Below is a model that you can use to calculate your GPA, which is a mathematical average of your course grades. It is easy to compute your current GPA by using the following procedure. For each course, multiply the number of credit hours by the number assigned to that grade you have received (A = 4, B = 3, C = 2, D = 1, and F = 0.). For example, if you received an A in a three-credit history course, you would multiply 3 x 4 = 12. The number 12 in this case represents the "quality points" you have earned for this class. Do this for each of your classes. Then add up the quality points and divide them by the total number of credit hours you took that semester. This is your GPA. See the example below.

Course	Grade	Credit Hours	Grade Value	Quality Points
History	B	3	3	9
Chem.	C	4	2	8
English	D	3	1	3
Math	B	3	3	9
Total		13		29

29 ÷ 13 = 2.23 GPA

overall plan. Read them carefully and be certain that you ask about any policy that is not clear to you, because it will be difficult to get an exemption from it. For example, if you wish to add or drop a class and fail to get your request in within the time set by the catalog, do not expect the school to allow ignorance of a published policy to lead to an exemption from that policy.

Your Academic Advisor

Your school will provide you with a faculty or professional staff member who will function as your personal academic advisor. He or she is your ally in designing and implementing an academic program that will help you accomplish your personal goals within the least amount of time and with the least investment of money. They are also aware of other support services offered by your school and may be able to assist you with personal challenges you face as well as those directly linked to academics. But as you read earlier, do not assume your advisor will be willing to do the planning for you or will intuitively know your needs. As the name suggests, an advisor is there to give you advice, not make decisions for you. Know what your professional goals are, know the academic program that will help you achieve those goals, know what you want to do in any given term, and then let your advisor edit and support your plan.

Your first advisor will typically be assigned to you by the school. If this advisor is a specialist in the area of your academic major, you may remain in that advising relationship for your entire college career. On the other hand, your first advisor may be a general advisor who will help you make the transition into college and then transfer you to someone in the area of your major. Of course, there is always the chance you will change your major. In the latter cases, you may need to interview and pursue a new academic advisor.

If that is the case, realize that no two people look for exactly the same qualities in their advisor, and advisors do differ considerably from one another. Some are very friendly and personal, willing to spend a great deal of time with you, hearing about your concerns and offering you direction and encouragement on both the personal and professional fronts. Other advisors will be more conservative in the use of their time and more businesslike. Some advisors will be very direct in the advice they give while others will take a more hands-off approach. Some advisors will be more knowledgeable than others. Some advisors will be very interested in helping you make professional contacts that either lead to a job interview or graduate school application and others will be less helpful in this way. The point is that advisors come in all shapes and sizes. Be sure that you select an advisor who has the qualities you would like. And if you do not have an advisor with the qualities you like, be sure that you begin the process of changing to an advisor more suited to your needs.

In all these cases, you will be more satisfied with your advising relationship if you follow a few simple guidelines in working with your advisor. If you have something to talk about with your advisor that is important to you, make an appointment to see your advisor rather than dropping in unannounced. You are much more likely to get the amount of time you need and the quality of time you require by following that simple rule. When you make an appointment, be sure that you show up and are on time. Advisors are very busy people who are typically glad to meet with you, but will have little patience for students who either do not show up for their appointment or come late. Be certain that you are prepared. If you are coming to talk about registering for classes, be sure that you have done as much planning as you can on your own. Do not expect your advisor to have the time or patience to work through planning steps that you could have accomplished on your own. In this regard, it is a good idea to come with questions written down that you need answered. This will prevent you from leaving the office only to remember an important question you had failed to ask during the session. It is also wise to write down the answers or advice you receive. With all the things you have going on in any one day, it is easy to forget helpful advice you have received. Taking notes during an advising session will not only aid your memory, it will also demonstrate that you are serious about the appointment. In general, treat your advisor as a professional who is there to help you. Your respect for them will earn their respect for you.

The Class Syllabus

*I*N EACH OF YOUR college classes, you will receive a class syllabus. This is a very important document that will outline the learning objectives for the class and the various ways your progress will be guided and measured as you work towards completion of those goals. Typically your class syllabus will include your instructor's name and methods for contacting him or her, the class attendance policy, a daily assignment schedule, and a schedule reflecting the dates for papers and exams. It is critical that you keep the class syllabus in a safe place and that you transfer the due dates for all assignments and tests to your weekly and monthly calendar.

Exercises for Success

The History of My School

The history of your college or university has played an important role in shaping the school you are attending today. Make a list of questions you would like answered about your school, questions like the following: What year was my college founded? Who were the people that supplied the driving force for bringing the school into being? What is the relationship between my Christian school and the tradition that founded it? What events were most dramatic in shaping the history of my school? After you have created your list of questions, ask a member of the history department what sources would be most efficient in helping you answer those questions. Prepare a two-page summary of what you find.

Our School Seal

The official school seal has something important to say about the unique nature of your institution in an artistic presentation. Obtain a copy of the school seal and study it carefully. Look at every detail and determine what message the artist is communicating about your school. Write a one-page paper that describes what the school seal says about the history and purpose of your institution.

World View Summary Report

This chapter offered you a very brief introduction to a variety of world views. Do a more detailed study of one of them: rationalism, romanticism, empiricism, pragmatism, or existentialism. Pursue questions like the following: What historical circumstances helped give birth to this world view? Who were the key individuals who championed this world view? How does this world view define what is to be true and cherished? How does this world view integrate or conflict with my Christian views? After you have completed your personal study of that world view, interview at least three faculty members at your school to get their impression of the last question. Summarize your findings in a four-page paper.

Ongoing Issues in Higher Education

Your experience in college is taking place in the middle of a continuing debate about how higher education should look and what it should be doing for our culture. Below is a list of topics presently being debated. Investigate the current state of one issue using library and Internet resources, and then present a two-page paper that summarizes the current state of the conversation in America.

Should students in higher education be more deeply immersed in liberal arts courses or in courses that are more narrowly designed for application in a profession?

How is the current relationship between the federal government and higher educa-tion, played out in matters like federal financial aid and the use of universities to do federal research, create a conflict of interest?

Given the expanding base of knowledge available to study, should higher education become more specialized in its course work or focus more on integrating all the knowledge on a topic that is available?

Is there a definite list of "Great Books" that every American college student should read or should education be more elective, allowing students to pursue areas of study unique to their own interests?

Identifying Key Campus Resources

Every university campus has an array of resources available to support the health and well being of its student population. This list may include services such as a health center, a counseling center, an advising center, financial aid office, etc. Consult your campus web page or directory and determine what campus services you think may be most useful to you. Pick six of those services and complete the resource out-line below.

Resource	Contact Person	Phone Number	E-Mail Address	Web Page	Hours	Location

Critical Dates

Your school catalog contains important dates that will affect your semester. Consult your current school catalog for the following dates and make certain that they are recorded in your semester calendar.

First day of class

Last day of class

Last day to add a class

Last day to drop a class

Date of final exam week

Dates of all holidays and breaks

Spiritual Reflection Journal

Read Daniel 1 and reflect on the higher education experience of Daniel and his friends. They were taken away from familiar surroundings and forced to meet a world view that challenged their spiritual beliefs. Where do you see similarities and differences between your experience in higher education and that of Daniel, Hananiah, Mishael, and Azariah (Belteshazzar, Shadrach, Meshach, and Abednego)? What attitudes and behaviors do you see in them that you wish to adopt as you pursue your education?

Time in Prayer

In your personal time in prayer or in connection with others in your class, pray for the following people and needs.

* For those in your class who are uncertain about their career plans

* For all Christian college students facing world view challenges to their faith

* For the church body that supports your Christian school

* For the faculty and administrators who work to define the world view presented by your college

* For your academic advisor

On the Net

The Internet can be a helpful resource for you as you look for ideas to make yourself a more happy and successful student. Visit the College Success page offered by Thomson Wadsworth for web links that will help you grow further on this topic. Go to *www.success.wadsworth.com* and click on Resource Web Links.

Making Time for Everything

There is a time for everything, and a season
for every activity under heaven.

Ecclesiastes 3:1

- How can I use my time more efficiently?
- How can I become better organized?
- How can I limit distractions?
- How can I avoid procrastination?

*T*IME IS A GIFT from God that can be used either well or poorly. This is illustrated in the story of Mary and Martha (Luke 10:38–42). When Jesus came to visit their home, Mary and Martha used their time in very different ways. Mary sits down and listens to Jesus as he teaches, but Martha scurries about investing herself in the household details that would make Jesus' visit comfortable. One could argue that both Mary and Martha were involved in activities that were worthwhile and meaningful. But when Martha expresses dismay that Mary is not helping her, Jesus replies that Mary has made a better choice by using this time to listen to his teaching. Certainly there are times when housework must be done. But since Jesus' time with them would be brief, the household preparations could wait. Mary seized an opportunity she would not always enjoy, so Jesus affirms her choice over that of Martha.

So how does your time-use habit look? Are you easily distracted from your work? Do you forget when assignments are due? Do you run out of time when working on a project? Some people mistakenly assume that they were "born" to be poor time managers or that they have less time to use than others. This is not the case. We all have 24 hours each day and we all make choices about how we use those 24 hours. That is why we are calling your use of time a *habit*, a habit that may be edited and changed if you so desire. This chapter invites you to carefully inspect your time-use habit at several levels to determine where your current habit contributes to your success as a college student and what portions of your habit may need improvement. This means looking at how you organize your time, how you manage distractions that challenge your use of time, and what you do when confronted by the appeal of procrastination.

Be warned ahead of time. The assessment of your habits may indicate the need to change and change is hard. But the need to edit your old time-use habits should not come as a surprise. As a new college student, you are in a very different learning environment. You will need to set aside more time for reading. You will have to manage assignments that are more widely spaced and that consume more time. And you will have more free time to manage. Some of your default time management skills will transfer easily to your college environment, while others will need to be changed.

If you are thinking that the best way for a college student to manage time is to just work all of the time, that is not the answer either. On the contrary, there is a right time for everything. The Gospels report that Jesus took time with his disciples to rest, to celebrate with others at weddings, and to pray quietly by himself. Balance is the key. So rather than seeing time management as your enemy, see it as a friend that will help you find time for all the things you want to do by improving your organization, prioritization, distraction management, and procrastination management.

My Perceptions

We will get started with a look at your perception of how you use your time. Estimate the amount of time you spend in a typical week in the following categories and then add up the hours at the end of the chart. Do not worry about being too specific. Just write down your general impressions of how a typical week looks.

Time in class	_____ hours
Studying	_____ hours
Work	_____ hours
Commuting	_____ hours
Family time	_____ hours
Volunteer work	_____ hours
Exercise	_____ hours
Athletics	_____ hours
Social time with friends	_____ hours
Sleeping	_____ hours
Eating	_____ hours
Worship services	_____ hours
Prayer and Bible study	_____ hours
Grooming, dressing, cleaning	_____ hours
Fun (TV, music, dating, video games, hobbies, shopping)	_____ hours
Other	_____ hours
Total Hours	_____
	(Do not exceed 168 hours!)

My Actual Time Use

Tracking your actual time use will allow you to see how closely your perceptions match your weekly reality. Use the following chart to record your use of time over one week. Take a few moments every four hours that you are awake and write down what you have been doing during the last four hours. Once the week is complete, add up the amount of time you actually spent in each of the categories and write them on the chart.

Calendar for the week of _____

	SUN	MON	TUES	WED	THUR	FRI	SAT
6:00 am							
7:00							
8:00							
9:00							
10:00							
11:00							
12:00 pm							
1:00							
2:00							
3:00							
4:00							
5:00							
6:00							
7:00							
8:00							
9:00							
10:00							
11:00							
12:00 am							
1:00–5:00 am							

Example of "Time Spent" Chart

Time in class	_____ hours
Studying	_____ hours
Work	_____ hours
Commuting	_____ hours
Family time	_____ hours
Volunteer work	_____ hours
Exercise	_____ hours
Athletics	_____ hours
Social time with friends	_____ hours
Sleeping	_____ hours
Eating	_____ hours
Worship services	_____hours
Prayer and Bible study	_____hours
Grooming, dressing, cleaning	_____ hours
Fun (TV, music, dating, video games, hobbies, shopping)	_____ hours
Other	_____ hours

How Is Your Habit?

You should now have a more accurate picture of your time management habits. Reflect on that picture and compare it with your perceived use of time. Where do your perceptions match your reality and where do your perceptions and reality part company? Talk over what you have discovered about your habit with a friend or teacher who successfully manages their time. Then write out three positive things about your time management habits and three things most in need of improvement.

Time Management Habits

LOOKS GOOD:

1.

2.

3.

NEEDS IMPROVEMENT:

1.

2.

3.

Building a Better Time Plan

Now that you have had a chance to reflect on your time use, it is the opportune time to make some changes. As you set about designing an improved time plan, it is critical to review the goals you established for yourself in Chapter One. Those goals will play an important role in shaping your time-use plan at every level. Just as those goals are unique to you, so the particular way you will design your time plan will be unique to you. But in general, a healthy time plan addresses the way you organize your time at three levels: the semester plan, the weekly plan, and the daily plan. Here we will explore suggestions and ideas that you can use to tune up your time-use habits.

THE SEMESTER PLAN

Not every week of your semester looks the same. One week, you may have a paper due. Another week, you may have two exams. Your best friend is getting married in April. A semester plan will help you keep track of those unique events that occur in any given month of your semester, events that can easily get lost if you focus only on the regular rhythm of your week. A semester plan calls for you to identify and place on a monthly calendar all the birthdays, weddings, athletic events, church meetings, and family gatherings that punctuate your year. Then carefully review all course syllabi for exams, papers, presentations, and the dates on which they will be due. Once you have placed everything on the calendar, you may even color code them by class or type activity for easy reference. A typical month might look like this.

FEBRUARY						
SUN	**MON**	**TUE**	**WED**	**THUR**	**FRI**	**SAT**
			1 History Exam	2	3	4
5	6 Persuasion speech	7	8	9	10 Sociology paper	11
12	13	14 Dad's birthday	15	16	17	18 Winter festival
19	20	21	22 Church meeting	23	24	25 Pat's wedding
26	27 English Paper	28				

Now consider what you do to manage these details in your life. If you would like to experiment with building this type of semester plan, obtain a calendar with room to write. Then gather information on your personal activities and meetings, extracurricular commitments like sport schedules or organizational meetings, and all your class syllabi. Place each of the items you need to remember in their appropriate place on the semester calendar and post that calendar for easy reference. As your semester marches forward and as you have more and more things you need to remember, you will come to value having a calendar like this that relieves you of the need to remember the date of every assignment and every birthday.

THE WEEKLY PLAN

The semester plan will help you remember the unique commitments of your month. The weekly plan is designed to help you organize the regular components of your week like studying, socializing, attending class, or going to a tutoring session. By being more intentional about the time you spend doing these things, you will be more likely to find the balance you are seeking in your weekly schedule.

As you plan your week, study time will be critical. Most college teachers expect you to invest between one and two hours of studying per week for each hour you are in class. You will want to distribute those 25 hours of study time throughout the week at times when you will be alert and energized for the task. Not only the time during the week but even the time during the day when you plan to study can be critical. Many students have found that working during daylight hours tends to be more productive than work done at night. But you know better than anyone else when your "prime time" occurs. That is the time during the day or week when you know you are at your best. As you prepare a weekly plan, be sure to exploit that time for studying.

Your happiness and success as a college student will be influenced greatly by the way you balance your time. All work and no play is a recipe for disaster. Plan to set aside regular time in your week for spiritual growth. When will you pray, read your Bible, have quiet time with the Lord, and worship with others? That weekly schedule will also need to be balanced with time for your social life and exercise. When during the week will you plan your aerobic workouts, time with friends, and time alone when you can rest and rekindle your energy?

As you think about your current time-use habits and consider editing what you are doing, do not view a weekly plan as enslaving. Think of it as a guide, not a task master. This is your plan and you will always remain in control of its composition. As you become more sophisticated in your understanding of college life, your weekly plan will go through several drafts. At a minimum, you will want to reevaluate your weekly time plan at midterm and make the changes that seem prudent to you at that time.

If you would like to experiment with a weekly plan, use the grid that follows to help you design it. First enter the fixed elements of your week. Put in things like your class schedule, work schedule, commuting time, and practice time for your athletic team. Then using a pencil (because you may need to erase) begin to enter the more flexible parts of your day like time for studying, worship, recreation, and exercise. It will be insightful to return to the time-

Example of Weekly Plan

	SUN	MON	TUES	WED	THUR	FRI	SAT
6:00 am			Breakfast		Breakfast		Sleep
7:00		Breakfast	Study	Breakfast	Study	Breakfast	↓
8:00	Breakfast	History	↓	History	↓	History	
9:00	Church	Study		Study			Exercise
10:00	Bible study	↓	Speech	↓	Speech		Study
11:00	Laundry						↓
12:00 pm	Lunch	Lunch	Lunch	Lunch	Lunch	Lunch	
1:00	Fun		Study		Study		Lunch
2:00			↓		↓		Family
3:00	↓	Psych.		Psych.		Psych.	
4:00			Exercise		Exercise		
5:00	Dinner	Dinner	Dinner	Dinner	Dinner	Dinner	
6:00	Work		Math	Work		Fun	
7:00		Tutoring			Tutoring		↓
8:00		Study			Study		
9:00	↓	↓		↓	↓		
10:00		↓		Bible study		↓	
11:00	Prayer	Prayer	Prayer	Prayer	Prayer	Prayer	Prayer
12:00 am	Sleep	Sleep	Sleep	Sleep	Sleep		Sleep
1:00–5:00 am	↓	↓	↓	↓	↓	Sleep	↓

tracking exercise you prepared earlier in this chapter as a guide. Do you need to increase the amount of time you are spending in some areas? Do you need to decrease the amount of time you are spending in other areas? Can you work out your schedule so that you are doing two things at once, like doing laundry and reading your history assignment?

Schedule for the Week of _____

	SUN	MON	TUES	WED	THUR	FRI	SAT
6:00 am							
7:00							
8:00							
9:00							
10:00							
11:00							
12:00 pm							
1:00							
2:00							
3:00							
4:00							
5:00							
6:00							
7:00							
8:00							
9:00							
10:00							
11:00							
12:00 am							
1:00–5:00 am							

THE DAILY PLAN

Even though you have designed a weekly plan for yourself, there are still portions of any one day that might be used in different ways. The third part of building a better time plan means creating a list of things you could do today and prioritizing that list so that you know which items are more important than others. Some days you might be using your designated study time to read an assignment, while other weeks that time might be used to start a term paper. One week your exercise time might be spent playing intramurals, while another week might find you lifting weights with a friend. Clearly you will have various ways of filling in the study time, social time, volunteer time, or fun time blocked out on your weekly calendar. That is where a daily plan can come in handy; for it not only can help you organize your day, it can also help you feel progress towards the larger goals you have committed yourself to that semester.

Of course, not everything on your list will be of the same importance. That is why it is helpful to divide your list into categories of significance. You can prioritize that list by thinking in terms of things that are critical, important, and possible. Give the highest quality time to critical items, filling in with the possible items only when you have extra time. A typical daily plan may look like this:

CRITICAL	IMPORTANT	POSSIBLE
☐ Prepare for history exam	☐ Outline Eng. paper	☐ Movie
☐ Bible study	☐ Birthday gift	☐ Call home
☐ Research on English paper	☐ Laundry	
☐ Exercise		

If you would like to experiment with this method of organizing your day, try this on for size. For the next five days, build a daily list of things you want to accomplish. Be sure to divide that list into objectives that are critical, important, and possible. Copy the grid that follows or make up your own. Remember there is no time management plan that fits everyone, so the more you customize these ideas to your personality the more success you are likely to have.

```
TODAY'S PLAN

DATE:

CRITICAL          IMPORTANT          POSSIBLE
  ☐                 ☐                  ☐
  ☐                 ☐                  ☐
  ☐                 ☐
```

Distractions and Procrastination

We need to make one last stop in our review of your time habit, because your careful planning may be undone if you are victimized by either distractions or procrastination. Distractions can come in all shapes and sizes. You may be distracted by your neighbors' music down the hall, by a phone call from a friend, by something that happened at work earlier in the day, or by your own physical exhaustion. You may procrastinate because you feel overwhelmed by the assignment or because you are waiting for just the right moment to start. What can you do to manage your distractions and procrastination?

DISTRACTIONS

Some of the distractions you face come from the environment in which you are trying to work. One way to minimize those distractions is to have a specific place set aside to study. When you discipline yourself to study in the same location, your body and mind become conditioned to that space and actually move into the study mode more quickly and attentively. That environment should be comfortable, well lighted, and away from sounds, sights, and memories that may distract you.

Your friends or family may also distract you from accomplishing your goals with invitations and conversations that invade the time you have set aside to work. The reality is that you are responsible for controlling the way you use your time. Either you will control your use of time or someone else will. Since you know what is best for you, learn to say "no" when their invitations or conversations prevent you from following your plan.

You may find yourself distracted by your own thoughts. Problems you are trying to manage in life can dominate your thoughts, even when you try to put them out of your mind. Unsettling news can come to us from many places: a relative may be seriously ill, the stress of work may invade our thoughts, or even lingering concerns over an argument with a close friend. If you find yourself distracted by a problem, it is unlikely you will be able to concentrate fully on your work. Take a few minutes to pray about the situation. Remember that God has promised to hear and to help. You may also find it helpful to write down the matter that is distracting you. By doing so, you can give yourself permission to set that topic aside for the time being. The written record will serve as a reminder to take it up again when the time is right.

Finally, old habits can be a distraction. Maybe you are in the habit of doing most of your studying at night after a full day of work and class. Perhaps you are in the habit of studying with music or in front of the TV. Maybe you find yourself surfing the Internet for fun whenever you are using your computer to write a paper. One way to identify and eliminate these kinds of distractions is by making a "not-to-do" list. Make a list of those habits you wish to avoid and post it in your study environment as a reminder of old habits you are willing to change.

PROCRASTINATION

Distractions can prevent us from accomplishing our goals and so can procrastination. Procrastination is the postponing of tasks that are perceived as unpleasant. Your procrastination may be caused by a number of factors working in isolation or combination with one another. Think about your situation for a moment and put a check mark by the items below that cause you to procrastinate.

Lack of confidence and frustration can be both a cause and a symptom of procrastination. One way to rebuild your confidence and defeat your frustration is to begin with a smaller task that you know you will achieve. The success you have with a smaller task will build momentum and help you break the procrastination cycle. And when you overcome the temptation to procrastinate and are successful in completing even a small task, celebrate that fact and reward yourself in a way that is meaningful to you. That will help you associate good time management behaviors with pleasure rather than pain.

Factors Affecting Procrastination

- I am not confident.
- I am easily frustrated.
- I am not motivated.
- I am bored.
- I have difficulty starting a task.
- I feel overwhelmed by this project.
- I think the task will take less time than it actually does.

Alternatively, you may have difficulty beginning a project because you lack motivation or feel bored with it. If that is the case for you, reread the section on motivation in Chapter One. Identify what it is that creates passion in you and link that passion to whatever project lies before you. That internal motivation will be more powerful than the pressure others place on you. But remember that you can ask a friend, a teacher, or a relative to help hold you accountable for tasks you are committed to completing.

Sometimes people have difficulty starting a task because they are waiting for just the right moment to begin. In general, that magic moment does not exist and this simply becomes an excuse to delay the project. When you are tempted to delay the start of a project, commit to sitting down for ten minutes of work on the project. After ten minutes, decide whether to continue. More often than not, the momentum you build during the first ten minutes will break the inertia and move you forward. As you get started, be aware of escape routes you have used in the past that have contributed to the delay. Do not let the habit of taking a nap, cleaning, or watching TV prevent you from getting started.

Perhaps you find yourself easily overwhelmed by the size and complexity of an assignment. But like the builder of a house, you do not do everything at once. The construction of a home is a very complex project with many dimensions to it. First the builder lays the foundation and then the frame of the house is erected. Electrical and plumbing components are added before the finishing work is done. When facing a big task, look for ways to break it down into small parts that you can manage and complete. This will help you overcome the feeling that the project is too large or complex to begin.

On the other hand, you might be prone to underestimate the size and complexity of an assignment. Consequently, you miscalculate the amount of time needed to complete a task and delay starting the work. If you do not catch this miscalculation early, you will be rushed to get it in on time. The result is often work that is of inferior quality or work that is handed in after the due date. In either case, you will likely receive a lower grade than what you could have earned. One way to address this problem is to set a starting date that is well before the time you believe you need to start the project. Of course, you may complete the assignment before it is due, but there is no penalty for completing a project early.

Time is a great gift from God that may be either used well or poorly. The story of Mary and Martha clearly illustrates that point. We have seen that time use is a habit over which you have great control. This chapter has given you the opportunity to reflect on that habit. Now is the time to experiment with changes in your habit that will improve your chances for success as a college student.

Exercises for Success

Create Your Plan

Throughout this chapter you have read suggestions on how you might assess and improve the way you organize your time. Pick one or two of the exercises suggested in the paragraphs above and look for a way to improve your semester planning, your weekly planning, or your daily planning. Again, it is critical that you tailor those exercises in such a way that you make them your own. You might choose to organize your weekly plan using a different scheme or you might choose to use technology like an electronic calendar or organizer to actualize your plan. Failure to plan amounts to planning to fail. This is the time to experiment with something that will improve your time planning.

Assess Your Weekly Plan

Because it is unlikely that you will get your planning absolutely right the first time, it is important for you to assess the outcome of your time management experiment. Assess the effectiveness of your weekly time management plan on or around mid-semester. How closely have you been able to adhere to your schedule? Have you allocated enough time for homework? Are there new commitments that need to be integrated into the plan? What adjustments could you make to your schedule? Are you spending enough time during the day on your studies? If necessary, create a new weekly time management plan that meets your needs.

Examine Other Plans

Find three people whom you believe are good time managers. They could be students, faculty, staff members, co-workers, friends, or family members. Interview them about their time management habits. How do they organize their commitments? How do they stay motivated to keep their schedules? What types of tools do they use (e.g. day planners, calendars, computer software, etc.)? Ask if you can examine their time management tools. What sorts of techniques and ideas can you incorporate into your time management plan? Write a brief summary report of your findings, and incorporate the helpful discoveries into your time management plan.

What Distracts You?

Keep a sheet of paper near you as you study. On the top of the page, write down the date, the time of day, and the location of where you are studying. Every time you find yourself distracted from your work, write the reason. Was it a phone call, a knock on your door, music down the hall, or a family member watching TV? Did you fall asleep? Did your own thoughts distract you from your task? Now, analyze and categorize your list of distractions. Knowing what distracts you is the first step in defeating them. Once you know your distractions, develop a plan to limit them.

Spiritual Reflection Journal

The Bible records many of the activities of Jesus. While most of this record reveals Jesus' teaching and preaching, it also records that Jesus spent his time doing activities that were necessary and healthy for a balanced life. Read the following Bible verses and write down the different types of activities in which Jesus engaged: Matthew 4:23, Matthew 8:23–24, Mark 6:31–32, Mark 14:32, Luke 5:29, Luke 6:12, John 4:6, and John 11:35. Now make a list of the different activities in life that call for your time. As you think about that list, consider how you have balanced your time. Write about where you have balanced your time well and where you feel a need to make adjustments.

Time in Prayer

In your personal time in prayer, consider praying for the following people and needs:

* For the ability to balance my time wisely

* For the ability to organize my time in a meaningful way

* For the motivation to stick to my time management plan

* For other students who may be struggling with managing their time effectively

* For change in my procrastination habits

* For a sense of peace when I feel overwhelmed

On the Net

The Internet can be a helpful resource for you as you look for ideas to make yourself a more happy and successful student. Visit the College Success page offered by Thomson Wadsworth for web links that will help you grow further on this topic. Go to *www.success.wadsworth.com* and click on Resource Web Links. You may also find it helpful to visit the Academic Skills Center website at Dartmouth, *www.Dartmouth.edu/admin/acskills/success/time.html*. You can also check out the following websites for Christian perspectives on time management: *http://www.faithwriters.com/article-details.php?id=4923* and *http://www.crosscreekcc.org/studies/time_management.htm.*

Defining My Style of Learning

I praise you because I am fearfully and wonderfully made.

Psalm 139:14

- Why does my friend have an easier time learning in lecture classes than I?
- What is my preferred style of learning?
- How can I use my dominant learning style to become more successful?

*T*HE DESIRE TO EXPLORE our world and to understand its complexity is found in every child that is born. We may not be curious about exactly the same things, but we all have a curiosity about our world that fuels our desire to learn. Why is the sky blue? How were the pyramids built? Why did my friend act the way she did? What happens to people when they die? Ever since their creation, humans have pursued questions like these. And the pursuit of those questions over time has produced a collection of answers that fills the books and articles accessible in any college library where curious people can work to find answers to their own questions.

God created people not only with this desire to learn but also with unique ways of learning. These are often called learning styles. Some of your fellow students would rather explore questions about the world using *words* while others would prefer to learn by *pictures*. One of your friends may be able to look at a graph and instantly interpret its value while another may puzzle over the same graph for hours before obtaining the same insight. You may prefer to learn by quietly thinking over the question yourself while another would prefer to talk about it in a small group. The same God who created humans with a questioning mind also created those same people with diversity in how they prefer to pursue answers.

Imagine that you have just purchased a vacuum cleaner. You bring it home and need to assemble the vacuum cleaner before it can be used. You open the box and remove the contents. What would be your next move? Check the box that describes your most likely course of action.

☐ I would read and follow the written instructions.
☐ I would study the diagrams and look at the picture on the box.
☐ I would pick up each of the pieces and assemble them by trial and error.

Although you may use each of these techniques at some point in the assembly process, chances are you have a certain preference for the way you would complete this task. There is no right way or wrong way to assemble the vacuum, but there is your preferred way.

In a small way, this exercise illustrates the unique way that God has fashioned you and how you prefer to learn. The role of this chapter is to deepen that insight so that you may learn more about your learning preferences and how you may use that knowledge to improve the quality of your work. It is certainly possible to learn and grow as a college student without a formal awareness of your learning style. But successful students typically know something about their learning style and know how to use it to their advantage both in and out of the classroom.

Initial Impressions of My Learning Style

Just as we are different on the outside from one another, so also are we different on the inside. Just as there is no "right" way to look on the outside, so there is no "right" way to learn. Consequently, this chapter is not about checking the correctness of your learning style but about exploring the way you learn more naturally. The learning style we are going to investigate is your preferred way of studying the world and of sharing what you have learned with others.

One way that internal difference becomes apparent is when you identify the type of exam you would prefer to take. Would you rather take a multiple-choice test or an essay test? In the box below, explain your choice in two or three sentences. When you have finished with your answer, pair up with another member of your class who selected the other type of exam and compare your answers.

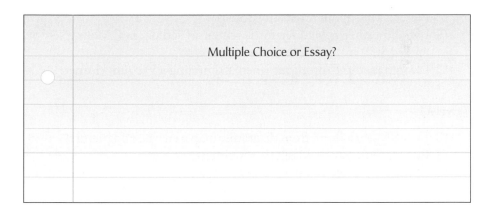

Multiple Choice or Essay?

Your answer gives you another clue about your preferred method of learning. If you prefer multiple-choice tests (or similar types) you are someone who feels more comfortable working in the world of facts and concrete examples. If you like essay tests, you prefer to move beyond the facts to the theory and abstract ideas behind them. Just because you are more theory driven does not mean you are unable to take a multiple-choice test. But it does mean that you will need a prepare for such an exam in a way that feels less intuitive and natural if you are going to be prepared.

Verbal, Visual, and Kinesthetic Modes of Learning

There are many ways to assess your learning preferences, but one way is to consider which mode of learning is more natural for you: verbal, visual, or kinesthetic. As you completed the exercise with the vacuum cleaner, you may have noticed that we offered options that appealed to each of these modes of learning. The typical student will employ all three modes of learning during any one month of school but will feel more natural using one or two of the following modes of learning. Check the statements that best describe you.

VERBAL

- ☐ I usually remember what I read or write down.
- ☐ I like to listen to my instructors talk.
- ☐ I would rather call someone on the phone than write a letter.
- ☐ I like talking about interesting topics.
- ☐ I would rather have directions written in sentences ("Make a left on Spring St.") instead of drawn on a map.
- ☐ I would read the directions when assembling a vacuum cleaner.

VISUAL

- ☐ I usually learn more from diagrams, maps, charts, and pictures.
- ☐ I would rather have a map than written directions.
- ☐ I usually remember what my instructor projects on the screen during class.
- ☐ I like textbooks with lots of colors and pictures.
- ☐ I like to put jigsaw puzzles together.
- ☐ I like to figure out mazes.
- ☐ I would rely on the diagrams to assemble a vacuum cleaner.

KINESTHETIC

- ☐ I like working with my hands.
- ☐ I enjoy classes that have a lab.

☐ I like to move around when I study.
☐ I like teachers who have us move about the room instead of sitting or standing in one place.
☐ I learn more by doing than by listening.
☐ I would assemble the vacuum cleaner by trial and error—putting the pieces together that seem to fit.

The exercise above will help you discover more about the modality of learning you prefer. Where did you place your checkmarks? Your approach to learning may be more balanced or may suggest a strong preference for one learning mode. In either case, check out the description of each learning mode that follows and read the suggestions below to see how you may exploit your preferred learning mode(s).

VERBAL LEARNERS

Verbal learners usually learn better with written or spoken language. They enjoy discussions and prefer verbal explanations and directions. Students strong in verbal learning also tend to take in more information by reading. Many college classes favor a verbal learner because many teachers rely on lecturing, class discussions, and reading assignments. If you believe you are stronger in the verbal area here are things you can do to help you study.

* Rewrite your notes so they are clearer.
* Create outlines for reading material.
* Recite your notes out loud.
* Discuss the class material with a peer or in a study group.
* Teach the material to another person.
* Ask someone to quiz you from your notes, study guides, or textbook questions.
* Rewrite your class notes while adding notes from the textbooks.
* When learning mathematic or scientific formulas, write out or talk through the steps in order ("First, do the necessary computations within the parentheses").

VISUAL LEARNERS

Visual learners usually learn better with information presented visually, as in pictures or images. Students stronger in visual learning are drawn to videos, films, maps, charts, diagrams, tables, and other types of visual presentation. If you believe you are stronger in this area, here are things you can do to help you study.

- Examine the diagrams and charts in your textbooks, add additional information to them, or redraw them in your notes.
- Think about how you can translate verbal information into visual pictures. For example, rewrite conceptual information using mind maps (see the chapter on taking notes) and historical information with time lines. If you have a list of statistical information like percentages, draw a pie chart.
- Highlight your notes and textbooks with different colors that are coded for specific information (for example, yellow for important facts or concepts, green for new vocabulary words, blue for definitions).
- Lay out your notes on your desk or post them on a wall to study them. Visualize the location of information on your desk top or wall when taking an exam.
- If you are trying to learn a sequence of steps or process, draw boxes around each concept and connect each step with an arrow. Visualize the boxes in your mind as you study and take a test.
- Create multicolored flash cards and use symbols and pictures on the cards.

KINESTHETIC LEARNERS

Kinesthetic learners usually learn better when they are physically moving about or actively doing as they learn. Students who favor kinesthetic learning are drawn to laboratory work, field work, demonstrations, and other types of "hands-on" activities. If you believe you are stronger in the kinesthetic area, here are things you can do to help you study.

- Recite your notes out loud while moving about your room.
- Create flash cards and study them while pacing. Be sure to recite the information out loud.
- Teach the material you are studying to another person. Use a chalkboard or large sheet of paper in order to write or draw some of the information for your "student."
- Draw mind maps or pictures to accompany your notes.
- Learn critical information by creating outlines, mind maps, or pictures on a chalkboard, whiteboard, or large sheets of paper.

For the sake of simplicity, we have discussed the learning modalities above as if they existed in isolation from one another. In reality, while favoring one style, you have the ability to learn by experiencing life in all three modes. Try the suggestions above that fit your learning style preferences. If you are a visual learner, use visual techniques to study. But remember that this is only a preference. Do not hesitate to experiment by tapping into various modes of learning. Try using some verbal and kinesthetic learning techniques to supplement your dominant preference. We believe that you will find learning information with a variety of techniques will create a more interesting learning experience and help you strengthen your retention.

"Professor Smith is driving me crazy . . ."

D O YOU FIND YOURSELF frustrated in a class and do not know why? Maybe your instructor's teaching style is at odds with your learning style. Instructors have a tendency to teach the way they learn. If you are a visual learner in a class with an instructor who only lectures, you probably feel a bit frustrated. It is critical at times like these to design personal study time that translates the material into a learning mode that is more amenable to your style of learning. Find a student in the class who is having similar difficulties. Together, you may be able help each other "translate" all the verbal information into a visual format that is easier for you to grasp. In this case, you might also consider asking the verbal learners in the room to help you identify the key concepts that you might not identify as quickly.

Learning Styles and Personality Type

Another way in which to investigate our preferences for learning is by examining the unique personality that God has given to each of us. In this portion of the chapter, you will be able to explore your learning style by studying the personality types described in the work of Isabel Briggs Myers and Katharine Briggs.[1] They developed a personality inventory based on Carl Jung's theory of psychological types. This inventory explores four aspects of personality preferences that combine to form sixteen distinct personality types. The

---

[1] Isabel Briggs Myers, *Gifts Differing: Understanding Personality Type* (Palo Alto, CA: Davies-Black, 1980).

following exercise is based on these personality preferences as they are related to learning styles. You will discover things like whether you prefer to work in groups or individually, whether you like to make decisions based on fact or feelings, or whether you prefer to plan or be spontaneous.

In the extended exercise that follows, you will be introduced to four scales with opposite personality poles. As you consider each scale, you will be asked to identify which of the opposite poles more accurately describes your current personality. Please do not feel that there is one side of the scale that is more appropriate than the other. Your success as a college student is not based on which side of the scale you find yourself. The "right answer" is the one that best describes you.

EXTRAVERT/INTROVERT SCALE

The first scale reveals where people like to focus their energy and attention. Some prefer the inner world of thoughts and ideas, while others prefer the outer world of people and action. Of course, we all function in both worlds, but we tend to have a preference for one or the other.

Extraverted people like to focus their energy on the outer world of people and activities. Are you outgoing and talkative? Do you like working with people? Do you feel energized at a party? Do you like to relax by talking with a group of friends? If you have a problem, are you most likely to "talk it out" with a trusted friend? Then you are probably an extravert. Extraverts focus on the world around them and enjoy interacting with the people in that world. Extraverts also draw on that energy from the outer world in order to "recharge" themselves. For example, extraverts will probably seek out a group of friends or make some phone calls when they need a study break.

Introverted people like to focus their energy on the inner world of thoughts and ideas. They are refreshed by time spent alone in quiet places. Do you enjoy quiet times and relaxing by yourself? Would you be more likely to ponder and think through a problem than discuss it? Would you prefer to work alone rather than in a group? Are you bothered by interruptions? You may be an introvert. Although introverts certainly like people, they usually prefer to work or study quietly by themselves. Introverts are not shy, as some may mistakenly believe. They "recharge" by spending time alone or engaging in mental activities rather than social interaction.

As stated previously, you are likely to be a blend of both introversion and extraversion, but one of these two preferences will be stronger than the other. Estimate what percentage of your personality is more extraverted and what percentage is more introverted. Combined they should total 100%.

EXTRAVERTED (E) _____ %

INTROVERTED (I) _____ %

On the left side of the circle below, place either an E (extraverted) or I (introverted) to reflect the higher percentage from the scale above. Place that percentage value in the lower right segment of the circle.

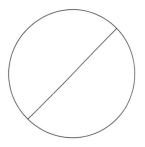

SENSING/INTUITIVE SCALE

The next scale expresses your preference for acquiring information. We all gather information that helps us understand our world and manage our lives within it. But we have different preferences for the way we gather information and the value we place on the information-gathering process.

Sensing people like to work with the facts that they have obtained from their five senses. Do you prefer to deal with present and concrete information like facts and figures? Do you see yourself as being practical? Are you good with details? Do people describe you as realistic? You are probably a sensing individual. Sensing people can engage in theoretical discussion, but they prefer the world of facts. They tend to place more importance on the information they gain from their experiences in the sensory world, value common sense, and realistic expectations. Sensors trust information that is based on concrete data drawn on what they hear, see, feel, or touch.

Intuitive people prefer to deal in the world of ideas. Do you enjoy a discussion about an abstract, philosophical concept or theory? Do you move quickly from the bare facts to their relationship to one another? Do you tend to look for the "big picture" and spend less time on the details? Do you have a tendency to think ahead to future possibilities and pursue nontraditional rather than traditional solutions to problems? You might be an intuitive person. Intuitive types understand details and facts, but prefer to find the relationships and meaning beyond the facts. They may gather information via their senses, but they tend to trust their intuition and will try to find the meaning beyond the data.

Again you are likely to see a bit of both the sensing and intuitive personality in you, but one of these two preferences will be stronger than the other. Estimate what percentage of your personality is more sensing and what percentage is more intuitive. Combined they should total 100%.

SENSING (S) _____ %

INTUITIVE (N) _____ %

On the left side of the circle below, place either an S (sensing) or N (intuitive) to reflect the higher percentage from above. Place that percentage value in the lower right segment of the circle.

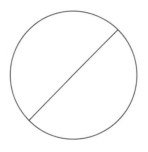

THINKING/FEELING SCALE

The third dimension reveals your preference for making decisions. Like the differences in gathering information, we differ on how we use that information to make a decision. The thinking/feeling scale shows the way we prefer to make decisions.

Thinkers prefer to make decisions based on logical analysis. Do you make decisions after carefully collecting and weighing all the facts? Do you try to remain objective when making a decision? You are probably a thinker. Thinkers obviously have emotions and feelings like everyone else. They just allow feelings a diminished role and prefer to base their decisions on facts and evidence. Thinkers place a high value on fairness and logic. They try to be objective and carefully analyze all the aspects of situation before making a decision that passes the test of being both logical and fair.

Feelers prefer to make decisions by considering values and emotions. Do you usually make decisions based on how you feel or how others may be impacted by your decision? Do you try to maintain harmony with those around you? You are probably a feeling type. Feelers take into account the logic and facts of a decision. However, the facts are a secondary consideration behind their own emotional cues. This does not mean that feelers are overly emotional or irrational. But they will place a premium on the personal consequences of a decision.

We all blend both the thinking and the feeling qualities as we make decisions, but one of these two preferences will be stronger than the other. Estimate what percentage of your personality is more the thinker and what percentage is more the feeler. Combined they should total 100%.

THINKING (T) _____ %

FEELING (F) _____ %

On the left side of the circle below, place either a T (thinking) or F (feeling) to reflect the higher percentage from above. Place that percentage value in the lower right segment of the circle.

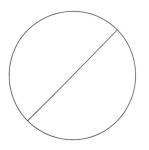

JUDGING/PERCEIVING SCALE

The last scale reveals your preference for designing your daily activities. Again, we are likely to be a blend of the following types. As you read the following, think about how you prefer to plan your life as a college student.

Judgers prefer to plan and approach life in a very organized way. Do you prefer structure to your day and week? Do you like organizing information and making concrete plans? Do you set goals and try to stick to them? Do you make lists of things to do? Do you have a carefully organized work space and closet? Do you have a calendar that keeps track of your assignments? Do you complete tasks you begin? Judgers like to live in an orderly world. They make plans and stick to them. When judgers have to make a decision, they are happy when the decision is made and will follow through with a plan to implement the decision. They often feel a strong sense of satisfaction at the completion of a project they have planned.

Perceivers like flexibility and spontaneity. Do you like to experience life without feeling the need to plan your day? Do you like to "go with the flow?" Do you put off decisions while you continue to gather information? Do you struggle with procrastination? Do you see yourself as flexible? Do you resist organizing your work space or closet? Do you find it easy to leave tasks uncompleted? Perceivers often feel unduly constrained when asked to live by a daily or weekly plan. They like the spontaneity of life and can handle changes or unusual circumstances without much problem. Perceivers like to gather a lot of information before making a decision and may feel tension if forced to make a decision before they feel ready. They often feel satisfaction when starting new projects, but because of their reluctance to create a schedule and their propensity to procrastinate, projects may be rushed, late, or forgotten completely.

Think about this dimension as it relates to your life. Again, you are likely to demonstrate a blend of both judging and perceiving traits, but one of these two preferences will be stronger than the other. Estimate what percentage of your personality is more judging and what percentage is more perceiving. Combined they should total 100%.

JUDGING (J) _____ %

PERCEIVING (P) _____ %

On the left side of the circle below, place either a J (judging) or P (perceiving) to reflect the higher percentage from above. Place that percentage value in the lower right segment of the circle.

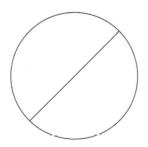

Now it is time to bring this information together. In the circles, you have placed a letter that represents your preference in each of the four scales noted below. Collect the letters from the four circles and enter each letter on the lines below.

_____	_____	_____	_____
E-I	S-N	T-F	J-P

This is how you see yourself at the moment. No personality is without strengths and weaknesses, so we can explore how your preferences impact the success of your learning. Examine the following box for possible strengths and weaknesses of your personality type.

Strengths and Weaknesses of the Types[2]

	Possible Strengths	*Possible Weaknesses*
Introvert	is independent	avoids others
	works alone	is secretive
	reflects	loses opportunities to act
	works with ideas	is misunderstood by others
	avoids generalizations	dislikes being interrupted
	is careful before acting	
Extravert	interacts with others	needs people to work
	is open	needs change and variety
	acts, does	is impulsive
	is well understood	is impatient with routine
Intuitor	sees possibilities	is inattentive to detail
	works out new ideas	is inattentive to practical matters
	works with the complicated	is impatient with the tedious
	solves novel problems	loses sight of here and now
		jumps to conclusions

(continued)

[2] Adapted with permission from Gardner, J. N. & Jewler, A. J. *Your College Experience: Strategies for Success.* Belmont, CA: Wadsworth, 2000, pp. 71–72.

Sensor	attends to detail	does not see possibilities
	is practical	loses the overall picture in details
	has memory for details/facts	mistrusts intuition
	is patient	is frustrated with complexities
	is systematic	prefers not to imagine future
Feeler	considers other's feelings	is not guided by logic
	understands needs, values	is not objective
	is interested in conciliation	is less organized
	demonstrates feelings	is overly accepting
	persuades, arouses	
Thinker	is logical and analytical	may not notice other's feelings
	is objective	misunderstands other's values
	is organized	is uninterested in conciliation
	has critical ability	does not show feelings
	is just	shows less compassion
	stands firm	
Perceiver	compromises	is indecisive
	sees all sides of issues	does not plan
	is flexible	does not control circumstances
	decides based only on data	is easily distracted from tasks
	is not judgmental	does not finish projects
Judger	decides	is stubborn
	plans	is inflexible
	orders	decides with insufficient data
	makes quick decisions	is controlled by task or plans
	remains with a task	wishes not to interrupt work

You and Your Instructors

Now that you are more aware of your own personality profile, see if you can guess the personality style of your instructors. They may have taken a similar personality inventory and can tell you what their own results were. But it is more likely that you will have to investigate their personality based on the evidence they have given you. Check out the syllabus and the classroom presentations of your teachers. Is this instructor more introverted or extraverted, sensing or intuitive, feeling or thinking, judging or perceiving? If your roommate says that she absolutely loved the professor that you find nearly intolerable, it may be because the personality style of your roommate and that instructor match more closely than your own. And that leads to some interesting facts about college students and those who teach them.

Research from the Center for Applied Psychological Type[3] (CAPT) indicates that first-year college students tend to be about evenly mixed between extraverts and introverts, but that college faculty are more likely to be introverts. In the general United States population, CAPT research indicates that sensing types make up about 65 to 70% of the population. This statistic seems to be fairly representative of most first-year college classes as well. Curiously, CAPT reports that the majority of college faculty are intuitive types. What is more, college faculty are also more likely to be judgers rather than perceivers.

Do not despair if you think you are feeling at odds with your instructors. First, you should note that the personality preferences revealed in the Myers-Briggs model only focus on four aspects of our personalities. There is much more complexity to our human natures than those four dimensions can reveal. What is more, having differing preferences on this measurement does not mean you cannot learn from that instructor. Also be aware that the personality preferences on these four scales are not cut into stone. We all change and grow. Having a professor with a more extraverted personality teaching you as an introverted personality may cause you to explore new ways of interacting and make you a stronger person in the process. In the same way, if you are a strong sensor, a highly intuitive instructor can provide you with opportunities to hone your conceptual and creative thinking skills.

Your God-given curiosity about life will continue to drive you in pursuit of new knowledge. And as you raise and pursue questions about your world, you will be using your preferred modes of learning and a learning personality

---

[3] *Estimated Frequencies of the Types in the United States Population* (Gainesville, FL: Center for Applied Psychological Type, 1996).

that is part of your learning style. Knowledge is power. The more you know about your personal learning style and the more you look for ways to exploit that knowledge, the more successful you will be as a college student.

Exercises for Success

Applying What I Know about My Learning Style

Throughout this chapter, you have been gathering information about your learning style. It is now time to put that information to work. Using the material from the chapter, describe what you have learned about your learning style. Which learning modes did you favor? What did the four scales teach you about your learning personality? Where does your learning personality favor your success as a college student and where do those habits threaten your success? Complete each of the sentences below to gain a clearer understanding of what you have learned.

My personality preferences and learning type is . . . .

When it comes to learning, I believe my greatest strengths are . . . .

When it comes to learning, I believe my greatest weaknesses are . . . .

Fitting My Style to My Classes

It is vital that you think critically about how your learning style will function in each of your classes. How has the instructor designed the class? Does the instructor's presentation favor a visual, verbal, or kinesthetic mode of learning? Does the class favor an extraverted learner or an introverted learner? Does the class require that I deal more with ideas or concrete facts? How does my preference for making decisions and organizing my life impact my ability to be successful in this class? Once you have answered questions like these, write out three specific techniques that you can use when studying for that class. Keep in mind both your learning style and the nature of the class.

Class:

The class presentation favors . . . .

The exams in this class favor . . . .

Because of the nature of this class, I plan to use the following techniques:

1.

2.

3.

Spiritual Reflection Journal

As God designed the very unique person that you are, he did not do so serendip-
itously but very purposefully. He designed you to fit in the world in a way that no
one else could. One of the goals of that unique design is to forward the message
and cause of the church. Read 1 Corinthians 12. What unique gifts do you have
that will advance the church of Christ?

Time in Prayer

In your personal time in prayer, consider praying for the following people and needs:

- For an understanding of your learning style
- To praise God for the unique person he has made you
- For the ability to successfully apply your learning style in your classes
- For a love for learning
- For wisdom
- For insights on the gifts you have for advancing the church
- For your instructors who can help guide your learning

On the Net

The Internet can be a helpful resource for you as you look for ideas to make yourself a more happy and successful student. Visit the College Success page offered by Thomson Wadsworth for web links that will help you grow further on this topic. Go to *www.success.wadsworth.com* and click on Resource Web Links. If you would like to investigate more how personality inventories can help you, visit the following websites.

www.keirsey.com.

www.metamath.com/lsweb/dvclearn.htm

www.rrcc-online.com/~psych/LSInventory.html

www.clat.psu.edu/gems/Other/LSI/LSI.htm

www.capt.org

Chapter 5

Pursuing Careful Thought

A simple man believes anything, but a prudent man gives careful thought to his steps.

Proverbs 14:15

* What does it mean to think well?
* How can I use my college experience to improve my thinking?
* What is critical thinking and how can I develop it?

*T*HERE IS A TIME for faith that is sure of what is hoped for and confident about what is not seen (Heb 11:1). God calls us to use such faith when he tells us that he is both three and one at the same time. This math stands outside the bounds of every human experience and defies all attempts at logical explanation. Yet in faith, we take God at his word. However, this call to faith is not a call to be gullible. God does not expect us to believe everything we are told. If the high school student delivering pizza to your residence hall room asserts that he is really the owner of the entire food chain, you would do well to be skeptical of the claim. The call of the Christian is not a call to stop thinking nor is it a call to abandon the quest for better thinking. In this chapter, we will see that the Bible not only contains examples of effective thinking but also contains the challenge to think carefully. "A simple man believes anything, but a prudent man gives careful thought to his steps." (Prov 14:15)

This axiom from Proverbs not only sheds light on your personal life but also illuminates the value of college in your pursuit of a career. The reason that certain careers are open only to college graduates and the reason that college graduates receive a higher wage for those kinds of careers is intimately linked to the fact that college, by design, produces better thinkers. While much of your formal learning to this point has been more about memorizing "facts" and returning them to your teacher for a reward, your college education will be about much more than that. For what is regarded as a "fact" in one generation of learners can quickly become a "falsehood" for the generations that follow. For example, there was a time in history when students like you were taught that human flight was impossible, that women were not capable of voting, that Native Americans needed to be civilized, and that computers would never replace the typewriter. In a world where the "facts" are edited so frequently, well-educated people will pursue thinking skills well beyond rote memorization so that they can be effective in the board room, in the city council chambers, and in parent-teacher meetings.

If being smart is more than just the ability to memorize facts, then what is it? Who is the smartest one in the classroom? A young teacher came to realize that this weighty, philosophical question was already being discussed among the members of her first-grade class. The students all claimed to know who the smartest student was in the room. Can you guess to whom they quickly pointed? These first graders claimed that the smartest person in the room was the girl who always handed in her quiz first! Assuming that you believe there is more to it than that, how would you complete the following sentence?

The smartest person in the room is the one who . . .

A. Answers the question correctly.
B. Asks the best questions.
C. Thinks beyond the boundaries of the question.
D. Questions all of the answers.

If you are feeling frustrated by the question, you are already thinking well. Because the right answer to the quiz question is not A, B, C, or D, but is "all of the above." The most effective thinkers are those who know how to frame a question, how to pursue the answer to the question they raise, how to think beyond the boundaries of questions others have asked, and how to carefully evaluate traditional answers for potential problems and weaknesses.

Your college education seeks to improve your thinking in each of those arenas: content knowledge of the facts, logical organization of the facts, creative thinking that goes beyond the facts, and critical thinking that examines the credibility of the facts. In this chapter, we invite you to do some careful thinking about thinking by exploring each of the four components of effective thinking. For the more you know about what effective thinking is, the better you will understand the goal of your college education and the individual assignments that are designed to improve the quality of your thinking.

Know the Facts

Effective thinking starts by knowing the facts as they are currently conceived. This process of learning the basics began long before you attended your first formal class in grade school. As you explored your world, you learned the relationship between pain and a hot stove as well as the social appropriateness of sharing your toys with others. Once you began your formal education, you began to meet more facts, long lists of "who," "what," "when," "where," and "why" facts in subjects like math and English. These basic facts have allowed you to function as a person balancing your checkbook, balancing your meals with food from each food group, and even reading the words on this page.

Being a college student does not mean that you will be free from increasing your knowledge of facts. It is assumed that well-educated people will have a grasp of even more "who," "what," "when," "where," and "why" facts than the average person who did not graduate from college. Of course, what facts should be taught to all college graduates is an ongoing debate in itself. But be confident that your college education will require you to know basic facts like the following.

The physics behind the operation of a lever

The grammatical components required in a well-formed English sentence

The rules that govern the balance of power between the legislative, judicial, and presidential offices of our government

The name of the waterway that links the Great Lakes with the world

The English meaning of words in your French class' vocabulary list

The location of the Sistine Chapel and the artist who painted its ceiling

The dates of the Civil War

The difference in musical value between a half-note and a quarter-note

The difference between modern and postmodern models of truth

Your school is full of specialists in areas like theology, art, politics, biology, physics, and literature. As you meet them in your general education classes and eventually in your major courses, they will expect you to learn the basic jargon used in their discipline and the truths currently held in their respective areas. As you are tested and evaluated, you will be asked to demonstrate an advanced knowledge of "who," "what," "when," "where," and "why."

This dimension of thinking that challenges you to remember certain important facts is reflected in a variety of Bible stories, but one stands out in particular. When God was ready to bring the Children of Israel out of captivity in Egypt following ten dramatic plagues, he established an annual festival, the Passover, which was associated with this event. This festival required the worshipers to reenact a portion of deliverance known as the Exodus from Egypt. Read Exodus 12 and you will see that the meal they ate, the way they ate the meal, and how they dressed during the meal were all choreographed to review the "facts" of the Exodus. God expected the younger children who participated in this ceremony to ask questions about this unique family behavior. The answer to their questions would bring the details of the Exodus to life in a new generation (Exod 12:26). Facts remain important. Good thinkers, careful thinkers are those who know those important facts.

Logically Organize the Facts

The second component of effective thinking is the logical thinking that organizes facts in a meaningful way. That organization may take the form of placing items in chronological order or of placing items together that have a similar theme or quality. It may mean determining the relative importance of facts or their degree of intensity, allowing them to be placed into a hierarchy. It may mean organizing an experiment into certain steps that must follow in order. Or it may mean deciding how best to design the structure of an oral presentation so that it may be more easily grasped by the audience.

Your college education will give you plenty of practice in improving your logical thinking skills. For example, learning a second language is one way for you to improve your ability to think logically. As you study the way another culture carefully structures its communication, you will come to a fresh appreciation of the unique way in which thoughts are structured and communicated in your first language. In a Bible history class, you may be asked to learn the chronological relationship of various Bible stories. Did the story of Noah come before or after the story of Abraham? In a political science class, you may participate in a formal debate that calls for the use of logic in defending your views on campaign finance reform against those who hold a contrary view. In a lab session, you may be asked to observe the reaction of various metals as an electric current is applied to them and then draw logical conclusions from your observation. And each time you are asked to write a research paper, you will practice the art of carefully organizing that presentation so that it pleases the reader with a logical and coherent flow. In these ways, college classes and assignments will give you many opportunities to improve your logical thinking skills.

When reading your Bible, you will see many examples of people demonstrating logical thinking skills. Consider the Apostle Paul. During one of his missionary trips, Paul found himself in Athens as he shared the Gospel with its residents (Acts 17:16–34). When Paul delivered his message in that city, he began a conversation with a group of Epicurean and Stoic philosophers. Their interest in his teachings led to an invitation; Paul was to speak publicly at a meeting of the Areopagus where the latest ideas were publicly discussed and debated. Paul logically deduced that these were not individuals who had had previous contact with the Old Testament so his traditional approach used when teaching within the Jewish synagogue was not going to work in this context. In fact, he knew that if he claimed to bring a message from God to them that was completely disassociated from their culture, they would be quick to close their ears. Consequently, Paul begins his address by observing that the citizens of Athens must be very religious people given all the idols that lined their streets. "As I walked around and observed your objects of worship, I even found an altar with this inscription: TO AN UNKNOWN GOD. Now what you worship as something unknown I am going to proclaim to you."

(Acts 17:23) He preached the same message of forgiveness of sins, but logically framed it in a way that was more winsome for this new audience.

Creatively Think Beyond the Facts

Effective thinkers are those who know the facts and who can logically organize those facts in a meaningful way. But effective thinkers are also those who can creatively think beyond the facts, seeing and exploring possibilities and connections that others have failed to see. In order to achieve this level of creative thinking, it is necessary to defeat the inertia placed in our path by the demands of conformity and the demands of time. Creative thinkers are those who look at the question before them and then look through the question and beyond the boundaries of the question itself. Creative thinkers release themselves from the bondage of searching for only one "right answer" and even from the bondage of needing a question before they begin to search. What is more, creative thinking requires time that is not easily given by a culture that is in a hurry for quick and simple answers. During this extended time, creative thinkers practice strategic daydreaming that unlocks their mind's eye, allowing it to wander and rove to new and unique places. The creative thinker is the artist who takes a formless lump of clay and turns it into a sculpture that once only existed in his or her mind. Creative thinkers are inventors who play with problems and think where others have not thought before, giving us products like self-sticking notes and microwave ovens. Creative thinkers are problem solvers who think outside of the logical box to see solutions in places others do not.

This creative thinking is evident in inventors like Orville and Wilbur Wright, who took time to lie on the beach and watch sea gulls in flight. In doing so, they conceived of an airfoil design that would allow them to become the first humans to enjoy mechanically powered flight. This creative thinking is alive in the fingers of Maya Angelou as she reflects on life and turns those reflections into poetic verse. This creative thinking is alive in the mind of George Frederick Handel, who meditated on the Word of God and then brought it to life in music of "The Messiah."

You too can further develop this creative thinking ability by carefully living your daily life. Remember that creative thinking requires time. Walk a bit more slowly as you go about your daily routines. Observe things and relationships that might have gone unnoticed before. Try to see and think about things in ways you have not before. And remember that conformity can be the enemy of creative thinking. If everyone is doing their class presentation in the same way, make it a point of communicating what you have to share in a different way. Learn to play the guitar or another musical instrument and spend quiet time playing combinations of notes that no one before you has played. Set aside time for strategic daydreaming when you are writing a paper. Think about how you might approach the topic differently. What have others missed that you may see during your reflective time? And take classes that formally develop the creative dimension of your personality. An art class, an acting class, a music class, or a creative writing class can give you the opportunity to develop your creative side.

Perhaps the most striking example of creative thinking in the Bible is Solomon's judicial ruling when two women came to him with an infant boy. Both woman asserted that the child was her own son (1 Kings 3:16–28). Solomon knew that one of the women was lying but he had to discover a way to reveal the real mother of the child. After careful reflection, he gave his judgment, causing all those who heard it to gasp. "Cut the child in half and give each woman one half of the child." His creative thinking on this topic led to this unorthodox verdict, assuming that the compassion of the true mother for the child would reveal itself in the face of such an unthinkable verdict. He was right. Immediately after hearing this verdict, the real mother of the child was overcome with compassion and immediately withdrew her claim to the child. Once the true mother revealed herself in this way, Solomon then returned this child to his rightful home. This remarkable demonstration of creative thinking caused all Israel to stand in awe of Solomon.

Critically Question the Facts

The fourth dimension of effective thinking involves what we narrowly define as critical thinking. Critical thinking is thinking that questions the answers. It does not see the first answer to a question as a stopping place but as a temporary resting place. It is skeptical thinking that asks the even harder questions. Is the answer true? Does it make sense? Are there other alternatives that have not been considered? Does it work in application? Critical thinking probes the presumed answer with these kinds of questions to test its value and validity.

As a student, you will have increasing amounts of practice with critical thinking in your advanced course work. But even in your first semester, you may be asked to refine this dimension of effective thinking. For example, your professor may very well assign you a critical response paper in which you are to react to an assigned reading or to the views of a speaker. Be careful that you do not fall into the trap of writing a summary paper rather than a critical response paper. Such a paper will, of course, require you to briefly summarize the main points of the reading or speech, but your professor is asking you to do much more than that. He or she is asking you to critically evaluate what you have read or heard.

Critical Thinking

1. Identify the thesis.
2. Identify the evidence used to support the thesis.
3. Evaluate the truthfulness, validity, and value of the evidence.

Consider using the following model as an outline for completing this kind of assignment. First of all, identify the thesis statement within the reading or speech. This is more than a topic. It is the "point of view" or the perspective that the writer or speaker is taking on that topic. For example, you may be asked to listen to a speaker who is addressing the president's foreign policy in the Middle East. That is the topic of the speech. But you will need to isolate the thesis of the speech, the point of view on that topic. "The president's current plan for peace in the Middle East is flawed." That is a thesis statement.

The second step in the process is to identify the evidence summoned to support the thesis statement. That evidence will often become evident to you by turning the thesis statement into a "why" question. "Why is the president's current plan for peace in the Middle East flawed?" The speaker may argue that the president's plan is flawed because it is based on a misunderstanding of Middle Eastern culture. Or she may argue that the plan is flawed because it is not as aggressive as it needs to be. This sort of evidence that is provided in support of the thesis statement needs to be identified.

Once those arguments have been identified, the third step in the process requires that you evaluate the quality of the evidence being used to support the thesis statement. This is where the hard questions need to be asked. Is the evidence being presented true? If it is true, does it really speak in support of the thesis? Are there other explanations that the speaker has not taken into account? Docs the entire argument make sense when it is assembled as a whole? Any evidence of logical fallacies will undermine the argument and should be noted in your response paper. Your paper will need to honor the fact that most thesis statements are supported by a collection of arguments that vary in quality. Acknowledge those with merit and critique those that fail.

Logical Fallacies

LOGICIANS HAVE IDENTIFIED AND labeled a number of arguments that are inherently weak. Hence they are called logical fallacies. A sample of those logical fallacies is included below with the Latin names that are often used as shorthand for them.

FALSE CAUSE-EFFECT (*Post Hoc Ergo Propter Hoc*)

This fallacious argument assumes a direct causal relationship between two events that occurred at approximately the same time. For example, you may assert that your stomach cramps are being caused by food poisoning since the food you ate at the local restaurant did not taste like it usually does. You have taken two events that are correlated in time and assumed that they were causally related. But in the absence of other evidence, your stomach cramps may be caused by a case of the flu rather than food poisoning. Correlation does not always equal causation.

APPEAL TO AUTHORITY (*Ad Verecundiam*)

This fallacy is in play when the authority being used to support a thesis has questionable credentials as an expert on the thesis in question. For example, the plea from a nationally known athlete to use a certain type of sports shoe in an advertisement may be a legitimate use of that person's expertise. But why should I take that athlete's advice on the type of automobile to buy from the local car dealer?

APPEAL TO PITY (*Ad Misericordiam*)

The appeal to pity seeks to divert attention away from the evidence and instead asks the evaluator of the thesis to respond with mercy toward the presenter of the thesis for mercy's sake. The college student who cannot afford to fail his or her first-semester history class may seek to divert the professor's attention away from the evidence found in failed quizzes and exams and instead ask that he or she not be failed because it would affect the student's financial aid package for the next semester.

(continued)

APPEAL TO FORCE (*Ad Baculum*)

The appeal to force, like the appeal to pity, seeks to divert the evaluator's attention away from the evidence. But in this case, the evaluator is threatened with the consequences of not agreeing with the thesis. Unfortunately, the Christian church used such an appeal to force when dealing with Galileo in the seventeenth century. Using his telescope, Galileo was finding growing support for the theory of Copernicus that identified the sun, rather than the earth, as the center of the solar system. Feeling threatened by this evidence, the church condemned Galileo as a heretic and threatened to burn him at the stake if he did not retract his thesis.

AGAINST THE PERSON (*Ad Hominem*)

This fallacious attack on a thesis is really not an attack at all on the ideas of the thesis but on the person who is presenting them. It assumes that if you can discredit the messenger, you will then have discredited the message. This popular fallacy often takes the form of giving someone a label designed to discredit them. For example, if a Democratic candidate for governor comes up with a sound idea for dealing with unemployment, she may be attacked as being a "bleeding-heart liberal," a label that is designed to turn people against her argument without engaging the argument itself.

ARGUMENT FROM IGNORANCE (*Ad Ignorantiam*)

The argument from ignorance presumes that a thesis is valid as long as it has not been proved wrong. Even if there is no evidence to support the thesis, it claims to be correct in the absence of any evidence that defeats it. If this form of argumentation is allowed, then I may assert that the oddly shaped cloud in the sky is actually a UFO. I may not have any evidence to support my thesis, but I can claim it true so long as there is no evidence to deny it.

HASTY GENERALIZATION (*Dicto Simplicitur*)

This fallacy occurs when one draws a general conclusion from too few cases or exceptional cases. For example, it has been argued that college athletes should be paid since they make money for the university. This argument fails because while some universities make money from their athletic programs, the majority of universities do not. The argument fails because it is an inappropriate generalization.

This kind of critical thinking is also encouraged and illustrated in the Bible. The Apostle Paul traveled extensively, sharing the message of God with people throughout Asia and Europe. But of all the places that he stopped, he was particularly happy with the reaction of those in the Greek city of Berea. These members of the Jewish synagogue listened carefully to the ideas presented by Paul, but then thought critically about them. "Now the Bereans were of more noble character than the Thessalonians, for they received the message with great eagerness and examined the Scriptures every day to see if what Paul said was true." (Acts 17:11)

Sometimes the Bible also records the failure to weigh evidence carefully. Following the death of Solomon, his son Rehoboam became king of Israel. At Shechem during his coronation, the people complained about the tax burden Solomon had imposed on them and asked for tax relief. In forming his response to the people, Rehoboam received conflicting advice from his advisors. The elder members of his cabinet realized civil war was imminent and so encouraged King Rehoboam to give the citizens of his country tax relief in exchange for their loyalty. The younger men with whom Rehoboam had grown up encouraged him to give a rhetorical show of force that would threaten the people into submission. He followed the poorly contrived advice of the younger men, telling the people, "My father made your yoke heavy; I will make it even heavier. My father scourged you with whips; I will scourge you with scorpions." (1 Kings 12:14) Rehoboam's uncritical acceptance of this poor advice led to a civil war that divided this kingdom for centuries.

Effective Thinking Is a Symphony

For the sake of this presentation, we have broken down effective thinking into four parts: knowledge of facts, logical organization of facts, creatively thinking beyond the facts, and critically questioning the truthfulness of the facts. In reality, we do not think in these little compartments. Our thinking is a symphony in which the sound of individual instruments is not noticed in the grand synthesis of sound produced by the orchestra. Such thinking allows us to look at a declared fact in a number of different ways.

For example, let's take the case of the Italian navigator, Christopher Columbus. You may have been taught that he discovered American in 1492. Consider how this "fact" might be addressed by the careful thinker. It can be examined logically to determine if such a journey would have been possible given the technology of the fifteenth century. Did the construction of ships in this period permit such a journey? Would there have been room for sufficient supplies to make this kind of journey? What methods were available to navigate effectively on such a trip? In the end, the logical thinker could come to a conclusion on whether such a trip and such a discovery seemed plausible.

The declared fact could also be explored creatively by thinking beyond the mere details of the trip to explore the character of a person like Columbus. What kind of personality did it take for a man to captain a ship on such a voyage? How did this man manage a crew and keep them motivated for such an uncertain voyage? The creative thinker thinks beyond the details of the thesis to explore regions of the topic that had not been explored by previous inquiry.

And finally, the same fact can be explored critically by questioning the truthfulness of the statement. Although for many decades the activity of Columbus was called a "discovery," the appropriateness of that description itself can be called into question. Did Columbus discover America, did he happen upon it by chance, or did he invade America to the harm of those already living there?

Grow as an Effective Thinker

This effective form of thinking on a topic is already at work in your life. But what is good can become even better through repeated practice. Let me give you an analogy to consider. As a college student, I enjoyed playing tennis in the summer with a close friend. Tim was an excellent tennis player who went on to play tennis professionally for a time. On all the afternoons we played together, I never won a match. From time to time, I would win a game and once or twice I won a set. But I never beat him in a tennis match. Still I kept playing because I noticed something about my tennis game. As I played against a partner who was better than I, the quality of my play improved.

There is an analogy between the author's experience with Tim and your experience in college. Your school has hired people to teach your classes who are expert thinkers. As you listen to their lectures, as you take their tests, as they grade your papers, you will improve your thinking week by week. Just as playing tennis with someone who is better than you can improve your tennis game, so thinking with people who think well will improve the effectiveness of your own thinking. That is the positive way of viewing research papers, critical reaction papers, lab assignments, and essay exams. They are all chances to improve your thinking.

"A simple man believes anything, but a prudent man gives careful thought to his steps." (Prov 14:15) The same God who created us with the ability to think has also challenged us to think more effectively as we take our steps in this life. In a world where so much changes, you as the future leaders in your professional fields, as the future leaders of your country and communities, and as the future leaders of God's church would do well to become as effective in your thinking as you can.

Exercises for Success

Analogies

One way to see and practice your thinking skills is to practice word puzzles called analogies. Below you will find four examples from the guidebook for the Miller's Analogies Test. To answer them all correctly you will need to know certain facts, think logically, creatively, and critically. Look for a relationship between the first two terms and then seek to replicate that relationship on the second side of the double colon by choosing one of the words found within the parenthesis.

Light : Dark :: Pleasure : (Party, Sunlight, Pain, Eyesight)

Centrifuge : Mixture :: Prism : (Water, Spectrum, Light, Sound)

Green : Blue :: Red : (Orange, Yellow, Brown, Pink)

Swan : Butterfly :: Dive : (Fly, Sink, Stroke, Smell)

Answers:

Light : Dark :: Pleasure : Pain

As light is the opposite of dark so pain is the opposite of pleasure.

Centrifuge : Mixture :: Prism : Light

As a centrifuge divides a mixture so a prism divides light.

Green : Blue :: Red : Orange

Green is the product of adding the color yellow to blue, so orange is the product of adding yellow to red.

Swan : Butterfly :: Dive : Stroke

The swan is a type of dive and the butterfly is a type of swimming stroke.

In order to get each of the analogies right, you had to practice the four forms of thinking described in this chapter. Go back and determine which forms of thinking were necessary to answer each of the analogies above correctly and where weaker thinking blocked your progress in solving these word problems.

Box Challenge

Using only four straight lines and without lifting your pencil from the page, connect all of the following dots.

Answer:

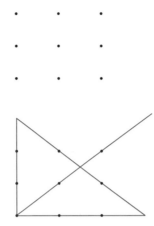

Had you assumed you needed to stay within the borders defined by the box of dots?

Creative Circle Sculpture

To work the creative side of the thinking process, make a copy of the circle below on a piece of cardstock. Cut out along the lines and color the shapes different colors. Place the shapes before you and manipulate them again and again to form figures that your mind has not yet seen.

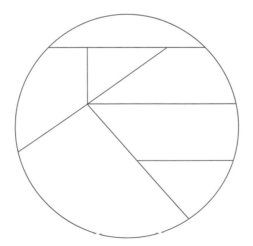

What Can You Do with That?

Another way to practice creative thinking is to think of uses for a common device that have not occurred to others. Take an everyday object like a paper clip in your hand. In three minutes, write down as many different uses for the paper clip as you can imagine. Of course, the obvious is for holding papers together. But what about using a paper clip as a screwdriver, as a twist tie, or as a hanger for Christmas ornaments? Have fun!

Critical Reaction to a Television Commercial

Television commercials are enacted thesis statements that seek to persuade you to purchase a product or service. Tape several television commercials and practice your critical thinking approach on them. Commercials in support of political candidates are particularly good. Identify the thesis of the commercial. Look for evidence presented that supports the thesis statement and then put that evidence to the test. Where does the logic fail in the evidence? Where do you see examples of logical fallacies at work?

Spiritual Reflection Journal

We have seen that effective thinking consists of knowing certain facts, thinking logically, creatively, and critically. When the Apostle Paul was called before the Sanhedrin with his teachings on trial, we see him thinking in all four categories of effective thinking presented in this chapter. Read Acts 23:1–11 and point to places in this story where you see each of those four components of effective thinking at work.

Now think about your own life as a Christian thinker. Which dimensions of effective thinking have you practiced the most? Which dimension of thinking do you enjoy the most? Where do you see places that you can improve your thinking and how will you do it? How do you see improved thinking in your life strengthening your church?

Time in Prayer

In your personal time in prayer or in connection with others in your class, pray for the following people and needs.

- For your professors that they might carefully design classes and assignments that will improve your thinking

- For God's blessing on your growth as an effective thinker

- For God's direction in using your thinking as a tool that will glorify him and advance the Gospel message

On the Net

The Internet can be a helpful resource for you as you look for ideas to make yourself a more happy and successful student. Visit the College Success page offered by Thomson Wadsworth for web links that will help you grow further on this topic. Go to *www.success.wadsworth.com* and click on Resource Web Links. See also *www.criticalthinking.org/default.html.*

Engaging in the Classroom: Listening and Taking Notes

So Jeremiah called Baruch son of Neriah, and while Jeremiah dictated all the words the Lord had spoken to him, Baruch wrote them on the scroll.

Jeremiah 36:4

* Why should I take notes in class?
* How can I improve the quality of my listening?
* What system of note taking will work best for me?
* When and how should I review my notes?

*I*T IS TOO HARD to remember everything that is important to remember. That is why we take the time to write down the things that are most important to us. We write down the time and location of our intramural basketball game. We write down the date of the midterm exam in history class. And we write down the phone number of that special person whom we intend to ask out on a date.

God also had things written down that were important to him. Rather than just count on the memory of eyewitnesses and the reliability of oral communication, God inspired writers to record events, laws, speeches, and poetry meant for our comfort and growth. Thanks to those notes, we know how we can find release from our guilt, how we can live more successfully in a sin-ruined world, and how we may have hope for a better life in eternity. Baruch was one of the men whom the Lord selected to record the Word of God for us. It was his responsibility to write down the prophetic message of Jeremiah.

Like Baruch, you too will take notes on the important things that you see and hear in your college classes. Of course, the notes you take during your classes will not have the powerful impact of the Bible. But they will impact your personal success during college since they will help you organize and recall critical details from your classes. In this chapter we will discuss how you can become more active as you engage with the lectures, discussions, and demonstrations that fill your week in college. This discussion will include an overview of strategies that will help you improve your attentiveness during class, the quality of the notes you take, and the effectiveness of the review process. Since you have been taking notes in class for years, you might assume that you will have nothing to learn from this chapter. It is true that you are likely to be affirmed in many of the things you are already doing. But since college classes and college exams are different from the ones you have experienced before, this is a good time to experiment with new approaches and practices. Make it your goal to find something new in this chapter that will advance your habits in a meaningful way.

Why Take Notes?

It goes without saying that taking notes during a class is a distraction. Clearly, it would be better if we could just listen to and discuss the topic without the burden of also keeping a written record of key points. The problem with that is our inability to recall the key elements of a class session even one day after we have experienced it.

One solution would be to audio record the entire class so that you could just listen during the session and take notes from the recording later. This particular approach may work well in the occasional class that is more challenging for you. But in most instances, this strategy is far from desirable. The recording and listening process will literally double the amount of time you need to spend "attending" any one class session. Consequently, it would be much more desirable to have a means of recording the key components of a class session the first time you experience it rather than create the time management nightmare of "attending" the class session twice. If you do elect to record a class session, be sure to ask the permission of the instructor before doing so. Since the class presentation is the intellectual property of the instructor, he or she may have a policy that prohibits such recording.

So is taking notes really that important? Yes, until someone discovers a better solution, the traditional practice of taking notes is still the most effective way to defeat the inevitable forgetting that occurs following a class session. Consider the following statistics. Most people can recall about 50 percent of what they hear, if they are paying close attention to the speaker. After two days they can only recall half of what they originally remembered. In essence, after two days most people can only remember about 25 percent of a message.[1] Would you feel confident going into a quiz knowing that you may only be able to recall 25 percent of the instructor's lecture? While it would be very desirable to just listen and discuss the material during your week in college, notes and note taking are a reality that you will live with as a college student.

Be Attentive

Since note taking is an inevitable part of the college student's life, we will now explore what kind of notes and note taking will best meet your needs. This begins by evaluating the level of attentiveness you bring to the note-taking process. Your attention is connected to your attendance, your pre-class preparation, and your ability to stay focused during the class session.

ATTENDANCE

Your ability to be attentive during the class session will be impacted first by your attendance pattern. Your commitment to be in class and to be on time

---

[1] Michael P. Nichols, *The Lost Art of Listening* (New York: Guilford, 1995).

sends an important signal to the instructor about your level of commitment. What is more, on-time attendance is also critical to your first-hand knowledge of what was said and done in that room. You may already know students who elect to skip class and then rely upon the notes someone else has taken or the notes they obtain from the instructor's web site. By doing this, they have missed out on a key step in the learning process. First of all, there is no guarantee that the notes they borrow truly capture the essence of the session they have skipped. But even if they do, their experience with the class session will lack the animation and emphasis of the real thing. Using someone else's notes may be helpful to you when you have to miss a class. But those notes are a weak second to being there. If you want to have the best notes possible, be there and be on time.

PREPARATION

The second key to attentiveness is pre-class preparation. Your instructors will typically assign reading and exercises that will set the context for that day's class. Complete all reading assignments and exercises before coming to class. It may be that you will more easily understand the reading assignment after a lecture or discussion. However, we still recommend that you familiarize yourself with the topics before coming to class. The pre-class preparation will provide you with an understanding of key landmarks you may expect to meet on the way. Knowing the general direction of the lecture and understanding the main issues will help you stay focused on the material presented in class. You will take notes with greater understanding because the information is not entirely new to you. And you will have the opportunity to listen carefully during the lecture or discussion for a point that was unclear to you in the reading that might be clarified during the class session. The moments right before a class session may be used in a variety of meaningful ways. One of them is to review the key points from the reading to improve your attentiveness when the session begins.

STAYING CONNECTED

Then there is the matter of staying connected during class and avoiding "thought vacations" that take you off topic. Staying connected begins by acknowledging that there is a difference between listening and hearing. You can hear sounds like a clock ticking, cars rushing past an open window, or someone shouting your name across a crowded room. But listening is more than hearing sounds move through the air; it is about actively attending and

Would You Like a Partner?

ONSIDER ASKING ANOTHER STUDENT in class to be your note-taking
partner. This is not a tag-team event where you trade dates going to class,
but an opportunity for two people who were in the same class session to grow
from each other's experience. Here is how it may help you.

* A note-taking partner provides you with a safety net to ensure you do
  not miss important information from the session.
* It may motivate you to take more complete notes since you know that
  you will be comparing notes with your partner.
* It will provide you with an alternative for learning the class content, if you
  must miss class due to illness or a family emergency.
* It may lead to a weekly review session with your partner.
* It may lead to phone conversations or electronic conversations about a
  class session that sharpen your understanding.

engaging with the words that are spoken and the demonstrations that are
given.

Complete honesty demands that we admit this can be a problem. Even
when we are in class, have prepared for the session, and have committed ourselves to paying close attention, we can find our focus drifting away. One of
the reasons this happens is that there is a big difference between how much
information our brain can process compared to how much information can
be delivered in oral speech. The brain processes 400 to 800 words in a minute,
but most people speak at a rate of 120 to 150 words per minute.[2] The difference between the brain's processing time and the average speaking rate can
work to your advantage because it means you will physically be able to keep
up with your instructors. But it also presents a problem. Because your brain
can process information so quickly, the comparatively slow speaking rate
gives your brain "lag time" in which to wander. And with some speakers and

---

[2] Florence I. Wolff and Nadine C. Marsnik, *Perceptive Listening*, 2nd ed. (Fort Worth, TX: Harcourt Brace
Jovanovich, 1992).

some classes, all we need is a brief lag in attention to send us off on an extended thought vacation.

So what can you do in light of that reality? First of all, acknowledge that staying connected in class is a habit. And if you are in the habit of being less attentive during class, this is something you are empowered to change. Here are some ways in which you can edit poor listening habits if you truly want to make a change in your ability to pay attention during class.

- Say to yourself "I am going to actively listen now" when the instructor starts. This calls your attention to focus and prevents you from getting started on the wrong foot.
- Create several questions from the reading assignment. By keeping a list of questions on your desk top, your presence in class can become an active quest for the answers. If it appears that the lecture is leaving the topic without addressing your question, this is the time to raise your hand and ask the question out loud.
- As you think about the subject matter being discussed, try to anticipate the next points. What line of logic is the presentation following?
- If you disagree with something that is being said, make a quick note of it so that you can think about it later rather than allowing it to consume your attention space during the lecture. Be sure to listen to the entire message before you respond.
- If the subject matter is difficult or you feel your attention starting to slip, remind yourself that this class is important to your success. Briefly recall the goals you set for this class and push yourself to listen.
- Watch for changes in the instructor's enthusiasm, intensity, and the use of visual aids. These are clues that will direct you to lecture content that is particularly important to your instructor.

Proceed with a System

Apart from paying attention, effective note taking in college classes also means proceeding with a system for taking those notes. By now you have discovered that not every class is the same. Not only are college classes different from high school classes, one college class differs from the next. If you are going to take notes in classes that differ so widely from one another, it makes sense to have more than one note-taking system. Compare it to the toolbox you have in your car or at home. This box is filled with different types of tools because it will be used to address different kinds of repair. One repair may require a screwdriver, while another may require a hammer. You would not think of trying to make one tool do every repair, so it is a stretch to assume that one form of note taking will work in every class. Here we will consider the options you have and how they may apply to different classes. As you evaluate an individual class' subject matter and the teaching style of the instructor, and as you consider the various note-taking systems that may be modified to suit your needs, you will find just the right tool for the job.

OUTLINES

Outlines work well with instructors whose lectures are clearly organized into major and minor ideas that flow in an orderly way. If your instructor offers a main idea, then expands on the idea with more detailed minor points, try taking notes using an outline format as illustrated below. The advantage of taking notes in this way is that you can rely on the structure of the outline to recall the key points and their relationship. This will diminish the amount of writing you need to do and present a visually appealing structure that can aid you in recalling the lecture.

PARAGRAPHS

Not all lectures can be easily recorded using an outline. What is more, some people find the outline a less helpful review tool. When you have an instructor who likes to present a main theme and then discuss examples and ideas that relate to the theme, a paragraph format may work well for you. These notes do not have to be grammatically complete sentences. However, they should capture the main elements of the idea being presented. Leave lots of space within your notes if you choose this style. Later when you review your notes, you can add extra information or rewrite sections to make your notes clearer.

CORNELL RECALL COLUMNS

This system is based on the Cornell format developed by Walter Pauk.[3] For each page of your notes, draw a vertical line the length of the page three inches from the left edge of the paper. This will create two columns, one wider and one narrower. During class, take notes only on the wider, right side of the page. This is called the record column. After class when you are reviewing

---

[3] Walter Pauk, *How to Study in College*, 6th ed. (New York: Houghton Mifflin, 1997).

Example of an Outline

Topic: Narrative Criticism

Date: September 21, 2004

I. What Is Narrative Criticism?

   Narrative criticism is the careful analysis of the author's artful
   selection of content and form when telling a story.

II. What Components of a Story Need to Be Analyzed?

   A. The Plot

      The plot is the organizing principle of the story. It has a
      beginning, middle and ending.

   B. The Characterization

      Authors invite us to meet characters in a variety of ways.

      1. The character speaks.

      2. The character is spoken about.

      3. The character acts.

      4. The character's appearance is described.

      5. The character is named.

   C. The Shaping of Time

      1. Duration

      2. Sequence

your notes, reduce the notes from the right side of the page to single words, phrases, or questions. Place them in the smaller column on the left side of the page. The item in this recall column may become the memory hook that serves as a path to the fuller discussion. After studying the record column of your notes, cover the record column and use the recall column to quiz yourself on the main points. Can you recite the information that is covered?

Example of Paragraph Notes

Topic: Narrative Criticism

Date: September 21, 2004

What Is Narrative Criticism?

Narr. criticism =   careful analysis of the author's artful selection

of content and form when telling story

What Components of a Story Need to Be Analyzed?

Plot is organizing principle of story . . . a beginning,

middle + ending.

   Ex: David and Goliath—tension of Philistine invasion moves

to victory of Israelite army.

Characterization

   How? Watch for the character speaking, spoken about,

acting, appearance, and naming.

   Ex: Goliath—writer of I Sam 17 gives description of Goliath

and directly quotes Goliath as he speaks to David

Shaping of Time

   How? Duration and sequence of time.

      Ex: time slows to emphasize the speech and character

of David

VISUAL MAPS

A fourth format for taking notes can be used on its own or in conjunction with any of the methods described above. Sometimes the information presented in class may be easier to remember if you turn the data into something with more visual appeal. One way to do that is by creating a visual map. If the instructor leaps from one point to another and then backtracks to what was

Example of a Cornell Recall Column

Topic: Narrative Criticism	
Date: September 21, 2004	
Definition	Narrative criticism is the careful analysis of the author's artful selection of content and form when telling a story.
Components:	The components of a story that need to be analyzed:
Plot	The plot is the organizing principle of the story. It has a beginning, middle and ending.
Characterization	Characterization is achieved when . . . 1. The character speaks. 2. The character is spoken about. 3. The character acts. 4. The character's appearance is described. 5. The character is named.
Time	Time is shaped by duration and sequence of events.

said earlier, it can be difficult to take notes using an outline or paragraph format. So instead try recording the information using a visual map. When creating a visual map, you will place the theme or topic in the very middle of the page. Draw a circle or square around it using a heavy line or bold color. Whenever a new point is introduced you can add that point to the picture and

Example of a Visual Map

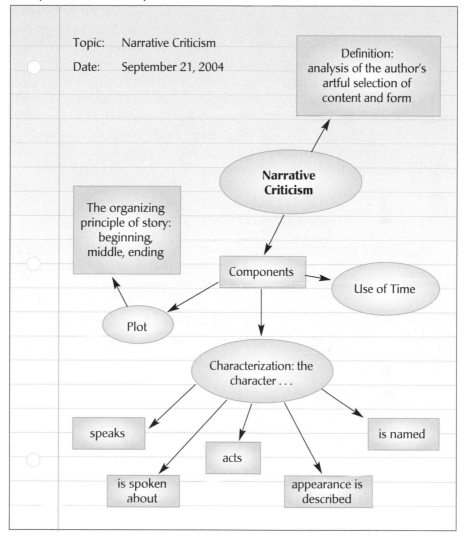

Topic: Narrative Criticism

Date: September 21, 2004

Definition:
analysis of the author's
artful selection of
content and form

**Narrative
Criticism**

The organizing
principle of story:
beginning,
middle, ending

Components

Use of Time

Plot

Characterization: the
character . . .

speaks

acts

is named

is spoken
about

appearance is
described

connect it with a line to the main point or one of the other subpoints you have
already put in place. In the end, your notes will look like a large spider web
with strands that connect various data to one another.

If you favor a learning mode that is more visual or kinesthetic, you may
find this a helpful way of turning a more verbal lecture into a picture that is

helpful for you. This is particularly the case if you experiment with various shapes and colors to differentiate between types or information or between information of various levels of importance. Some of our readers might feel hesitant to use this technique as their primary technique since it is so different from what they have done before. If that is the case for you, try converting some of your notes into a visual map as part of the review process. Nothing will be lost in the experiment and you may discover another tool that will function well for you in certain class settings. Remembering has much to do with seeing relationships, and visual maps easily illustrate relationships between concepts. Thus you may find yourself recalling information more easily when using a visual map rather than an outline or paragraph form.

GENERAL TIPS FOR ANY NOTE-TAKING SYSTEM

As you consider the various systems you may modify to meet the needs of your current classes, here are general tips that would be helpful and applicable to any general method you might select.

Always date your notes. Dating your notes leaves no doubt regarding the chronology of the information presented in class. This is particularly helpful if the pages of your notes get mixed up or if you miss a day of class. In the latter case, you will be able to easily identify which day is missing so that you can fill in the gap with a classmate's notes.

Write on one side of the paper. Writing on both sides of a piece of paper means that you must consult both sides of the paper when reviewing your notes. The greatest advantage to writing on just one side of the paper will come during the review process. If you write your notes just on one side of the page, you will be able to lay your notes out in front of you on a large surface and be able to see everything at once. This can be of great help to you when you are attempting to define a chronology or logical flow that would be interrupted by flipping the page. At times, you may even remember an item from your notes by its position on the tabletop.

Leave blank space. Always be generous with the blank space you leave in your notes. This will prevent your notes from feeling crowded even when you add additional insights you gain from a review session or when comparing your notes with those of another classmate.

Record information from boards, overheads, or computer-generated images.
Since the creation of visual aids takes time and energy, your instructor will
typically create these visual aids only for the important information. Make
sure you take note of them.

Ask if you do not understand something. Your education is important to
you and you deserve to understand all that you can. If the class session heads
in a direction that is not clear to you, ask for help either during class or after
class. You can even use electronic mail. As long as you do not fault the instructor for your failure to understand, you are likely to find the classroom leader
ready to help you in any way that he or she can.

Use a "lost" signal. If you get lost in class and are unable to complete a section of your notes, mark your notes so that you know where they are going to
be incomplete. The "lost" signal will remind you to recover what you had
missed either from the instructor or a classmate. Failure to mark such a location is a recipe for review frustation.

Develop your own shorthand. There are many words or concepts that will
repeat when you take notes in a class. Save yourself space and writing time by
developing shorthand symbols for commonly used words and concepts.

Record main ideas, not each word. Class lectures are typically structured to
have several major points with supporting evidence and examples. Your goal
in note taking should not be a word-for-word transcription of the lecture.
Instead, your goal is to record the main points of the class and any evidence
or examples that help you understand those main points. If you are having
trouble figuring out what to write, listen for important themes. At some point
in your college experience, you are likely to meet an instructor whom you
have difficulty decoding. This is the time when an informal study group, Sup-
plemental Instruction group, or note-taking companion can be of help to
you.

Should I use a laptop? Laptop computers are portable enough to take to
class, but there are advantages and disadvantages to their use during class. We
recommend that before you try taking notes on a laptop in class that you
practice transferring traditional notes you have taken to the computer. You
may find that pen and paper have some advantages that you will not wish to
lose.

Should I Take Notes Now? Yes!

L EARNING EXPERIENCES COME IN many shapes and forms. Just because today's class is not a traditional lecture hour does not mean that it is a good idea to leave your notebook in your backpack. Clearly, it is better to have notes that you might not need rather than realizing you need notes you do not have. The following are examples of learning experiences that your instructor may offer in connection with a college class. Do not be fooled into thinking this is "time off" when you can let your note-taking guard down.

- Guest speakers: People who are invited into a classroom generally bring some expertise, knowledge, or unique experiences to share. Note new concepts they bring to class and note how their perspective relates to what you have read and heard from your instructor.

- Videos or other electronic media: The information presented through videos could be brand-new information or examples that reinforce class readings and lectures. In either case, be sure to create a written record of those things that are important to you.

- Class discussions: Since college is about developing your communication skills as well as your listening skills, expect to be involved in group discussions. It may be more difficult to take notes and participate, but it is worth the effort. Pay particular attention to times when the instructor enters the conversation and expresses a criticism, compliment, or different point of view. Furthermore, if your instructor makes statements like "that is an excellent example of . . ." or "that is the key to . . ." be sure to note it. Those are verbal cues that your instructor finds those comments important.

- Lab experiments or demonstrations: Lab experiments and demonstrations provide hands-on experience for students. Keep your notebook within arm's reach to record any important information that can supplement your lecture notes.

- Student presentations: Some instructors involve students in the learning experience by assigning individual or group presentations. Take notes during these presentations just as you would if your instructor lectures.

- Field trips: Bring along some type of notebook that is easy to carry as you engage in out-of-classroom experiences. You never know when something memorable will be said on a field trip.

Taking Notes during Science and Math Classes

Taking notes in a math or science class is different from taking notes in a history or theology class. Math and sciences courses communicate more information through formulas, equations, graphs, charts, and pictures. Just the mere recording of the formula, equation, or picture may, in this case, not be enough to give you the understanding you seek. If you have math and science classes, we suggest the following.

- Be prepared: Complete all reading assignments before each class. Familiarize yourself with new vocabulary and new math or scientific symbols. Study examples of equations and formulas. This will give you a head start when they are used during class.
- Get a three-ring notebook: It is especially important that all your course materials stay organized. We suggest you use a three-ring notebook for math and science courses. This way, you will be able to keep handouts, your own class notes, and homework problems in one place and grouped by topic.
- Think big, write large: A page that is densely filled with marks is one that is less inviting to review. Give your eyes a break by writing larger and by leaving white space on the page. This is particularly true when recording diagrams, formulas, or pictures.
- Review previous material: Higher level math and science concepts usually build on basic information. If the foundation starts to erode over time, you will find it very hard to understand the advanced concepts. Refresh your memory by routinely reviewing the basics.

End with Review

Class is over and you have a set of notes in hand, but the most important part of the learning process still lies ahead, the review. It is vital to review your notes because this is where you will do the majority of the encoding that will secure the information in your long-term memory.

WHEN?

Since much of the lecture will be forgotten within a day or two, plan to do the first review of your notes within 24 hours of taking them. Designate review sessions into your time management plan if you have not done so already. Do not recoil too quickly from the idea because we are not talking about a significant block of time. Ten minutes per class session, set aside the same day the class has met, should do it. Even a busy schedule will be able to manage this brief review time to revisit the key points of the class. In addition to those brief sessions, we would recommend a longer period of time each week during which you review and assimilate the data from that week's class. We will have more to say on that topic when talking about exam preparation. But an early review coupled with regular review will beat cramming every time.

HOW?

You have produced a valuable study tool. But the real value of that tool will not be realized unless you design creative ways in which to revisit the material during your review time. If you have been in the habit of just rereading your notes, we could understand why the idea of reviewing your notes might seem a burden. Since you are in charge of how you use this time, make it as active, interesting, and diverse a time as you can. Here are a few suggestions that you can creatively combine and modify to meet your needs:

- Enter key words in the recall column of your notes and give yourself a quiz.
- Create a visual map to supplement the notes you took in class.
- Combine insights you obtained from the readings with your class notes.
- Recite your notes out loud.
- Try teaching what you have learned.
- After reciting them, try to describe the concepts in your own words without looking at your notes.
- Review foundation material for math and science courses.

Whatever you choose to do, make your review time an active learning time. And if you get bored with your routine, change it. You have the power to design this time in a variety of ways.

Baruch had an important job to do as he recorded the words of Jeremiah. Since his note taking was under the inspiration of the Holy Spirit, his notes could not be improved! That is not true of us. Since you will be taking notes every semester that you are in college, this is a great time to experiment with ways that could improve the quality of your work. Try out new techniques that allow you to improve your attentiveness in class. Experiment with a different system of taking notes, finding one that fits the style and content of each class. Then design a review plan that is both timely and interesting. Old habits are hard to change. But changing old note-taking habits can be very worthwhile since this change has the potential to improve your education across so many classes.

Exercises for Success

Stare and Compare

Pick a class that requires a lot of note taking. Ask three of your classmates for photocopies of their notes from one of the class sessions. Look at the product they have produced. When compared to your notes, did they record the same content? Compare their note-taking system to your own. How is it similar? How is it different? In which ways are their note-taking systems weaker or stronger than your own?

Defeating My Distractions

Not paying attention during class is a habit. You can blame the instructor, the class subject, or the person across the aisle, but the reality is your level of attention is also a habit. If you are in the habit of becoming inattentive during class, try the following exercise. Put a blank sheet of paper next to your notes on the desk. Put a check mark on the page every time you catch your mind wandering from the lecture. At first, you may have a lot of marks on the page because you do not realize how often you give in to distracting thoughts. But if you try this technique, you will find that the number of marks will decrease over time. By thinking more actively about where your attention lies during class, you will begin the process of defeating distractions.

Fit the System to Your Class

College classes differ from one another in terms of content, presentation technique, and testing. In this exercise, we challenge you to find a system of note taking and review that fits the uniqueness of each of your classes. Using the grid below, identify each class you are taking. Then give careful thought to the method of note taking and review that will allow you the best opportunity for success.

Class:

The best system for taking notes in this class would be:

The best time to review my notes for this class is:

I will review my notes using these methods:

···

Class:

The best system for taking notes in this class would be:

The best time to review my notes for this class is:

I will review my notes using these methods:

···

Class:

The best system for taking notes in this class would be:

The best time to review my notes for this class is:

I will review my notes using these methods:

···

Class:

The best system for taking notes in this class would be:

The best time to review my notes for this class is:

I will review my notes using these methods:

Note-Taking Experiment

Nothing ventured will result in nothing gained. Now is the time to experiment with some dimension of your note-taking habits. After completing the previous exercise, pick one class and try the new approach you have described above. Spend two weeks using the new techniques for note taking and reviewing. Then evaluate how successful your approach is and make adjustments as needed. Write a two-page paper that summarizes both your experiment and its outcome.

Spiritual Reflection Journal

Read Jeremiah 36:1–4 and Luke 4:1–20. What was the function of the written word in each of these passages? How do these inspired notes impact your well being and perspective today?

Time in Prayer

In your personal time in prayer, consider praying for the following people and needs.

* For the ability to focus and listen during classes

* For the diligence to study your notes on a daily basis

* For the ability to keep personal problems from distracting you during class

* For students who are feeling homesick and overwhelmed with work

On the Net

The Internet can be a helpful resource for you as you look for ideas to make yourself a more happy and successful student. Visit the College Success page offered by Thomson Wadsworth for web links that will help you grow further on this topic. Go to *www.success.wadsworth.com* and click on Resource Web Links.

Reading to Remember

Then Philip ran up to the chariot and heard the man reading Isaiah the Prophet. "Do you understand what you are reading?" Philip asked.

Acts 8:30

- What types of reading occupy the time of a college student?

- How can I read so that I do not become tired and distracted?

- Where and when is it best for me to do my reading?

- How can more intentional reading improve the quality of my reading time?

- How can I recycle my reading in ways that improve what I remember?

"*D*O YOU UNDERSTAND WHAT you are reading?" The high ranking, Ethiopian official from Acts 8 was a very frustrated reader.
This well-educated man was attempting to read the Book of Isaiah
and find significance in the passage before him. He knew the meaning of all
the individual words in the text and he was correctly decoding each of the
grammatical structures. But he still had difficulty comprehending the passage
before his eyes until Philip stepped up to his chariot and helped him understand what he was reading. Many first-year college students have a similar
experience. College textbooks are very different from the textbooks used in
high school and from popular publications like newspapers and magazines.
They are written at a higher reading level, with more complex sentence structure, and with less familiar vocabulary. Like the royal official from Ethiopia,
college students can turn every page in the chapter and read every word but
still be frustrated in their bid to comprehend and remember what they have
read.

Do you understand what you are reading? If you find yourself answering
this question with "no" on a regular basis, that can spell trouble for you as a
college student since so much of college homework involves reading textbooks. Think about the assignments that you have for any one week and you
will likely find that textbook reading accounts for more than half the homework you have been assigned. Those numbers can really add up. A typical
undergraduate student can expect to read 2,500 or more pages every semester. That is over 150 pages of reading every week! Consequently, anything you
can do to improve your textbook reading will have a significant impact on
your success.

If you saw the adults in your family reading regularly and if your family
read to you as a child, then the thought of reading 150 pages this week may
not seem so daunting to you. On the other hand, reading may be new and
uncharted territory, even something you dislike or dread. Perhaps you have
been out of school for a while and so are not in the habit of setting aside time
for assigned reading. In any case, you can improve your reading skills by
learning more about your own reading habits and how to improve them using
the methods described in this chapter.

Of course as with all changes we make in old habits, changing your reading habit will take time and effort. You may feel frustrated during the process
and want to quit, but we encourage you to stick with it. Commit yourself right
now to improving the reading habit you have. Sample the ideas from this
chapter, experiment with a new approach for several weeks, and then evaluate it. There is no magic bullet. Not everything you read in this chapter will

work for you. But as you consider where and when you read, as you experiment with a new system for reading that is more intentional, and as you explore a method for recycling your reading, you will find something new that will help you read those 2,500 or more pages of assigned reading this semester more effectively. That prize alone is worth reading this chapter and experimenting with a method to use when reading your college assignments. Take heart, because effective readers are made, not born.

Not Every Kind of Reading Is the Same

The first step in growing as a reader is realizing that a one-size-fits-all method for reading does not do justice to the wide variety of reading you do. Different types of reading invite different methods of reading. Consider the different approaches that may be taken when doing devotional reading, recreational reading, and analytical reading. The Lord invites us to hear his voice in our daily lives through the reading of his Word. In your quiet time, you may read and then meditate on the meaningfulness of what you have read in God's Word. In contrast to this style of devotional reading, you will employ a different reading style in the recreational reading you do. This style is used when you sit down to read a popular magazine on a Saturday afternoon, when you read the daily newspaper at the breakfast table, when you pick up an adventure novel, or when you surf the Internet for a good deal on a used pair of rollerblades. This form of recreational reading is faster and lighter than analytical reading. Analytical reading is very careful and slow reading whose goal is to get every last detail just right. If you are attempting to troubleshoot a problem with your computer using the help menu, or if you are reading the contract you will sign for a student loan, or if you are reading a recipe for making a new dinner, you will employ this slow and careful form of analytical reading.

Textbook reading is different from devotional reading, recreational reading, or analytical reading in that it combines a higher level of concentration, a greater amount of time, and a greater need to retain what has been read. Textbooks are written using language that is more difficult than the language we encounter in a newspaper. The readings are longer than most magazine articles and yet textbooks must be read more quickly than we would read a contract. Once you see that college textbook reading is different from the other types of reading you do, you will see that it is important to have a distinct method and style that will help you read those textbooks for the valuable information they contain without committing more time than necessary to the task.

Primary and Secondary Sources

*Y*OUR COLLEGE READING ASSIGNMENTS will take place both in primary and secondary sources. Primary sources are the original documents or records that display the prominent thinking of a notable individual or group from the past or present. The Bible, the US Constitution, the letters written by Dr. Martin Luther King, and the audio tapes of President Richard Nixon are all examples of primary documents. When reading a primary document, it will be your goal to learn as much as you can about the views and perspective of the author or speaker. Sometimes it is helpful to read such documents out loud, changing your volume and tone to replicate the voice of the author to get a feel for the flow of language being used.

By contrast, secondary sources are those sources that comment on and critique primary sources. They reflect the opinion and views of a subsequent reviewer who is analyzing and interpreting the material from the primary source. A commentary on the Book of Romans, an essay that discusses the application of the First Amendment to Internet pornography, or a book on the Watergate scandal are examples of secondary sources that use and seek to interpret primary resources. When reading secondary literature, it is important for you to understand the perpsective being argued in the secondary literature and to evaluate the evidence that the author is using to support his or her view of the primary source.

Picking the Right Time and Place to Read

As you create a plan for reading your textbooks more effectively, it will be important for you to pick the right place and time to do that kind of reading. Remember that going to college is a full-time job and reading is the primary responsibility you have in completing that job. That makes picking the right place and time for doing this work critical. It goes without saying that some types of reading can be done in almost any place and at almost any time. You can surf the Internet in a noisy café or you can read a romance novel in a crowded bus that keeps stopping and starting. But neither place would be conducive to reading a textbook assignment that requires a higher amount of focus and concentration. Read your textbook in the wrong place or at the wrong time and you open the door for frustration due to the many things that can distract your attention from the task. Think about your own habits for a moment. When you take a thought vacation from your textbook reading, what is it that most likely causes that distraction? Below is a list of items that could be the culprit. Circle each item in the list below that has proven to be a problem for you and list any others we may have missed.

Television

Children

Music

Video games

Temperature

Lighting

Eye fatigue

General noise

Uncomfortable seating

Worry

Headache

Checking and rechecking the length of the assignment

Feeling drowsy

RIGHT TIME

One way to address these distractions is to be particular about when you plan to do your textbook reading. Reading at different times during the day will result in varying levels of success for the time you invest. Given the importance of reading your textbook effectively, it will be vital for you to pick times for your textbook reading when you are well-rested and most alert. That prime time of the day will not be the same for everyone. Some will have more energy and focus in the morning and others will find they are more alert and focused at night. By setting aside those hours during the day when you are at your peak and reserving them for reading, you will accomplish two things. That regularly scheduled time will keep you from rushing through a reading assignment because you did not get around to reading it until just before it was due. Secondly, you will be able to read at those times of the day that will give you the best results in the least amount of time, lowering your level of frustration with the task.

Selecting the time you read will give you some control over the level of competing noise you will experience when reading. Some students report that they require absolute quiet when they read. Others find that absolute quiet itself can distract them from their reading. Background noise is not necessarily harmful to your reading so long as the background noise does not change in volume or intensity. For that reason, it may be helpful to listen to very quiet background music while you read. But the noise associated with television, radio, and video gaming will be harmful to the reading process.

Studying with Sound

*I*F YOU HAVE BEEN in the habit of studying with the television or radio playing in the background, you may be studying less effectively than you could be. Most students report that they can study better with some background noise than with absolute quiet. But studying with the television or radio on in the background can impede your focus and concentration. Programs on television and the radio are sponsored by people who want you to listen to their advertising. Thus they design the advertisements to recapture the lagging attention of the listening and viewing audience by changing the volume and intensity of the sound of their commercials. You can grow accustomed to having a television or radio playing in the background, but you will not be able to avoid the distraction that such advertising causes.

Using your prime time of the day for reading will also allow you to have more control over the length of time you will read in one sitting and thus shorten the time of the reading session during which you will read less efficiently. Reading your textbooks in an unscheduled way may force you to read your assignments too quickly and for extended periods of time without taking helpful breaks. The pressure of reading through a college assignment shortly before it is due is a recipe for frustration, frustration that may even lead you to skip reading assignments altogether. Consequently, it is wise to set aside specific times during the week when you plan to do your textbook reading. As you plan that time, be honest and realistic about how long you are able to read without taking a break. It is not wise to plan a two-hour reading session without breaks because most students find that they are more effective if they read for 35–45 minutes and then take a 10–minute stretch and concentration break. If your current habit allows you to read for only 10 minutes without taking a break, do not be discouraged. You will be able to lengthen the reading time you invest before taking a break by increasing the time slowly. Start with 10 minutes, if that is your habit, and then increase it to 12, 15, 20, and so on until you are able to sit and read for 35 minutes or more without a break.

LENGTH OF TIME

It is to your advantage to increase your reading time between breaks as much as you can, since each break you take will introduce some inefficiency into the reading process. You may already have noticed that when you begin reading an assignment, you are reading with less focus and flow than after you have been reading for several minutes. The more often you take a break, the more often you will go through the cycle that begins with several minutes of less focused and less effective reading. Consequently, if you reduce the number of breaks you take during any hour of reading, the more efficiently you will be reading. Of course, there is a limit to how much time you can read in one sitting before you need to stand up and take a break. Consider 45 minutes to be a realistic mark after which fatigue can diminish reading effectiveness. Once you have read for 45 minutes, it is wise to take a ten-minute break that rejuvenates you mentally and physically. Just be cautious about how you use that break time. If you engage in an attractive alternative to reading like watching TV or playing a game on your computer, that brief break could turn into an unintended hour distraction. Get up and stretch, walk around, get some fresh air, and you will be ready to engage your reading again. If you will be taking a longer break or not resuming your reading until the next day, make a quick note to yourself about what you have been reading and what you expect to encounter next in the reading assignment. This will diminish the warm-up time and allow you to get back into the more effective reading zone more quickly.

RIGHT PLACE

Selecting an appropriate place for reading can be as important as selecting the right time to read. By defining one location where you plan to do all your textbook reading, you will be able to control environmental factors that will help you read more efficiently. At base, the place that you select to read should be one that has comfortable seating, adequate lighting, and a temperature that is just right for you. Do not assume that just because your residence hall has a desk and chair that it will be the best spot for you to read. Be strategic and intentional about the choice of location. It could be the patio, the kitchen table, or a desk in the library. By selecting a spot designated exclusively for studying, you will be able to control the noise and other distractions that prevent you from reading most effectively. Furthermore, when you study in the same place time after time, you move into a more effective study and reading mode more quickly since you have unconsciously associated that location with studying. For this reason it is unwise to read in bed or to nap in your reading spot since that can cause role confusion. If you are accustomed to socializing while sitting at your desk, try reading in a different location. As you rethink the method you will use in reading your textbooks, give careful thought to the time and place you choose to read. You will be more efficient in your reading if you follow a routine and study in the same place and at the same time every week. Let that spot be one that is environmentally comfortable, with the tools you need at arm's reach, and free from as many distractions as possible.

Rereading Is a Habit

MANY STUDENTS REPORT THAT they become frustrated when reading a textbook because they end up having to read a page more than once. If you are reading very difficult or technical language, rereading can be helpful. But if rereading is your regular habit here are some things you can try. If you have eliminated all the other distractions in your reading area that could impede your focus, then it is time to address the habit you have of rereading a page of your textbook. You may have gotten into the habit of lowering your attentiveness the first time you read a page because you know that you always go back and read the page again. Here is one way of breaking that habit. The next time you read a page, place a piece of paper on the page and slide it over the sentences that you have completed reading. As you move your eyes from the top to the bottom of the page you will be covering up sentences that you have already read. You may need to employ this technique for a while before you notice that your habit is changing. But by using this method you are continually reminding yourself to pay attention to what you are reading the first time.

Reading with Intention

Once you have determined the best place and time to do your reading, it is time to check the method. Just as there is more than one kind of reading material, so there is more than one method that can be used when reading. That variety in method may be compared to the various ways in which people shop. At times, you may travel to a store to do some recreational shopping. When you do recreational shopping, you are not really shopping because you need something from the store; you are there for the fun of it and would be content to leave the store without making a purchase. Consequently your feet will wander through the aisles and your eyes wander from one shelf to another in a more haphazard way. By contrast, you may be shopping in a more thoughtful way with the intention of purchasing a special gift for someone you care deeply about. You may not know exactly what you want to buy but your feet will be traveling in a more intentional way past the lawnmowers, past the refrigerators, and on to the jewelry department. As your eyes light upon an item that might be right, you pick it up and turn it over and over in your hands. You may set it down and walk away only to return later to reflect and mull over its merits as a gift for this special occasion. This thoughtful, reflective shopping not only looks different than recreational shopping, it also looks very different from the intentional shopping you might do in the grocery store. As an intentional shopper, you are not interested in browsing or mulling, you are interested in efficiency. You have made a list of things you need and your feet will travel in a very direct line between the front door of the store, the shelves on which the items lie, and the checkout line. No time is wasted as you get what is on the list and nothing else.

Of course, there is nothing right or wrong about each of these shopping methods. They are simply different approaches that you would use on different types of shopping trips. Just as you use a different method for different types of shopping, so it is important that you use different methods of reading for the different types of reading you do. The recreational shopping method is similar in style to the method you might use when doing your recreational reading. When reading the Sunday morning paper, your eyes glide haphazardly from one place to the next looking at this or that article and advertisement between sips of coffee with no concern for time or efficiency. By contrast, the thoughtful shopping for a gift is comparable to the devotional reading we do in God's Word. We may be reading a passage of Scripture because it promises to offer us a word of direction or encouragement that we could immediately apply to our day. We read the passage thoughtfully, pausing to reflect and meditate on it. Finally, there is the intentional shopping that is done with a list. This form of shopping is most analogous to the style of reading we may best employ when reading a textbook chapter. If we read the textbook assignment with a list of questions we are pursuing, we will convert our reading from an aimless journey into a focused quest for information. We believe that this kind of intentional reading will save you time as well as the frustration of reaching the bottom of the page completely unaware of what you have just read. This more intentional form of reading can be done in more than one way. But here we will offer you a process of reading that has three steps: preview, question, and pursue.

PREVIEW THE READING

In the first step of this process, we encourage you to spend at least five minutes previewing the reading assignment. This time will help you warm up your mind and clarify the context of all that you read. Before you engage in any form of serious physical activity, it is important that you warm up your body. The drills you do before your athletic team practices or the stretching you do before running prepares the muscles in your body so that they are switched on and ready to go when you push them more aggressively. The same is true of your brain. Just a bit of warming up will help you think more effectively and efficiently when you get aggressive in your reading.

In addition, this preview will provide you with a context for the steps that follow. Consider the following short story: "A man left home, ran for a while, and then turned left. After a brief pause, he started running again and again he turned left. He continued running and turned left just before meeting a masked man. Nevertheless, he arrived back home safely." If you are unclear about the meaning of this story, it is not because you do not understand the vocabulary and the grammar, but because you do not understand the context of this communication. Now reread the story but do so in the context of watching a baseball game. Suddenly the message being communicated is clear. Someone has just scored a run! Context is critical to reading a textbook chapter and a preview of the reading can get you that context.

During this five-minute preview, turn the pages of the chapter quickly and look for clues about its contents and organization. Read the chapter title and the subheadings within the chapter. Look at the pictures, charts, or illustrations. Read the introductory and concluding paragraph of the chapter. In these five minutes of preview reading, you will not get everything you need but you will have a clearer idea of what the author is talking about in that chapter and how the ideas are organized. Remember, context is critical to your understanding of every sentence and paragraph in that assignment. If you fail to get a grasp of the context before you read it, you are requiring your mind to do two things at once—figure out the context and figure out how what you are reading applies to that context. This will require you to read more slowly, to back up, and to reread portions of the assignment that were less clear. The first step in reading your college textbook with greater intention is to conduct a preview reading of it.

QUESTION THE READING

Once you are warmed up and have set the context with a preview, now it is time to question the reading. By that, we mean that you will develop a list of things you will want to learn from the reading assignment. That list will take the form of questions. Look again at the chapter heading, the subheadings within the chapter, the introduction and conclusion, the words and phrases that are in italics or bold. These smaller segments of information related to the overall theme of the chapter can then be turned into questions that the chapter promises to answer for you.

For example, consider the chapter in your Old Testament history book that discusses the Book of Leviticus. As you previewed the chapter, you noticed the following subheading, "Sacrifices and Offerings." During this step of the reading process, you can turn that subheading into two questions related to the larger context of the chapter topic: "What sacrifices does God request of his people in Leviticus?" "What offerings does God request from his people in Leviticus?" A further subheading in this section is entitled, "The Significance of Blood." This also can become a question. "What is the significance of blood in the Levitical worship rites?" Perhaps the author of this chapter has also put some important terminology in italics, phrases like *whole burnt offering* and *peace offering*. These words can also become questions: "What is a whole burnt offering?" "What is a peace offering?" When you have finished this step of the reading process, you will have identified the most important topics the chapter will discuss and have turned them into questions.

Watch Your Speed!

T HE TYPICAL COLLEGE STUDENT has an average reading speed of about 240 words per minute. If you are attempting to do all of your textbook reading at the same speed, whether it is faster or slower than that, you are making a

(continued)

strategic error. The most effective college readers are those who can change the pace of their reading and make a point of varying their reading speed to the type of assignment they are reading. For example, preview reading and reading of literature assignments may be done at a faster than average pace. By contrast, more technical reading for a science or math assignment may demand a slower pace and strategic rereading of certain paragraphs. Successful college students watch their reading speed and vary the speed with which they read from one assignment to the next.

PURSUE THE ANSWERS TO THE QUESTIONS

The preview and question phases of this method are followed by the pursue phase. With the questions in hand, it is now time to read the chapter. That does not mean that you will read every single word in the chapter. That is no longer your goal. Now you are pursuing the answers to your questions, reading only those portions of the chapter that are necessary to complete that task. Consequently your reading has become more intentional, directed, and focused. And each time your pursuit is successful, you will feel the reward.

Your search for the answers will also become more efficient if you read with an awareness of the way most textbook paragraphs are organized by the author. Typically a textbook paragraph will have a topic sentence that introduces the topic or thesis that paragraph will address. The topic sentence will be followed by sentences that offer either supporting evidence for the statement or illustration. You can use that organization to your advantage by knowing where to look within a paragraph for the most likely location of the answer to your question.

One word of caution is in order here. As you begin to use this approach to reading your textbook, you may fall into the unhealthy habit of stopping too soon and too often. Remember that context is important so you will want to read an entire section of the chapter before you pause to write down the answer to one of your questions, otherwise you may miss the larger picture the author is attempting to convey. This can result in the frustration of landing on either wrong or incomplete answers to your questions. Be sure that you read an entire section and then articulate the answer to the question that section promises to offer.

Recycle Your Reading

If you read with intention in the way described above, you will get more out of the textbook than you would otherwise. But the information that you encounter in that reading and the answers to the questions you have raised will not stick with you unless you also recycle that reading. The method of review we suggest will require that you have made a record of the questions and answers discussed above and then actively review that material by making use of a recycling plan.

DESIGN A READING RECORD

The first step in recycling your reading calls for you to design a way to record the questions you raised and the answers that you have found when you did your reading. This reading record can be generated in any number of ways.

Textbook Marking   For example, you may choose to write the questions you want to answer right in the margin of the textbook itself. As you read through a section and discover the answers to your questions, you can mark the textbook in a way that calls attention to those answers. If you are using a highlighter, you may highlight the answers to the questions in different colors in order to discriminate between major and minor points. If you do not want to highlight the text, another way to mark the answers to your questions is with a shorthand method of notation you devise. Answers to your questions could be double underlined. Critical points could be marked with a "!" and matters that you want to clarify later could be marked with a "?".

This system has its advantages and disadvantages. It does permit you to write the questions and mark the answers right in the book. This saves time rewriting the answers. But on the other hand, there is a distinct advantage to taking the author's ideas and putting them in your own words as is required in the other recording systems noted below. The marking of the textbook with a highlighter also comes with the risk of marking too much of the text. A textbook page that is colored completely in yellow is of very little value to you! So if you elect to use this way of identifying the answers to your questions, be sure to read the entire section of the chapter before you mark. And then only mark those items that are critical to you in answering the questions you have raised.

Example of Textbook Marking

Psychoanalytic Psychology

As mainstream psychology grew more scientific, an Austrian physician named Sigmund Freud was developing his own theories. Freud believed that mental life is like an iceberg: Only a small part is exposed to view. He called the area of the mind that lies outside personal awareness the **unconscious**. According to Freud, our behavior is deeply influenced by unconscious thoughts, impulses, and desires—especially those concerning sex and aggression. Freud's ideas opened new horizons in art, literature, and history, as well as psychology (Westen, 1998). Freud theorized that many unconscious thoughts are threatening, which causes them to be **repressed** (actively held out of awareness). But sometimes, Freud said, hidden thoughts and wishes are revealed by dreams, emotions, or slips of the tongue. ("Freudian slips" are often humorous, as when a student who is tardy for class says, "I'm sorry I couldn't get here any later.") Freud believed that all thoughts, emotions, and actions are determined. In other words, if we probe deeply enough, we will find the causes of everything we think, feel, or do. Freud was also among the first to appreciate that early childhood experiences affect adult personality ("The child is father to the man"). Most of all, perhaps, Freud is known for creating psychoanalysis, a method of psychotherapy that explores unconscious conflicts and emotional problems.

what is the unconscious?

what is unique about Freud's psychoanalytic psychology?

From D. Coon, *Introduction to Psychology: Gateways to Mind and Behavior*, 9th ed. (Belmont, CA: Wadsworth, 2001), p. 12.

Note Card or Self-Sticking Notes A second way in which to record the questions and answers is through the use of note cards or self-sticking notes. As you question the reading, write the questions you have raised on one side of the card or sticky note. When you begin to read for the answers, you will be able to write those answers on the back side of the card or sticky note.

This system has several advantages. First of all, it gives you the opportunity to write the answer to the questions in your own words. This is much more valuable to you than if you were to just reread the answer or copy the exact words of the author onto your card. Secondly, it allows you to manipulate the information on the desk or wall in front of you. You can create separate piles for separate topics in the chapter. You can stick the answers on the wall and create patterns of association that may help you recall the answers to the questions. You will be able to quiz yourself by asking the questions and then flipping the card or note to see the answer. But most of all, it allows you to put the textbook aside when you are done reading and focus instead on those parts of the reading that are of the greatest value to you, the ones that you yourself have written on the cards.

What does the Book of Leviticus mean when it talks about holiness?

(front)

Something that is holy is "set apart" from things that are common or ordinary in order to be of service to the Lord.

Example: furniture and utensils used in the Tabernacle.

(back)

Reading Notes A third way to design a record of your reading employs the use of regular note paper. Take a sheet of paper and draw a vertical line three inches in from the left-hand margin, leaving a smaller column on the left side of your page and a larger column on the right side of your page. As you question the text, write your questions on the left side of that page; and when you hunt for the answers and find them, place the answers to the right of the line you have drawn in the larger column.

Like the card or note system above, this has the advantage of allowing you to put the answers to the questions in your own words. It also allows you to put the textbook aside when you are done reading and focus on the work you have written. And it allows you to quiz yourself by covering the right side of the page and asking yourself the questions in the left column. The one disadvantage to this approach is that it prevents you from mixing up the questions when you quiz yourself or maneuvering the questions around on your desk top. But if you find that you study from a page of notes better than from smaller cards, this system may be more effective for you.

What was the role of the person who wanted to make a sacrifice?	1. Present the animal for sacrifice. 2. Place hand on the animal's head to personally identify with the animal. 3. Take animal's life.

DESIGN A RECYCLING PLAN

If you have read your textbook using the plan that is described above, you will now have a record of your reading that is ready for recycling. The plan you develop for recycling your reading will require you to spend additional time with the information and concepts you have already met. As you plan your review time, be aware that it will be most advantageous for you to review what you have written shortly after your reading was completed and regularly in brief sessions after that. Multiple review sessions over a longer period of time are worth much more to you than one long review session right before an exam. We would recommend that once you have finished writing and answering your questions that you review for at least half the time you spent in the reading process. For example, if your preview, questioning, pursuing, and recording took 40 minutes, it would be wise to dedicate another 20 minutes of time that same day to recycling your questions and answers.

Be careful how you plan to use that time, because a poorly designed recycling plan will cause you to lose interest and focus. Create as much variety in this time as you can, while giving special time to techniques that work best for you. For example, during this recycling time, you could quiz yourself by using the questions you raised. You could rearrange the questions in different ways on your desk top or wall. You could recite the information out loud. You could work with a partner to develop a game where you challenged one another to answer the questions from the reading. You could reformat the answers to the questions by making a visual map or a timeline. The point is that there are many ways to review what you have gained from the reading. Do not let your recycling time fall flat due to a lack of creativity in its design.

Do you understand what you are reading? A considerable part of your homework time will be claimed by textbook reading. If you are having trouble understanding or remembering what you have read, consider adjusting your reading habits. Realize that different types of reading require different approaches. Select the time and location for your textbook reading that minimizes distractions and optimizes your chances for successful reading. Check your reading method for the level of intentionality that it requires. Establish the context of your reading with a preview of the chapter before you establish the questions that will turn your textbook reading into a pursuit for answers. Then design a recycling program for your reading that allows for brief but frequent contact with your reading record. A system like this will go a long way toward building better understanding of what you read as well as help you remember what you need to know.

Exercises for Success

Design Your Own Textbook Reading System

Within this chapter you have read about a system that you could use when reading a college textbook assignment. Since one size never fits all, use the system described in this book as a starting point and design your own reading system. Be sure to provide as many details about that system as you can. How long will you spend in pre-reading the text? How will you record the questions and answers you will raise and answer in that reading? On what schedule and in what ways will you recycle the reading assignment?

Now pick one of the classes in which you regularly have a reading assignment. For the next two weeks, experiment with the reading system you have just designed.

Following your two-week experiment, write a two-page report for your instructor that both describes your experimental reading system and the results of your two-week experiment in using it.

Develop Your Vocabulary by Building a Word Wall

As a college student, you will be encountering new vocabulary on a weekly basis. Many of those new words will first come to you in the reading assignments you complete. Your professors will expect you to become familiar with these new words used in their area of specialty and to use them in papers you write for their classes. You can be certain that you will meet them again in the exams just ahead. One way that you can work to build your vocabulary is to make part of the wall in your study room a "word wall." Each time you encounter a word you do not know and want to remember, write it on a sticky note. Put the word on one side and its meaning on the other. Post those notes on the wall and look at them from time to time. As you review them and meet them again in future reading and class discussion, you will add to your vocabulary base. You can even turn this into a game with your roommates. Select five words and quiz each other on their meaning. Loser cleans the room!

Spiritual Reflection Journal

God has chosen to communicate with us using the written word. When we read that Word, we are being carried forward in faith to an extraordinary eternity with him. As the Apostle John has said, "These are written so that you may believe that Jesus is the Christ, the Son of God, and that by believing you may have life in his name." (John 20:31) Consequently we hear of people from Moses to Paul who are either reading God's Word or challenging others to do so (Exod 24:7, Neh 8:1–8, Luke 4:13–21, Col 4:16, 1 Tim 4:13, and Rev 1:3). Read those passages and then consider the time you spend in reading God's Word. Write about your Bible reading habits and how you want to improve them.

Time in Prayer

In your personal time in prayer or in connection with others in your class, consider taking time to pray for the following people and needs.

- For the courage to speak with the faculty members in whose classes I am having trouble

- That I, like Philip, may be ready to help someone read God's Word more effectively

- That I would improve on my own Bible reading habits

- That I define a method through which I might read my textbooks more effectively

- For my seminar instructor and the well being of his or her family

On the Net

The Internet can be a helpful resource for you as you look for ideas to make yourself a more happy and successful student. Visit the College Success page offered by Thomson Wadsworth for web links that will help you grow further on this topic. Go to *www.success.wadsworth.com* and click on Resource Web Links.

Scoring on Your Exams

*When the queen of Sheba heard of Solomon's fame,
she came to Jerusalem to test him with hard questions.*

2 Chronicles 9:1

- How can I design an effective preparation plan?
- What can I do during the exam to improve my grade?
- How can I control the anxiety that washes over me before and during an exam?
- What can I do when I am tempted to cheat on an exam?

*T*ESTS HAVE BEEN AROUND since the beginning of time. After God had created Adam and Eve, he invited them to eat from the plants in the Garden of Eden but instructed them not to eat from the tree of knowledge of good and evil. Satan measured their confidence in God's directive by asking them this test question: "Did God really say, 'You must not eat from any tree in the garden'?" (Gen 3:1) After Joseph was sold as a slave by his older brothers, he had every reason to wonder if they would also do harm to his younger brother, Benjamin. So he tested his older brothers to see if they would abandon Benjamin when he came into harm's way (Gen 44). When the queen of Sheba heard about the incredible wisdom that God had given to King Solomon, she came to test him with hard questions (2 Chr 9:1). And when Daniel and his colleagues were required to eat food that was forbidden in their diet, Daniel made a request. "Please test your servants for ten days: Give us nothing but vegetables to eat and water to drink. Then compare our appearance with that of the young men who eat the royal food, and treat your servants in accordance with what you see." (Dan 1:12–13)

Your life has also been filled with tests. From the time you were in grade school, the week was punctuated by tests and quizzes measuring everything from your ability to spell "luxury" to your skill at summarizing the achievements of Eli Whitney. Those early tests, like your college exams, are designed to give you and your instructor feedback on your progress. But college exams will look and feel very different from the previous exams you have taken. In college you will be tested less often, so each exam will cover significantly more material and have a greater voice in determining your course grade. What is more, your answers will be evaluated against much higher standards. For that reason, it is important for you to rethink and to edit both the way in which you prepare for your college exams and the strategies you use in taking them.

This chapter will give you the opportunity to do just that. When reading this chapter, you may find a number of techniques celebrated and encouraged that you are already using as you prepare for and as you take an exam. On the other hand, you will encounter ideas that you have not tried but that are worth exploring. For some, anxiety associated with exams can interfere with the demonstration of their knowledge and skills on the tests. So here you will also read about the anxiety that attends the college exam and how you might best manage the stress that you encounter. Finally, each exam you take in college will also be an opportunity to demonstrate your integrity. So we will discuss cheating on exams and how to manage the temptations to cheat that will most certainly come your way. In the end, we believe that by checking and editing your approach to college exams, you will be able to score better grades on them.

Design an Exam Preparation Plan

At the moment, you have an exam preparation habit whether you formally call it that or not. Portions of that habit may date back to the very first exams you took in grade school. But it goes without saying that if you try to prepare for a college exam in the same way that you prepared for a grade school exam, you would not meet with the success you desire. In this portion of the chapter, we offer you an exam preparation plan that you can edit to suit your needs. It has several steps: define the scope of the exam, know the type of exam, establish a preparation schedule, employ effective review techniques, and improve your memorization skills.

DEFINE THE SCOPE OF THE EXAM

It is the privilege of your college instructor to determine what knowledge or skills will be evaluated on an exam, but it is the student's right to know on what they will be tested. A good place to begin defining the scope of any college exam is the class syllabus. Reread the goals of the course to remind yourself of what outcomes the instructor is pursuing with you. Then check the course schedule to determine the chronological organization of the course and just where in the scheme of things this exam lies. Listen carefully to the description that the instructor gives during class to define the scope of the exam and write it down. Since your instructors will want you to prepare effectively for the exam, he or she may even invite you to ask any questions you have about the exam. Get all the information that you can. Will the exam be based on the assigned reading, the lectures, the discussion, the handouts, the guest speakers? Will the exam be cumulative, testing you on all your learning experiences to date or limited to the last unit? Defining the scope of the exam is the first step in the preparation process.

DETERMINE THE TYPE OF EXAM

Exams differ from one another not only in their scope but also in terms of their format. Since you will prepare differently for an essay exam than you would for a true/false exam, it is critical to determine the type of exam that lies ahead. As a college student you will see exams in many different formats.

True/false	Brief essay	Open book
Multiple-choice	Extended essay	Test bank
Matching	Take home	

If the exam is going to have more than one type of question, attempt to find out how many points of the exam will be associated with each type of question. Your teacher may or may not be comfortable in disclosing this kind of information. But there certainly is no harm in asking and learning all you can about the way your teacher is going to design this evaluation tool. Towards that end, make sure that you attend the last class before the exam. College instructors will often spend at least part of that time in reviewing for the exam and often give further clues about the exam's content and format. You will not want to miss that!

The All-Nighter

SOME COLLEGE STUDENTS EMPLOY a test preparation technique they call the "all-nighter." The night before an exam they literally stay up all night and use the time they would normally be sleeping to prepare for the exam. This technique is destined for trouble at more than one level. First of all, this technique assumes that study time is of the same quality no matter when during the day it is invested. It goes without saying that studying after 2:00 AM, when you have already experienced a full day of work and play, will not be high-quality study time. You may be going through all the motions of exam preparation, but studying with a tired mind will not produce strong results. Secondly, since learning continues during sleep as our brain consolidates and further deepens our recollection of those things met just before going to sleep, you rob yourself of a critical part of the learning process. And finally, the student who stays up all night will be both mentally and physically exhausted at just the time when they need to be most refreshed. The all-nighter may sound appealing, but it promises only to disappoint those who rely on it.

ESTABLISH A PREPARATION SCHEDULE

As soon as you know the date or approximate date of the exam, it is time for you to establish a preparation schedule. That schedule of activities may not kick into gear the first day of class, but the first day of class is the time to identify the dates for the exams and establish the schedule that will guide your preparation. This approach stands in contrast to the more serendipitous approach of studying for an exam when there is nothing better to do or leaving all the preparation until the night before the exam.

The reality is that there is a limit on how much information we can acquire and master in any given amount of time. Furthermore, there is a limit to how long we are able to maintain the high level of concentration needed for test preparation. So it makes the most sense to design a preparation schedule that extends back several days before the exam to allow you to process and digest the information you need more slowly. We do the same thing physiologically. There are a certain number of nutrients we need in any given week to remain healthy and to function normally. But rather than attempt to eat and drink everything that we need for one week in one day, we eat and drink smaller portions over several days. This is analogous to what we are suggesting you do as you prepare for an exam. Reintroduce yourself to the information over an extended period of time. This gives you the opportunity to reflect on that information, organize it, consolidate it, and so master it in preparation for the exam.

One week prior to the day of the exam is the latest that a daily review of the material should begin. Depending on the exam's difficulty, set aside one to two hours of time each day for the first six days. Put this time into your weekly schedule and defend it against all intruders. You may elect to spend a bit more time than that the day before the exam, but be cautious that you do not wear yourself out mentally or emotionally on that day. It is wise to keep the day before the exam looking as typical as possible, putting your final review as close to the time you will be going to sleep as possible. Even when we are sleeping, our mind will continue to process and work with the information most recently added. Because of that, you will wake up better prepared than when you went to sleep!

The last day before the exam is also a day to be careful with your sleep and diet patterns. If you have been preparing for the exam over the previous week, you will not need to stay up later than usual the night before the exam and you will benefit from being physically rested when you take the test. What is more, be careful about your food and liquid intake. Eat fruits, vegetables, and foods that are high in complex carbohydrates. These foods will help you achieve a more balanced physical and mental state and will help you avoid the peaks and valleys that can occur after using stimulants or foods with an abundance of simple sugars.

Cramming

*I*F YOU ARE CRAMMING for a college exam, you are working at a disadvantage. Because we are able to assimilate only so much information in a given amount of time, this technique will always prevent students from achieving true mastery of the material. The only time we would recommend this technique is in

(continued)

an emergency when some preparation is better than no preparation at all. If you are forced to cram for an exam, be aware that you will have to dramatically limit the scope of what you can effectively learn. Focus your time and energy on the big points and on those topics where you feel most vulnerable. And be ready to accept a lower grade for your efforts since cramming costs you learning.

EMPLOY EFFECTIVE REVIEW TECHNIQUES

If you are not in the habit of setting aside an hour or more a day to prepare for a coming exam, you may find it difficult to try this approach unless you are aware of the various review techniques you may employ during that time. Hours and hours of just rereading your notes is a recipe for boredom that will not give you the results you are seeking. Early in the exam-preparation week, we recommend that you begin a process of reducing, reorganizing, and reformatting your notes. Not every experience you have with a given class will be valuable to you on the coming exam. Thus it is necessary for you to reduce the large amount of information that you have read, listened to, written, and discussed into a smaller quantity of information you will review. Once you have reduced the data, it is time to reorganize and reformat it. You may use summary sheets, flashcards, or visual maps. By re-experiencing that meaningful core of information and manipulating it in this way, you will be on your way to remembering it.

Once your educational experience in this class has been reduced, reorganized, and reformatted, it is time for you to create repeated encounters with it. Vocal rehearsal (recitation of that information) will deepen both your recollection and your understanding of it. Use flashcards and test yourself out loud. Get together with others in the class who are as serious as you are about success and teach the material to one another out loud or go for a private walk during which you talk out your review.

Apart from reciting the information out loud, written practice will further deepen your total preparation. If the exam will require you to use mathematical formulas, practice using those formulas. If the coming exam will have you write essay questions, practice writing essays you make up or try answering the questions raised at the end of the textbook chapter. The week before you take an exam can be filled with meaningful practice if you employ review and recitation exercises like these that keep you interested and animated throughout the process.

IMPROVE YOUR MEMORIZATION SKILLS

While effective thinking is more than just the ability to recall data, the ability to recall data is a critical part of effective thinking. Consequently, most college exams will require that you hold and maintain a significant amount of information in your memory. Anything you can do to improve the memorization process will help you prepare for your college exams.

First of all, realize that God has created us with more than one kind of memory. Psychologists speak about short-term memory and long-term memory. Short-term memory is very helpful in the short run. It allows us to recall five to nine items for 30 seconds or so. This form of memory is wonderful for recalling our meal selection at a restaurant after closing the menu but is inadequate for remembering all the vocabulary needed to translate a paragraph of French literature. Long-term memory is what we need for the latter task. Such long-term memory is the product of a process that consists of encoding information, storing that information in a meaningful way, and then retrieving that information when we need it. If you have taken your French vocabulary through this cycle, it will be there when it is time to translate.

There are several principles associated with placing items in long-term memory that are helpful to know if your goal is to improve your memorization. First of all, it is easier to memorize something we understand than something we do not understand. For example, college students will have a much easier time recalling the words to a German song they are memorizing if they are able to translate it than if they are just memorizing a series of unfamiliar sounds. In addition, the laws of primacy and recency confirm that we are more likely to recall things early in a learning experience and late in a learning experience than those items in the middle of a learning experience. If your goal is to place something in long-term memory, it takes a simple mathematical calculation to see that multiple review sessions spaced over time are better than one long session since there will be more cycles with first and last items in them. Those multiple review sessions also give you the opportunity for repetitive practice. And such repetition will also speed the process of memorization. In this regard, many educators suggest that key concepts should be overlearned. Overlearning occurs when material is reviewed past the point of mastery by 50 percent. For example, if it takes you 30 minutes to master your German vocabulary list, study that vocabulary for an additional 15 minutes and you will have gone to the point of overlearning.

Memory is also enhanced by the addition of multiple senses into the learning process. Students in a German class will learn more quickly that the word, *Tür*, means "door," if they tape the word, *Tür*, to their residence hall room door and say it out loud each time they touch the door. Finally, we are more apt to recall things that are organized for us. A random series of names or dates is much harder to remember than a carefully organized list. If the items do not organize easily on their own, try using mnemonic devices to aid your recall of random lists.

Memory Aids

*P*OEMS AND ACRONYMS MAY help you recall concepts or lists of facts that are hard to remember. When you needed to figure out how many days there are in the month of April, you may have relied upon the poem, "Thirty days hath September, April, June, and November, all the rest have thirty-one." Here is a poem to help you recall the resignation of President Nixon in 1974. "In 1974 Richard Nixon found the door."

An acronym can help you recall lists of things. AROW helps pilots remember which documents they need to have in their airplane to fly it legally. AROW stands for airworthiness certificate, registration, operating limitations, and weight and balance information. You may have difficulty recalling the different forms of chemical bonds if you had to recall the list of ionic bonds, covalent bonds, and polar bonds. Forming the acronym, "PIC bonds," can help you remember that information.

Success on exam day is closely associated with the type of plan you use to prepare for that day. Check the design of your plan. Do you define the scope of the exam? Do you learn all you can about the type of questions you will meet during the exam? Do you establish a preparation schedule that allows you to reduce, organize, consolidate, and review the data? Do you employ review techniques that are both effective and keep your interest? And are you honoring the principles of memorization that will help you recall the data?

Design an Exam-Taking Strategy

The time to plan for a successful test session does not end when you arrive in class the day of the exam. There are also key things that you can do during the exam that will improve your grade. This portion of the chapter will talk about effective ways to use the first five minutes of your time, strategies for writing different types of exams (e.g. true/false, essay, take home), and how to manage the anxiety that attends an exam session.

THE FIRST FIVE MINUTES

On the day of the exam, arrive early and take a few minutes to get comfortable in your seat. Make sure that you have all the tools you will use during the exam like a calculator, exam review sheet, and extra pen or pencil. You may also consider bringing a snack to eat, particularly during a long exam period. We are not suggesting you attempt to eat an entire meal, but a quick snack or beverage during the exam can reanimate your focus and energy level. Before you receive the exam, take time to pray that the Lord will help you to think clearly during the exam, to limit your anxiety, and to write at the very highest level that you can.

Once the exam reaches your hands, listen carefully to any oral instructions and guidance that is given. If you direct all your attention immediately to one of the questions, you may miss valuable help being offered by your teacher. After the instructor is done speaking, take several minutes to survey the entire exam and read the directions for each section. You may find that you have options that are different from those you had expected. For example, you may be asked to answer two of the three essay questions offered. Or you may find that in the true/false section, you are to correct answers that you mark false.

This is also the time to determine how many points are associated with each portion of the exam and decide on how much time you will spend in each area. Consider writing down specific times in the margin of the exam to indicate when you intend to start and finish each section. For example, you may plan to do the multiple-choice questions from 8:35–8:45 and focus on the essay questions from 8:45–9:15. Of course, having a watch or clock in plain view will help you keep track of your progress. As you plan your time, be sure that you allow yourself time to return to any questions that gave you difficulty and to do a final check on all the answers. This strategic use of the first five minutes of the exam will delay the time between receiving the exam and writing your first answers, but it will improve the quality of the time you do spend in writing down answers and leave you feeling much more in control of the effort.

WRITING THE FIRST ANSWERS

With that plan in hand, it is time to answer the first question. In almost all cases, there is no rule that says you must begin by answering the first question on the very first page. During your survey of the exam, you may have identified a section of the exam about which you are very confident. This is the place to start whether it is on the first page of the exam or the last. Completing that portion of the exam will give you a positive start, making you feel more confident about yourself as you move into the portions of the exam that challenge you even more.

As you move through the rest of the exam, expect to encounter questions that are more difficult for you. When you come to a more difficult question, decide if it is best to wrestle with it now or leave it for later. Many students find that if they mark such a question and leave it for later, another portion of the exam may give them an insight that will help them answer the question they have set aside. This is particularly true of essay questions. When you first encounter an essay question that will be more challenging for you, write down as much as you know at the moment and then move through the rest of the exam. Clues quietly given in the rest of the test may help you further develop the answer to that troubling essay question.

STRATEGIES FOR DIFFERENT FORMATS

The goal of all tests is to measure your progress towards an educational goal. But educational goals differ from one another and so you will meet tests that differ in format from one another. Tests like true/false, multiple-choice, and matching are primarily designed to measure your knowledge of the facts. Essay tests and take-home tests are designed to measure both your knowledge of the facts as well as your ability to use higher forms of thinking as you compose your answer.

True/False Exams When you are asked to mark a series of statements as either true or false, consider the following. It is difficult to write a persuasive false statement, so expect that more of the statements in a true/false test will be true. As you approach one of the statements, make the assumption that it is true and stay with that point of view unless you can find something wrong with it. As you do so, watch out for little words that can turn an otherwise good statement into one that is false, words like, "always," "never," and "only." And keep a sharp eye on the statement for words like "not" and "except" that completely reverse the meaning of the sentence. For example, the following statement is true. "Jesus healed the sick on the Sabbath." But it becomes false when the word "only" is added. "Jesus healed the sick only on the Sabbath." Or it becomes false the word "except" is added. "Jesus healed the sick except on the Sabbath." Do not become consumed with attempts to find patterns or sequences of true or false statements in the test that predict where a true or false statement has been placed. Focus on each statement one at a time. Assume that it is going to be true unless you can find something false with it. And if you are absolutely uncertain about an answer, guess that it is true. Remember there are usually more true statements on an exam than false statements.

Multiple-Choice Tests Multiple-choice questions typically consist of a stem (an incomplete sentence) and several answers that would finish that incomplete sentence. Among the possible answers are one or more correct answers that would build a true statement when linked to the stem. Usually there are also one or more distracters, answers that when linked to the stem create a sentence that has the appearance of correctness but creates a false or an incomplete statement. Multiple-choice tests can be written in one of two ways. Either you will be asked to find just one correct answer or you will be asked to mark all answers that are correct. Be sure to read the directions carefully to make sure you know which of the two is required.

The best approach to answering multiple-choice questions begins with reading the stem and proposing an answer before you look at the possibilities presented to you. Then rather than searching for the right or most complete answer(s), identify and cross out the answers that are wrong or incomplete. This process of elimination will leave you with the best answer(s) while lowering your risk of being taken in by an appealing answer that is either wrong or incomplete. Consider the following multiple-choice question.

Abraham's son, Isaac, had two sons. Their names were . . .

A. Jacob and Esau.
B. Isaac and Ishmael.
C. Jacob and Joseph.

Be sure to read the stem carefully so that you can imagine the right answer before looking at the options. What were the names of Isaac's two sons? Once you have visualized the answer, try to discredit each of the options. Option A sounds correct. Option B is attractive since Isaac and Ishmael were brothers. But these were the sons of Abraham, not the sons of Isaac. The third option sounds attractive since Jacob was one of the sons of Isaac. But Joseph was the son of Jacob, not the son of Isaac. Thus you can return to option A since it is most correct and complete.

As with the true/false portion of the exam, do not waste time looking for patterns in the answers. Rather look for words like "always" or "never" that can turn a good answer into a bad answer by implying a level of consistency that rarely exists in this world. Again be alert for the introduction of a negative like the word "not" into the stem since this will completely reverse the direction of the question. If you are uncertain about an answer, attempt to identify at least one of the three options as incorrect to improve your odds in making an educated guess.

Matching Exams College instructors will sometimes use a matching exam to check your understanding of factual information or your knowledge of technical vocabulary. The first step in completing a matching exam is to determine whether or not the answers in the answer column may be used more than once. If not, then proceed to match all the items that you know for sure, crossing out the items in the answer column when they have been used. Once you have narrowed the options in this way, you can return to the items you are less sure about with a narrowed field of possible answers. Here is an example of a matching quiz that might be given in your Bible history class to assess your knowledge of the families in Genesis.

_____ 1. Wife of Abraham	A. Joseph
_____ 2. Brother of Esau	B. Leah
_____ 3. Son of Jacob	C. Tamar
_____ 4. Wife of Jacob	D. Sarah
_____ 5. Daughter-in-law of Judah	D. Jacob

Essay Questions Essay questions can require either a brief or longer answer. In either case, they are designed to measure not only your knowledge of the information but also your ability to think logically, creatively, and critically. The first step in answering the essay question is to make sure that you are in fact answering the question that is being asked. College professors often report reading wonderful essays that had little or nothing to do with the essay question they had asked in the exam! In order to answer the question effectively, you will need to identify and mark three components of the question: the key word, the limiting word, and the topic. The topic of the sentence is that part of the learning experience that your instructor wants to evaluate. The key word or words will ask you to do something specific with that topic, for example analyze, describe, compare, and contrast. The limiting word or phrase reduces the topic to a more manageable size. Consider the following essay question.

> Identify and describe the geographical features of ancient Israel that led the Lord to select this land as the Promised Land.

In this essay question, the topic you are to discuss is the geography of ancient Israel. The key words are "identify and describe." The limiting phrase reduces the discussion to the geographical features of ancient Israel that made it particularly attractive for selection as the Promised Land.

Key Words and Essay Questions

HERE ARE THE TASKS that instructors may ask you to perform in the key-word dimension of an essay question:

Analyze	to break the topic or problem into its parts in order to understand it. Discuss and examine each part and show how the parts work together within the larger framework of the topic.
Compare	to examine the characteristics or qualities of several topics and identify their similarities and differences.
Contrast	to examine differences between topics.
Critique	to evaluate the quality of a statement or an idea. A criticism will acknowledge positive and negative qualities. You may need to supplement your opinions with support from recognized experts.
Define	to give the accurate and concise meaning of a word or phrase. Providing an example may help to clarify a definition, but an example is not itself a definition.
Describe	to give a verbal account of something. This can be in a narrative or other form of description that lists characteristics or qualities.
Discuss	to examine important characteristics of a topic or issue. Discussion often includes identifying the main points and the important questions within the topic.
Evaluate	to weigh the strengths, weakness, merits, worth, or truthfulness of a topic or argument.
Explain	to make a concept or topic understandable. Explanations often treat how and why things develop.
Illustrate	to give concrete examples of something. This may be either in written form or in a diagram or picture.
Interpret	to explain the meaning or meaningfulness of something.
Justify	to argue in support of a position by giving evidence or reason in its favor. Provide logical reasoning and concrete examples to support your argument.
Narrate	to tell a story or describe a series of events in chronological order.

(continued)

Outline	to give the main points of a topic in appropriate order, focusing on broader concepts.
Prove	to demonstrate the truth of a statement by providing facts or logical arguments.
Relate	to identify the connections or relationships between topics or events.
Review	to summarize the main parts of a topic. Evaluation may also be included.
Summarize	to briefly cover the main points of a topic, omitting details. A summary covers all the most important points, yet remains a condensed account of the topic.
Trace	to describe the order of events or the development of an idea.

Once you have identified the precise question you are to answer, outline your response before you write. This will help you organize your thinking, avoid rambling, and balance the contents of your answer so that you give fair treatment to each component. In connection with the essay question above, you might have two parts to your answer:

   I. Location
  II. Absence of natural resources

Once you have identified those two features as the major points of your answer, you would then outline the subpoints under each. That outline might look like this.

   I. Location
     A. Key international crossroads
     B. News spread effectively via the merchants and travelers
     C. So the Land of Israel facilitated the spread of the Gospel
  II. Absence of natural resources
     A. Illustrate that Israel is a land void of natural resources
     B. The absence of natural resources increases dependence upon God
     C. Thus the Land of Israel nurtures faith in God's promises

At times, an essay question may require that you introduce your own opinion into the answer, but generally in an undergraduate class your instructor will be asking you to represent the scholarly view of others. If a scholarly consensus was presented on the topic, be careful not to wander far from that in your answer unless you are absolutely convinced you can make a case that will be impressive and convincing. In doing so, your instructor will expect you to use the jargon of his or her discipline in the answer, so be sure that you know the language and use it correctly.

Remember that the answer you give will be evaluated on the basis of its accuracy, clarity, and logic. Your instructor will further be impressed by an answer that is succinct, legible, and free from grammatical and spelling errors. The answer to an essay question that makes the corrector work too hard will receive a lower grade. Thus, unnecessarily long answers or answers that are difficult to read will receive a lower grade even if they are generally correct in their direction.

Take-Home Exams Certain essay tests will not be assigned for completion in class but for completion out of class. These take-home exams can be addressed in the same way as the essay exam described above but will also have some unique expectations associated with them. When an instructor allows you to write your essay exam outside of class, he or she will also expect you to have an answer that is higher in quality than one you would write in class. Follow the instructions you are given carefully, for the take-home exam may require you to use resources apart from your textbook and notes. You may be required to cite your sources as you would in a research paper. And you most assuredly will be evaluated against higher standards for the completeness, accuracy, and organization of your answer. Be careful about how you plan your time for writing a take-home exam. Typically such an exam will require you to spend more time writing than you would if you had done the exam during the class hour.

Open-Book and Open-Note Exams At other times, you will take exams in college that permit you to use written resources during the class hour when you take the exam. Some college students have been lulled into a false sense of security when they hear that they will be able to use their textbook and notes during the exam. Consequently, they have been disappointed in the experience because they ended up spending too much time researching answers and ran out of time for writing effective answers to the questions. Look at it in this way: the class hour for an open-book test is not the time to be learning the material but the time to be demonstrating your knowledge of that material.

Like the take-home exam, this type of exam will likely contain more difficult questions that carry higher expectations from the instructor. So it is critical that you prepare for such an exam by memorizing and familiarizing yourself with key information just as you would for a closed-book test. Think of the book and notes you bring to class as tools with which to supplement your answer rather than as tools that you will use to create your answer from scratch. In this regard, prepare those tools carefully. Use self-sticking notes and color coding to mark portions of the textbook you are most likely to use and organize your written notes in a similar way so that you can use these auxiliary tools efficiently and effectively.

Math and Science Exams College exams in math and science courses also have some unique expectations. They demand that you be competent in using scientific terminology and require that you accurately perform mathematical calculations. When taking a science exam, be certain that you are well acquainted with the terminology that your instructor and textbook have used. Your ability to answer the questions begins with your ability to understand the scientific terminology that is used to frame the questions. When science and math exams require mathematical computations, be sure that you practice the computation process and formulas many times before you demonstrate them on the exam. Be sure to check whether or not you are required to memorize formulas or if you are able to bring them along on a note card. And be certain that you allow yourself time to check each of your answers carefully. Does the answer you have make sense? Have you applied the correct formula? Have you completed each step of the formula in the correct order? Have you made any basic mathematical errors in the calculation process?

Hot Topics Card

A s you prepare for an exam, you will always find some piece of information or idea elusive and more difficult to understand. Consider carrying around a "hot topics" card. On this small card write down the formula, the vocabulary item, or term you are having difficulty recalling. During the slow moments of your day, waiting for a bus or waiting in line for lunch, do a quick review of the hot topics on your card.

Manage Your Anxiety

Exams and anxiety go hand in hand for most people. All of us would like to do well when we are evaluated and that creates a level of anxiety that is natural and normal. The symptoms of stress vary from one person to the next but may include the following: butterflies in the stomach, difficulty sleeping, irritability, nausea, loss of appetite, diarrhea, and headaches. If these symptoms become so acute so as to interfere with your ability to live a normal life or if they significantly impact your ability to demonstrate your capabilities on an exam, it is critical that you seek the direction and support of a professional counselor. The following suggestions for managing anxiety are not meant to replace such professional assistance, but they may help you to manage milder forms of exam anxiety.

The place to begin managing anxiety is with the one who has created us and who has promised to hear and answer our prayers. Read and take to heart this promise from 1 Peter 5:7, "Cast all your anxiety on him because he cares for you." There is nothing we can experience that exceeds God's power. And in love, he has promised to use that power to bring us peace in the midst of our worry.

A second way to address the anxiety you feel in connection with an exam is to prepare effectively. We tend to worry about those things we do not know about or are ill prepared to meet. The early pages of this chapter speak about a method of exam preparation that empowers you with knowledge and a preparation plan. Following such a plan is another step in limiting the worry you may feel about a coming exam. Remember that information and preparation translate into empowerment.

Thirdly, be careful that you do not give an exam more power than it is due. Exams are meant to measure a very limited amount of who you are as a person. They have no power to define your value or worth as an individual. They have no ability to absolutely predict your future success. And their outcome can be compromised by your physical and emotional state on the day you take the exam. Let the exam be a tool that measures your growth and provides feedback on how to improve, but do not let exams define you as a person. You are much bigger and more wonderful than the grade on an exam may suggest.

This is particularly important to keep in mind when you encounter a question in the exam that has caught you by surprise. Go into every exam assuming that there will be at least one question that will give you trouble. Do not let one or two questions derail your confidence and precipitate negative self-talk. It is entirely possible to pass most exams with a good grade even if you are unable to answer one of the questions.

Good company can help you diminish anxiety. But there is one kind of person you will want to avoid before an exam. We are talking about the person who panics every time there is an exam. He or she roams the halls forecasting the doom of all who will take the exam. This person will not be of help to you and is best avoide i until after the exam is completed.

Finally, realize that you have power over your anxiety. On the day of the exam, arrive in class early. Sit in the seat and focus on the task ahead. Use the stress reduction techniques that will be discussed further in Chapter Twelve. Visualize your success and then get to it.

Keeping It Honest

Each time you take an exam, you have a chance to give evidence of your integrity by avoiding the temptation to cheat. Such cheating can take any number of forms. Some students have intentionally been absent on the exam day forging claims of illness so that they can obtain information on the exam from others who have taken it. Other students have smuggled illegitimate information into the room and worked to keep it hidden from the instructor's eyes. Still others have devised systems to exchange answers during the exam, even making use of electronic communication in the process.

Students who have resorted to this dishonest behavior do so for a variety of reasons. They may have managed their time poorly or dealt with a very difficult personal situation that prevented them from preparing for the exam. They may be angry at the instructor and wish to do well in his or her class despite the perceived unfairness they have experienced from the teacher. Or they may be placing so much emphasis on their grade that they are willing to sacrifice their integrity by cheating to obtain a higher grade.

To be caught cheating on an exam carries with it significant consequences. Typically college faculty are empowered to handle the cheating student in a variety of ways. Such a student may be given a failing mark on the exam or may be given a failing mark in the course. And in certain cases, those found cheating will be expelled from the school. Such official consequences, along with the humiliation of failing this character test, are a burden to carry. Cheaters who are caught are clearly harmed, but so are cheaters who are not caught. Those who misrepresent themselves on an exam have lowered the value of their education. They have received a grade that has no connection with their knowledge or skill. What is more, those who cheat on exams rightly feel the guilt of sin and the personal humiliation of claiming to be someone they are not.

Keeping it honest on all your exams will not be easy but it will be possible because of the promises that God has extended to you. Assume that you will be tempted to cheat on an exam at some point during your college years. Preempt that temptation of Satan by writing out Hebrews 4:15–16 and placing it in your study area. In this verse, the inspired author reminds us that Jesus has been there. "For we do not have a high priest who is unable to sympathize with our weaknesses, but we have one who has been tempted in every way, just as we are—yet was without sin. Let us then approach the throne of grace with confidence, so that we may receive mercy and find grace to help us in our time of need." (Heb 4:15–16) When Jesus was beginning his earthly ministry, he too was tempted to take short cuts that were only paths to failure (Matt 4). He knows what you are feeling when tempted to cheat and has promised you the power to remain honest and true. If you are tempted to cheat, pray for his help, seek the support of a Christian friend, and even be ready to take a lower grade on the exam rather than misrepresent yourself. If your life has been complicated by personal tragedy, speak to your instructor about delaying the demonstration of your ability. And if you fall victim to this sin, confess it and find peace in the forgiveness of Jesus (1 John 1:9–10).

Test preparation is not new to you. You have been doing it for years. But as you consider your habits related to taking college exams, look for ways that you might strengthen yourself as a student. How can you improve the process you use to prepare for an exam? How can you strategically use the time during the exam to produce the best results? What can you do to lower your level of anxiety? What are you doing to prepare for the day when you are tempted to cheat on an exam?

Exercises for Success

Find Your Challenges

Most students find one type of exam to more challenging than another. Review the last four or five exams that you have taken and determine on what kind of questions you are losing the most points. Then do some further investigation on that type of exam question that gives you difficulty. Look for new preparation or test-taking strategies associated with that type of question that will produce more positive results for you.

Type of Question	*Test #1*	*Test #2*	*Test #3*	*Test #4*	*Test #5*
Multiple-Choice					
True/False					

Type of Question	Test #1	Test #2	Test #3	Test #4	Test #5
Matching					
Essay					
Other					

Build an Exam Plan

The ideas offered in this chapter need to be edited and made your own. Pick an exam that is coming up in the next month and draft a preparation plan. Experiment by starting your preparation earlier or using different review and recitation techniques. After the exam has been taken, you will have a better sense of what worked or did not work for you.

Exam Plan

Course:

Date of Exam:

Scope of Exam:

Type of Exam:

Study Schedule:

Day	Time	Content	Review and Recitation Technique
Day 7			
Day 6			
Day 5			
Day 4			
Day 3			
Day 2			
Day Before			

Dissecting an Essay Question

Below are two essay questions related to the contents of this chapter. Identify and mark the key word(s), limiting word/phrase, and topic. Then write an outline that would be the framework on which you would build your response.

> Compare and contrast the techniques that may be used to answer an essay question versus a multiple-choice question on a college exam.

> Explain why a college student needs to be proactive to avoid cheating on exams and relate what steps you plan to take in avoiding that temptation.

Interview a Successful Upper-Class Friend

Many of the best suggestions on how to be successful on the tests given by a particular professor may be obtained by asking an upper-class student who has successfully completed the class you are taking. Pick two of your classes and identify competent students who have already completed those courses with high grades. Interview them and find out what techniques they used both in and out of class to do well on those exams.

The Price of Dishonesty

Investigate the student conduct code on your campus under the topic of cheating on a college exam. Write a brief summary of what you find. How is cheating defined in the conduct code? What penalties are assessed to those who are caught? What can you do if you are charged with cheating when you are in fact innocent?

Spiritual Reflection Journal

Since you will face the temptation to cheat on a college exam, now is the time to arm yourself with prayer and the Word of God to combat it. Read Genesis 22 and Matthew 4. Describe the ways in which Abraham and Jesus met their spiritual tests. What do you learn from their experience that you can apply to your life?

Time in Prayer

In your personal time in prayer or in connection with others in your class, consider taking time to pray for the following people and needs.

- That God would motivate you to improve your exam preparation habits

- That those who are thinking about cheating on their next exam would be able to resist that temptation

- That you might find effective ways to keep anxiety from interfering with your ability to be successful on your college exams

- That God would bless the person in your class who is struggling in a relationship

On the Net

The Internet can be a helpful resource for you as you look for ideas to make yourself a more happy and successful student. Visit the College Success page offered by Thomson Wadsworth for web links that will help you grow further on this topic. Go to *www.success.wadsworth.com* and click on Resource Web Links.

Chapter

Saying It Just Right: Writing and Speaking Successfully

A word aptly spoken is like apples of gold in settings of silver.

Proverbs 25:11

- What can I do to improve my writing?
- How can I become a better public speaker?
- What kinds of research tools are available that will assist me in writing and speaking more effectively?

*I*N GENESIS 1, we read that God "spoke" and the world came to be. On a much smaller scale, we too have the ability to *create* using language. Through our use of language, we are able to shape the knowledge, perspectives, and attitudes of those touched by our words. This effective use of language is celebrated in the Bible. The poet in Proverbs writes, "A word aptly spoken is like apples of gold in settings of silver." (Prov 25:11) Your future employer will also celebrate your ability to communicate effectively. According to the National Association of Colleges and Employers, communication skills consistently rank at the top of the list used to evaluate prospective employees. That makes effective writing and speaking a priority for you.

But the mere ability to speak does not necessarily entail the ability to communicate effectively. This is a skill that can be developed. Consequently, you can expect to have a lot of practice refining those skills as a college student. For the mark of a well-educated man or woman is not only that they are able to think well but that they are also able to communicate that good thinking effectively in both written and oral form. That practice will come in a variety of assignments and opportunities as a college student, from writing research papers to giving presentations in class. Each time you develop a thesis statement, gather supporting evidence, argue for a solution, advocate a point of view, analyze a piece of literature, or offer a well-grounded opinion, you are in the process of honing your speaking and writing skills. It is likely that you will even have classes during your first year of college wholly dedicated to the topics of writing and public speaking. This chapter is not designed to be a substitute for them but serves as a tool to support your development at a basic level. Here we will discuss strategies for improving your writing projects, strategies for improving your public speaking skills, and tips for doing basic college research.

Improve Your Writing Skills

College trains you to be a better thinker, and writing has been a traditional player in accomplishing that goal. For there may be no better way for you to see and evaluate the quality of your thinking than through the medium of writing. What is on paper will reveal before your eyes both strengths and weaknesses in your thinking that you may not have noticed. You will see clarity or lack of clarity in your word choice. You will see the logical flow of your thinking or a tangled web of disconnected factoids. You will see a thesis that is persuasive or a presentation that is unconvincing. Since good writers are made and not born, we can discuss the practices that will help you become a better college writer. This begins with understanding the assignment, but quickly moves to the topics of establishing a writing schedule, engaging in meaningful prewriting tasks, writing the initial draft, and revising the initial draft.

UNDERSTAND THE ASSIGNMENT

The first step in the writing process is understanding the assignment. This might surprise you if you have never thought about the variety of writing assignments that you may be asked to do. Understanding the assignment means more than knowing the mechanics, such as the number of assigned pages or that the paper must be typewritten. It is about the very nature of the project itself. As you consult the syllabus, written guide, or instructor, you will be able to determine the precise nature of the writing assignment and will not waste time on an assignment that was never assigned in the first place. Here are some common types of papers an undergraduate may meet.

Position Paper Sometimes called an essay, the position paper requires you to discuss your views on a certain topic. For example, your political science teacher might ask you to write an essay about your position on a recent election issue.

Critical Reaction Paper After discussing a topic in class, reading an article, or visiting a Web site, your instructor may ask you to write a reaction paper, which typically requires that you briefly summarize and then evaluate what you have heard or read. Write about where you agreed, where you disagreed, and why. Study the evidence. Does it clearly support the conclusions? You may have several reactions to the topic, so be sure to organize your reactions clearly in the paper.

Case Study Perhaps your instructor wants you to conduct an in-depth review of a person or an event—a case study. Although the parameters of this type of paper vary, be sure to provide ample details and anecdotes.

Research Paper This is the most time-consuming writing project you will do as a college student, because it requires that you develop a thesis statement and conduct a significant amount of research. You need to gather information and organize it into a well-crafted presentation. Because of the complexity of this project and the amount of time it consumes, the research paper usually counts more heavily towards your final course grade. An early start on this type of paper is essential.

CREATE A WRITING SCHEDULE

It is important to create a schedule for each paper, particularly the longer research paper assignments where you have a large number of tasks to perform. This means breaking up the project into smaller steps and assigning your own "due dates" for each step in the writing process. Here is an example of a schedule that might be used for a research paper:

September 25:	Pick a topic and check it out with the instructor.
October 15:	Complete initial research on the topic.
October 20:	Create thesis statement and working outline.
October 27:	Complete additional research.
November 10:	Complete first draft.
November 15:	Revise first draft.
November 22:	Go to the writing center for feedback on paper.
November 30:	Complete final draft.
December 3:	Paper due in class.
December 4:	Reward myself with dinner and a movie.

Even if the assignment does not entail extensive research, you can still set due dates for those steps in the project that must be accomplished, including a working outline, first draft, and revisions.

GET READY TO WRITE

Long before you write the first draft of your paper, you have a variety of tasks to complete. These include selection of the topic, completing the initial research on the topic, forming a thesis, and designing a working outline. Each of these prewriting steps will have an impact on both your motivation for the project and its final quality.

Skimming for a Topic Sometimes your instructor will assign a specific topic for your paper. Other times, you will have the freedom to select your own topic. This freedom can present a problem for some students. Because there are so many different directions a paper might go, the choices can be overwhelming. If you are subject to procrastination, this may be the only excuse you will need to delay the start of the project. There is no right way to search for a topic. But consider the following approach if you are stuck. Go to the library and start skimming newspapers, magazines, indexes, or journals associated with the larger theme of the project. As you skim these sources, be aware of times you stop skimming and start reading an article with interest. Keep a list of the topics that you read. After an hour of skimming, look at your list of topics. Chances are something on that list will spark your interest.

Brainstorming After you have chosen your topic, spend some time thinking about it. What do you already know about the topic? And more importantly, in which ways can the topic itself be investigated? Ask the pertinent who, what, when, where, why questions as you brainstorm and begin to write down the various facets of the topic you discover in the process. Do not worry about spelling, grammar, punctuation. Just keep your fingers moving! Set a timer and free write for 10 minutes. Through this process you will not only gain a sense of context for the topic but you will also begin narrowing the topic into a size that is manageable for you and zeroing in on that facet of the topic that you find most interesting.

Let us say that you want to do a paper on the death penalty. That is an enormous topic. Brainstorm by yourself or with a friend. *Who* is affected by the death penalty? *What* forms of execution are used? *When* was the death penalty last used in this state? *Where* do the executions take place? *Why* do some states have the death penalty while others do not? Write the topic in the center of a piece of paper and explore all the dimensions and issues related to the death penalty. Your notes might look like this.

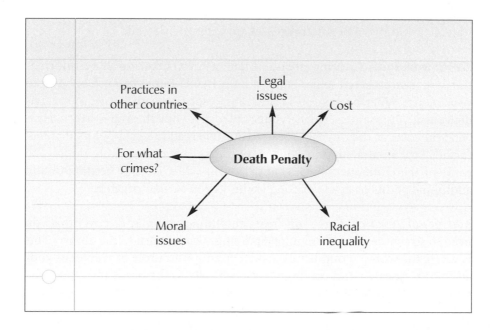

Initial Research   Once you have identified and narrowed your topic, it is time to do the initial research on it. The amount of research you need to do for a writing project will vary greatly depending upon the type of assignment you have. While a reaction paper will require little research, other writing assignments will require you to interact broadly with the thinking of others before you write. Your goal for this stage of the research is not to go into detail on every facet of your topic but to get a general overview. What are the main points? What are the basic issues and arguments? Who are the major representatives of the various positions? While you clearly will need to research in tools other than an encyclopedia, an up-to-date encyclopedia article (particularly in a subject-specific encyclopedia) can be a good starting point for getting a general overview of the topic.

Thesis Statement   Once you have narrowed your topic and done the initial research on that topic, it is time to take a stand. Your topic needs to become a thesis statement. Write out a sentence that captures the particular point of view that you will argue in the paper. For example, let us say you have been assigned a research paper related to World War II. After brainstorming, you decide you want to focus on the role of women during the war effort. After doing your initial research, you elected to focus on the topic of the Women's Airforce Service Pilots. That topic becomes a thesis statement when you take a point of view on it. "The development of the Women's Airforce Service Pilots (WASP) was critical to the success of the United States' Air Force during World War II." Note that a thesis statement is more than a topic. A thesis statement assumes a position that you are willing to defend.

Working Outline   Creating an outline will help you organize all the information you have gathered so far. Start with the main points you wish to cover in your paper. What background does your reader need to know? What evidence will you use to persuade your reader that your thesis is correct? How will you counter the opposing arguments? Then add the subpoints that will further explain and support your main ideas. This is a working outline, so some of the components will change as you write. Do not hesitate to add additional points or delete existing points as you further organize.

Additional Research   Once you create an outline, you may discover that you need to strengthen your own understanding with a return to the library. This is where the working outline plays such an important role. It will focus your additional research and reading very specifically to the needs that you have. Once this step is complete, you are ready to write.

WRITING THE FIRST DRAFT

When you follow the ideas and steps above, writing the first draft will not seem like such a daunting task. You have done a great deal of work already. Simply follow your outline and refer to your research notes as you write each section. Above all, write this first draft knowing you will revise it later. There is no pressure on you to write perfect paragraphs. Consider the following tips you may use in writing the first draft.

- Do not criticize your work or linger over one sentence with which you are struggling. Save the final polish for later.
- Although the introduction contains the first words your reader will read, it may not be the first words you write. If you do not have a clear introduction in mind, let it go. As you write the paper, ideas for the introduction will occur to you.
- If you have information from outside sources, cite these sources in your paper. Any words or ideas that are not your own need to be credited to the original author. Be sure to find out what preference your instructor has when it comes to citing outside sources in the paper (e.g., American Psychological Association, Modern Language Association, or Turabian). Check your library, learning center, or bookstore for the most recent edition of the style manual you will use.
- Do not let your conclusion fizzle. This is a crucial part of the paper. Give yourself time to really work on this section. This is the last thing your instructor reads before assigning a grade, so end the paper with a strong conclusion that revisits and confirms your thesis.

REVISING THE DRAFT

After your first draft is complete, it is a good idea to take a short break from the material. Put it away for a day or two. When you return to the paper to revise it, you will be able to look at it with a fresh perspective. The more time you spend revising your papers, the better your writing will become. Use the following suggestions to revise your initial draft.

Be a Critical Reader As you wrote your first draft, you were concerned with getting all the necessary information on paper. Now it is time to put yourself in the shoes of your reader by critically reviewing your paper. Do the sections flow logically or do you need to rearrange the material? Do you have transitions between the main points of the paper so the reader can easily comprehend the organization? Can you rewrite sentences using the active voice rather than passive voice? Do the quotations fit smoothly into the text of the paper? Are your arguments well supported by your research? Are you using gender-neutral language? Try to read the paper as if you were your instructor assigning a grade to it. What are the strong points? Where are the weak points?

Read It Out Loud One of the best revising techniques is to read your paper out loud. You will be able to identify awkward phrases and sentences much more easily. You wrote the paper. If you stumble over an odd choice of words, you know for certain that your reader will too.

Check for Grammar and Spelling Errors Since you want your reader to focus on your ideas, you do not want your reader distracted by spelling and grammar errors. Proofread your paper with a dictionary and grammar rulebook by your side. Use the spell checker on your computer, but remember that it will not catch every spelling error. For example, it will not indicate a spelling error in the phrase "Form 1950 too 1960 the United States . . . ." If you have a tendency to make these kinds of mistakes, ask a friend to proofread your paper too. But remember, you are ultimately responsible for cleaning up the spelling and grammatical errors.

Go to the Writing Center If your campus has a center where students can get feedback about their papers, take advantage of this opportunity. You will receive some very valuable advice from students who have refined the art of evaluating their own writing.

Revise Again Once you have revised the first draft, revise it again in a few days. Your writing will continue to improve through each draft. Weigh the strength of your paper using the following checklist:

- ☐ I have an introduction that catches my reader's attention and previews the main points of my paper.
- ☐ I have logically organized the main points of my paper.
- ☐ I have appropriate transitions between paragraphs.
- ☐ I have supported my arguments with convincing evidence.
- ☐ I have given the appropriate citation to any outside material I have used.
- ☐ I have correctly used the appropriate citation format.
- ☐ I have written a conclusion that summarizes the main points.
- ☐ I have checked for spelling and grammar mistakes.
- ☐ I have taken my paper to the writing center for feedback.

High-quality papers require careful research, writing, and revision. Be sure to understand the assignment and create a writing plan. Know what you want to say and how you want to say it before writing the first draft. When your first draft is complete, revise and revise again. College is the time to develop your communication skills, so use each writing assignment as an opportunity to improve.

What Grade Did You Get on Your Paper?

*M*ANY OF YOUR INSTRUCTORS will return papers to you with more than just a grade. They will also write comments about the quality of the paper. If your pride has prevented you from hearing that critique or if you have been in the habit of ignoring these comments, it is time for a change. The comments written on your paper not only tell you why you received the grade but also how you may improve your writing. For example, they may indicate a problem with your organization, they may point to problems with grammar, or they may indicate a weakness in citing resources. Look for patterns in the comments that you receive on returned papers. They signal ways that you may improve your writing. If the comments are not clear, be sure to ask your instructor to clarify those comments so that you can incorporate them in your next writing assignment.

Improve Your Speaking Skills

The practice of public speaking enjoys a rich heritage in the Bible. Consider the powerful speeches delivered by Jeremiah and Peter (Jer 7 and Acts 2). Although the advent of the computer and other technological communication devices allows us to connect with people by video images and teleconferences, there is still no substitute for the interaction between a speaker and the audience during a public speaking engagement.

UNDERSTAND THE ASSIGNMENT

Your public speaking opportunities will vary in nature and purpose, much like the various writing assignments you will have. Like your writing assignments, it is critical that you understand the objective of your presentation.

Speakers have various goals when they present a speech. Just think of a graduation ceremony you attended during which you heard a speaker deliver the graduation address. This type of speech, called ceremonial speaking, honors and celebrates the graduates. It is a well-known form of address, but it is not the type of speaking you will be called upon to do in college. Your speaking tasks typically aim to inform or persuade an audience.

Speaking to Inform Consider this type of speech an opportunity to expand your audience's understanding of a topic. Your task is to present information in a way that is interesting and understandable. It is a good idea to gather information from a variety of sources. Even if you do not use all the information you gather, you will become familiar with the material and more at ease discussing it in front of an audience. Like your research papers, it is critical that you orally cite your sources within your speech. You dare not claim an idea as your own when it is not. Giving credit to the authorities you consulted will add to your own credibility as a speaker as well. Since the task of informative speaking is creating a presentation that is interesting and understandable, consider using visual aids to enhance your speech.

Using Visual Aids in Your Speeches

VISUAL AIDS LIKE PICTURES, graphs, charts, and objects can give your speech a lot of impact. But it is important to use visual aids in a way that enhances your presentation rather than distracts from it. Before you spend time creating visual aids for a speech, make sure you have a clear purpose for them. Are you using a lot of statistics in your speech? Then a chart with all your statistics clearly written out will help your audience understand your argument. Is the speech topic complicated? Then a diagram of the different subpoints of the speech will help your audience to remember your speech. Are you speaking about different styles of artistic expression? Then pictures of different works of art will help your audience to see the various styles. Once you have created your visual aids, be sure to keep the following guidelines in mind:

- Does it look good? Poorly written charts, graphs, or posters look as if you did not care enough to spend time on the assignment. Use the technology available to you in order to create professional looking visual aids. If you must write out a visual aid by hand, plan it carefully and make it as neat as possible.

(*continued*)

- Will everyone be able to see it? Small-print charts and posters may be unreadable even in a small classroom. Test your visual aids by standing as far from them as the people in the room will be. Also, think about how you will display your visual aids while you are giving your speech. Is there an easel available? Will you need to bring tape in order to secure your visual aid to the wall?

- When should I use it? Generally, visual aids should be covered or placed face down until they are needed during the speech. Do not let your visual aid distract from your message when you are not using it.

- What about media aids? Always cue video and audio tapes ahead of time. If you are using computer images like a PowerPoint presentation, be certain you know how to use it during your presentation. It is a good idea to come to the classroom before your speech and set up any media equipment you will be using. This will help you prepare for your presentation and ensure that all the equipment is working properly.

- Will the visual aids be cumbersome to use while speaking? Not if you practice your speech with your visual aids. The visual aids should fit smoothly into the flow of your speech; therefore, you will need to practice holding, manipulating, or referring to the visual aids just as you would normally practice your speech.

- What if my visual aid gets lost or breaks down? Even professional speakers occasionally have a visual aid mishap. An overhead projector light bulb burns out, a VCR eats a videotape, or a chart is missing. While this may be nerve-racking, the show must go on! The quality of your speech will not be fully linked to your use of a visual aid. Use the speaking notes you have prepared and do not apologize for your missing visual aids.

Speaking to Persuade On the other hand, you may be asked to deliver a persuasive speech. Here, your goal is to encourage your audience to change their opinions or motivate them to action. As with speaking to inform, you should gather a variety of resources in order to be familiar with a subject matter. However, your task is not simply to present interesting material; you need to advocate a position and support it with evidence. Again, you must cite your sources within your speech, not only because it is required and adds to your own credibility, but because it also creates a persuasive impact.

The Thief in the Library

PLAGIARISM IS STEALING. When people use someone else's words or ideas as their own, they steal someone's "intellectual property." You use people's intellectual property all the time when you gather research for your papers and speeches. They help you understand facts and perspectives with which you yourself may not have a personal experience. During your presentation, it is critical that you give credit to those sources. If you pass off someone else's experience or thoughts as your own, you steal their intellectual property just as taking someone's bicycle would be stealing their physical property. You must give credit for any words, phrases, sentences, or ideas that are not your own. Furthermore, just changing a few words from another author's work is not sufficient to avoid citation. It is still considered plagiarism because you are using the author's structure and most of the words. Most instructors and colleges have stiff penalties for plagiarism, so it is important you understand what it is and not risk it. Not only are you stealing another person's intellectual property, you also risk severe academic penalties or possible expulsion from your school.

BASIC STRUCTURE OF SPEECH

The old public speaking adage, "Tell them what you are going to say, tell them, and tell them what you said," is still true today. Clear organization is critical during a presentation. Your audience has one chance to hear your message, so you must be clear the first time. In general, you should have an introduction, the main body of the speech, and a conclusion.

Introduction In order to inform or persuade your audience, you need their attention. The introduction should gain the audience's attention and preview your main points. Do not start your presentation with the words, "Today I'm going to talk about . . . ." That statement is overused and unimaginative. Start your speech with a short story, a question, or a shocking statement. Once you have introduced your topic, preview the main points of your speech. For example, a statement like "Nuclear, solar, and wind power are three sources of energy that our nation has yet to use to their fullest potential" outlines your three main points and the position you will be taking in your speech.

Main Body Here is the heart of your speech, where you will offer the bulk of your research. Organization is critical if you want your listeners to follow you through your major points and supporting points. Toward that end, you might organize your material in a problem/solution format by first offering evidence of a problem and then advocating for a specific solution. Whatever method you use, make sure it can be clearly followed by your listeners.

Conclusion The final segment of your presentation should review your main points and provide a short but eloquent closing. Professional speakers know that the last words can often make the most impact. Summarize the main points of your speech, then wrap up the speech with thoughtful closing lines or a call to action. Do not end your speech with the words "that's it" or "that's all." Speakers who do so have not developed a thoughtful summary and conclusion. Leave your audience with a clear and memorable ending to your speech.

DELIVERY

It is unfortunate, but all of us can probably recall a presentation where the impact of the message was diminished because the speaker had distracting physical or verbal mannerisms. It is important that your delivery, that is your physical and verbal presentation, supports your message. You do not need to be the most dynamic of speakers; those great public speakers that can inspire us have spent years honing their delivery skills. Your delivery needs only to be confident and polished.

Your delivery will improve with experience, but there are some things that you can keep in mind from the start. Direct eye contact with your audience is an important component of your delivery. You should know your material well enough that you can maintain eye contact with your audience for approximately 70 percent of your speech. If you were taught to "look over the heads of your audience" you were given poor advice. Speakers who do not maintain direct eye contact appear disconnected from the audience members.

Your posture and stance during your speech should appear relaxed and confident. While you may feel neither, there are things you can do to diminish those habits that might be distracting. Avoid hanging on to the podium or leaning against it. Let your hands gesture naturally as if you are having a conversation. Also, try to stand with your weight equally distributed on both legs so you do not shift your feet.

When you begin practicing a speech, you might have a tendency to stumble over your words or add sounds like "ah" and "um" to your sentences. The more you practice, the better you will know your material and the less likely you will be to stumble on words or rely on word fillers. If word fillers like "ah" and "um" are a problem for you, try to discover why. Is it just a habit? If so, you may not even hear yourself doing it. Have someone listen to your speech and ask them to signal you when you use a word filler. This may be disheartening at first, but it will help you become more aware of this distracting habit. Do not feel the need to completely eliminate sound fillers because this is an unrealistic goal. An occasional "um" will not diminish your message.

In general, your vocal delivery should include the natural variations in pitch, rate, and volume that you normally use while conversing. It is typical for beginning public speakers to speak quickly because they are nervous. If this is a problem, remind yourself to relax by writing cues like "slow down" in the margins of your speaking notes. Again, your vocal delivery, like your physical delivery, will improve with practice.

ANXIETY

Even seasoned public speakers feel nervous before giving a speech, so it is perfectly normal for you to experience anxiety before a class presentation. Your level of nervousness will vary with different situations, but learning how to respond to speech anxiety will help you cope with speaking situations that you face in college and in the workplace.

People react to fear with physiological and psychological responses. You might feel tension in your stomach, you might perspire more than normal, or your hands might shake. These are common physiological reactions of anxiety. If you are experiencing physiological symptoms of anxiety, try responding to them with physiological coping techniques. Do some stretching exercises before class. If you are experiencing these symptoms while waiting for your turn to speak, try a series of slow, deep breaths. Breathe in deeply, hold your breath for a few seconds, and then slowly exhale. You can also try tightening and relaxing your muscles. Tighten the muscles in your legs, hold the tension for a few seconds, and then slowly release. Continue to do this with muscle groups in your arms, neck, and shoulders. You may not be able to completely stop your hands from shaking or perspiring, but keep in mind that the symptoms you are experiencing may not be very noticeable to your audience. Concentrate on your message, not your symptoms, and you should start to feel some of that anxiety decrease.

Psychological reactions to fear and anxiety are usually manifested in the desire to flee a situation or in negative self-talk. Skipping class to avoid your speech because you are too anxious is not a good idea. If your anxiety is so overwhelming that you skip class, go to the counseling center on your campus. A counselor can provide strategies that will diminish more intense anxiety. You may also need to defeat the negative self-talk that can attend your anxiety. You might tell yourself you are a poor speaker or that you will perform badly on your speech. This kind of talk is exactly what you should not do when preparing to speak. Too often people focus on their nervousness and not on the task. Instead, try to focus on the goals of the speech and the learning experience. Yes, you may make some mistakes during your speech, but your goal is to learn in giving the speech, not be perfect. Focus on the opportunity to improve your public speaking skills. Focus on the goals of your message and the interaction with the audience and not on your anxiety.

PRACTICING

You can also reduce your anxiety through practice. Practice is what makes the difference between mediocre public speakers and good ones. You cannot become a better speaker without practice. Perhaps you, like many other people, think that good public speakers were born with that ability. That is simply not true. Dynamic public speakers have achieved their success through practice. They prepare their speeches, and they practice those speeches before attempting to deliver them in front of an audience. You have spent time gathering your material, developing an outline, and writing speaking notes. But you are not finished. Like the final editing of a paper, you are not finished preparing for a speech until you have spent time practicing it.

It is important to practice the speech in the same manner you will be presenting it in class. If you are part of a panel of presenters who will be sitting at a table in the front of the classroom, then practice the speech sitting in front of a table with your notes spread in front of you. If you will be standing to deliver your speech, then practice your speech while standing holding your note cards or placing them on a podium. Whatever the environment, try to simulate it as much as possible when you practice. Not only will this improve your presentation, but simulating the actual environment as much as possible may also calm your nerves.

As you practice your speech, there are several techniques you can use to improve your performance. If you want to focus on your physical delivery, you could practice in front of a mirror. This technique is helpful when you want to improve your eye contact, posture, and other physical aspects, but it is harder to focus on your verbal delivery when you are looking in a mirror. If you want to focus on your verbal delivery, you might try audio taping your speech as you practice. Videotaping your speech will give you the opportunity to examine your verbal and physical delivery. But be prepared for some discomfort when you watch yourself on tape, especially if this is a new experience for you. People tend to focus on the negatives when they see themselves on a screen, so make a point of looking for positive qualities that you can maintain. Finally, you can practice in front of your friends or family. If you choose this method, be sure to give your audience specific qualities to evaluate. For example, ask them if the organization was clear or if your eye contact was consistent. Give them specific instructions before you start in order to avoid general and less helpful comments such as "I liked it" or "It was fine."

You may discover other creative methods for practicing and improving your speaking skills. We encourage you experiment with the techniques above and engage in your own exploration of practice methods. But most importantly, do it. Practicing is the only way you will become a better public speaker.

Research Tools You Can Use

The library at your college will be different from the library at your high school or local community. High school and community libraries try to offer a variety of popular and academic material, but libraries on most college campuses are collections of scholarly books and articles. Here, well-educated people are able to access scholarly work for the papers and speeches they are required to do. If you are not familiar with the library at your college, we strongly suggest you attend a library tour or orientation. Becoming familiar with the variety of research materials in your library and their points of access in the library is essential to your success. In general, libraries will have the following resources.

REFERENCE MATERIALS

You might recognize several basic encyclopedias, dictionaries, atlases, and other such materials you have used in the past. General reference materials like *Encyclopedia Americana* and *Webster's Dictionary* are probably in the holdings, but you will also find more focused subject-oriented reference materials as well. For example, resources like *Black's Law Dictionary* and *The Encyclopedia of Religion* are reference materials that provide information in highly technical and specific subject areas.

POPULAR MAGAZINES AND NEWSPAPERS

You will be able to find information about current events from the popular press. These resources are helpful for locating basic information and are good sources for editorials and opinions on national issues. However, keep in mind that some publications openly advocate from a particular political position. This does not mean they are unworthy of your attention. It does mean that you should read with the knowledge of the publication's political preference in view. In addition, magazines and newspapers rarely offer the depth of analysis you will find in scholarly journals and books.

SCHOLARLY JOURNALS

Every academic discipline has journals in which experts and scholars publish their work. In most cases, the journal articles you gather have been thoroughly reviewed by editorial boards. Furthermore, not every article submitted to a journal is published and no initial draft finds its way into print without revision. These resources will report on the most current research being conducted and will present critical reaction to that research. Journal articles can be accessed by electronic indexes and databases available through your library's computer system or by paper indexes like the *Humanities Index* and the *Social Sciences Index*.

BOOKS

Books are a critical source of in-depth information. Because of their length, they can provide a good synthesis of a topic along with a historical background that might be lacking in a journal article or brief overview in an encyclopedia. They usually have extensive bibliographies that will identify resources you may not have discovered. However, because of the time involved in writing the material and producing the actual product, books will not always present the most current state of the discussion.

INTERNET SOURCES

The Internet has given people access to an enormous amount of information. Although some of this information is excellent, the mere presence of a website does not automatically imply that the author is an expert. When you are using the Internet to search for supporting materials for your papers and speeches, it is important that you learn to discriminate between websites that are credible and websites that are not grounded in research or produced by scholars. Go to "On the Net" at the end of this chapter for a list of Internet sites that are produced specifically for academic research.

REFERENCE LIBRARIANS

Reference librarians may be your most useful "tool" while researching a topic. Your reference librarian will be able to guide you to resources that you did not know existed. They are trained to find information and can quickly access resources in many different venues. If you are unsuccessful in locating information on a topic, cannot find a resource, or need help getting started on a task, ask for help.

Communication skills are essential to your academic success. Your ability to locate information from various sources is critical to writing papers and presenting speeches. Remember, each time you write a paper and deliver a speech, not only are you learning more about a subject, you are also becoming a better communicator.

Exercises for Success

Create a Writing Schedule

Choose a paper that is currently assigned for this term and experiment with creating a writing schedule like the one presented earlier in this chapter. The worksheet below will help you structure your writing plan. Edit it as necessary to meet your needs.

The Paper Plan

Class:

Paper:

Final Due Date:

Task	Date for Completion	Done
Know the purpose of the paper		
Select a topic		
Do initial research		
Create a thesis statement		
Create a working outline		
Complete additional research		
Complete the first draft		
Revise the first draft		
Revise the second draft		
Final draft		

Find the Writing Center

If your college has a writing center, go to the center and find out how to take advantage of the help they have to offer. When are they open? What types of services do they offer? What are the busiest times during the semester? In what stage can you bring in a writing project? In other words, do they prefer a final draft, or are they willing to assist you in the early stages of the writing process as well? Find out this information and write it in your day planner or keep it posted near your work area.

Study Speaking by Other People

Check your library's holdings of videotapes or DVDs for recordings of public speeches. These could be speeches by famous politicians, activists, or entertainers, but there might also be speeches by college students. If any types of speeches are available for your viewing, watch and evaluate how other people present their ideas. How is their delivery? How is their organization? What do you like about a certain speech or speaker? What do you not like? What can you learn from these speeches in order to become a better public speaker?

What Is the Penalty for Plagiarism?

Within the college catalog or student conduct code of your school, you will find both a definition of plagiarism and the possible penalties for it. Consult the source recommended by your instructor and learn all you can about the definitions and consequences of this illegitimate borrowing.

Take a Library Tour

Your college library will offer guided tours or orientations to students during the semester. Go to your library and find out the dates and times when these tours are offered. More importantly, attend one or more of the orientations. If your library does not offer something like this, ask the reference librarians for any written material that explains basic library holdings and procedures. Also, check if there is an online computer tutorial that can take you through basic research skills. Your goal will be to learn about the different types of sources in the library, their locations, and their access points.

Try Out Your Research Skills

Identify a topic that you will need to research in the near future. This might be for a paper or a speech, or it may simply be of interest to you. Your goal in this exercise is to find information on your topic from a variety of resources. Use what you learned from your library orientation to create a bibliography that includes categories of material like these:

* Subject-oriented encyclopedia
* Book
* Magazine or newspaper article
* Journal article
* Internet site

Spiritual Reflection Journal

Read Matthew 28:18–20, Luke 1:1–4, and Acts 17: 1–4. Think about how important written and verbal communication skills were to the spread of Christianity in the early church. How important are these skills to Christians in this century? How important are these skills to your own future profession?

Time in Prayer

In your personal time in prayer, consider praying for the following people and needs.

- For friends whom you have not seen in a long time
- For the courage to speak your beliefs
- For the ability to cope with speech anxiety
- For the ability to organize your writing projects
- For the wisdom to receive criticism and use it to improve yourself
- For the motivation to start your writing projects when they are assigned

On the Net

The Internet can be a helpful resource for you as you look for ideas to make yourself a more happy and successful student. Visit the College Success page offered by Thomson Wadsworth for web links that will help you grow further on this topic. Go to *www.success.wadsworth.com* and click on Resource Web Links.

There are several Internet subject directories that are useful tools when researching on the Internet. These directories and search engines access material that is more scholarly, and therefore more credible sources for your research:

http://lii.org
http://library.sau.edu/bestinfo/
http://infomine.ucr.edu/

For information on how to critically evaluate websites check:

www.library.cornell.edu/okuref/webeval.html

For a tutorial on how to search the Internet, go to the following website and click on "Web Searching Tips":

www.searchenginewatch.com/

Chapter 10

Making the Tough Decisions: The Role of Christian Values

He has showed you . . . what is good. And what does the
LORD require of you? To act justly, to love mercy, and
to walk humbly with your God.

Micah 6:8

- How can I be sure that I am making a good decision?

- What are personal values?

- What role does my Christianity play in making important decisions?

*W*HAT CAREER SHOULD I PURSUE? Should I use alcohol when I am in college? Should I copy that paper off the Internet and turn it in as my own? Decisions, decisions, life is absolutely full of decisions. As a college student, important decisions like these can consume vast amounts of time while generating significant amounts of anxiety. And once you have graduated from college, imposing new decisions will be there to replace the old ones you have already made. Should I think about getting married now or wait until my life is more settled? Can I afford the payments on that house or should I continue to pay rent to someone else? Should I take the new job I am being offered and move to the other side of the country or should I be content with a lower salary and stay where I am? Should I declare that income on my tax return or hide it?

Since important decisions like these will continue to be part of your life, your time in college is a great time to practice and refine your skills in making them. You will have plenty of practice during any week of college doing just that. As a college student, every week will bring decisions that require you to assemble options, weigh advantages and disadvantages, and come to conclusions. Through this repeated practice, you will hone the speed and accuracy of your decision making.

In this chapter, you will have the opportunity to reflect on the different types of decisions you make in life. You will see that a decision-making system is not necessary for many of the mundane choices you make every day. But for those really important decisions, this chapter will challenge you to design a decision-making process that honors the critical role Christian faith plays in making weighty decisions. Furthermore this chapter invites you to reflect on your personal value system. It will help you clarify the foundation that lies beneath your view of life and it will challenge you to check the content of your value system against the one outlined in Micah 6:8. Decisions, decisions, life is full of decisions. After reading this chapter, you will feel more comfortable and confident in addressing them.

Not All Decisions Are the Same

It goes without saying that all decisions are not created equal. Some decisions are vastly more important than others. For example, if you do a poor job of selecting a meal at a restaurant or if you do a poor job of harmonizing the color of the clothes you wear to school today, the consequences of those decisions are minimal and will fade quickly. On the other hand, there are decisions that have enduring power. Whom you chose to marry, what occupation you elect to pursue, and how you manage your credit card debt are decisions that have the power to affect your well being for a very long time. Clearly, decisions vary in terms of their weight and the consequences that attend them.

Additionally, it is important to note that simply being a Christian is no guarantee that you will always make the right decision. In the Bible, we see believers making a variety of important decisions with varying degrees of success. For example, when the sons of Jacob see their younger brother Joseph approaching them, they immediately begin to discuss how to handle their upstart brother. After carefully weighing their options, they elect to kill this man with the fancy coat and fancy dreams, to hide his body in a cistern, and to tell their father that a wild animal had attacked and killed him (Gen 37:17–20). Within a short time, the brothers changed their mind. Instead of killing Joseph, they conspired sell him as a slave and pack him off for an unknown future in Egypt. This narrative clearly illustrates that believers can make very poor decisions when they do not follow a careful process that honors the influence of biblical principles.

By contrast, the Bible also contains stories about believers who make very good decisions. Consider the subsequent experience of Joseph. After he arrived in Egypt, Joseph became the slave of a ranking Egyptian official named Potiphar. When Potiphar was away from the house, his wife came to Joseph demanding that he participate with her in a sexual affair (Gen 39). The biblical author celebrates the honorable decision that Joseph makes when he rejects the repeated advances of his master's wife and stands as an example of a believer making a very good decision, one that we will explore in greater detail shortly.

A Decision-Making Process

While simply being a Christian is no guarantee that you will always make the right decision, the careful application of Christian beliefs can go a long way toward improving the quality of the decisions you make. This portion of the chapter will present a process that may be used when you are confronted by a significant choice. This process lengthens the time required to make such a decision, but we believe that critical decisions are best made over an extended period of time. While less important decisions may be made more quickly, relying upon intuition and past experiences, more important and unique decisions require careful thought, time, and a process that honors one's status as a member of God's family.

STEP ONE: CLARIFY THE CIRCUMSTANCES AND THE QUESTION YOU NEED TO ANSWER

The first step in the process requires that you come to greater clarity about the circumstances that surround your decision and exactly what question you are attempting to answer. Take a pen and paper in hand or sit down at your computer. Write down as much as you can about the circumstances surrounding the decision. Who is involved and affected? What has happened to bring this situation about? What do you control and what lies outside your control? Where would you like to be at the end of this process? Once you have done that brainstorming, filter all that you have written into a single question. As you reflect and write, you will come to greater clarity about the circumstances that surround this decision and you will focus on the core question that needs to be answered.

Consider how this may have looked if Joseph had used this technique in determining his course of action with Potiphar's wife. His time in reflection may have looked like this: My name is Joseph. I have been separated from my family and am living in a household with a cultural and spiritual orientation that is different from the one I have known. I am a slave in this house and so I am not free to pursue certain courses of action. Yet the senior member of this household, who is a high-ranking Egyptian official, has great confidence in my management style and abilities. Over time, I have been placed in a position of high personal responsibility overseeing everything my master owns. God is blessing everything that is happening in this household through my leadership. I am also a very good-looking man who has attracted the sexual interest of my master's wife. I have sexual desires of my own. How should I respond to the sexual advances made by my master's wife?

STEP TWO: CLARIFY THE OPTIONS

The second step in making an important decision is thinking through the various ways in which the question you have raised may be answered. Again, writing down your options will help you see your thinking more clearly. Keep the notes you made earlier close at hand, for the brainstorming you did in connection with the first step will prove helpful to you here.

This is how that could have looked for Joseph as he clarified his options. How should I respond to the sexual advances made by my master's wife?

I could have sexual relations with her just once.
I could have sexual relations with her as often as she would want and try to keep it a secret.

I could ignore her repeated invitations and try to avoid her.

I could run away from this household.

I could refuse her advances and hope that she would respect my point of view.

STEP THREE: IDENTIFY THE PROS AND CONS OF EACH OPTION

Every option you list in the second step of this process will have its own advantages and disadvantages. In the third step of this decision-making process, it is time to honor that reality by formally listing the advantages and disadvantages of each option. This is clearly the time to pray for clarity of thought, to pursue God's Word for direction, and to consult with trusted Christian friends who may be able to see advantages and disadvantages to your proposed choices that are less clear or absent from your own thinking. The Bible may or may not speak directly to the options you have listed, but the Lord will speak to you when he is invited to be part of the process. Remember the promise that Jesus makes, "Ask and it will be given to you; seek and you will find; knock and the door will be opened to you." (Matt 7:7)

We can again explore how that may have looked in the decision Joseph needed to make. We will look at just one of the options he had, "I could have sexual relations just once with Potiphar's wife." This option boasts several advantages:

If I follow this course of action, I could gain favor with a very influential member of the household.

I could have my own sexual experience.

And by giving in just once, I could get past the distracting invitations that keep interrupting my day.

By contrast, there are some grave disadvantages to pursuing this option:

If my master finds out, I am sure to lose the high rank I have in this household or be put in prison.

I have no guarantee that she would leave me alone if I give in just once.

But what is most important of all, having sexual relations with her would be a sinful act that my God has forbidden.

Watch Out for Dualism

ANY STUDENTS LEAVE HIGH school with a very dualistic way of looking at life. They see issues as having only two sides and statements as completely true or completely false. Most matters in life are much more complex than this. To be sure, we need to define some matters in clear terms of right and wrong. But most matters in life are not that clear cut. For example, a proposed state law that would allow the carrying of concealed weapons defies dualistic thinking. The issue is very complex, with persuasive arguments being made on behalf of each position. Dualism is an excuse to stop thinking about a topic before you have thought your way completely through it. If you have been trained to think about the world in these limited terms, watch out for this form of dualism that stunts your successful thinking on a topic.

STEP FOUR: DECIDE AND PROCEED IN CONFIDENCE

Once the matter has been carefully brought to this point, through prayer and meditation on the Word, it is time to proceed confidently with the option that appears most reasonable and that honors the leading of God. That is precisely what we see Joseph doing in Gen 39. In the end, Joseph refuses the advances of his master's wife, hoping that she would respect his point of view. After every option was considered, this was clearly the best course of action, the one that allowed him to remain faithful to his earthly overseer and to his heavenly Lord. Once the decision has been made, Joseph proceeds with confidence and announces his decision to Potiphar's wife. "With me in charge my master does not concern himself with anything in the house; everything he owns he has entrusted to my care. No one is greater in this house than I am. My master has withheld nothing from me except you, because you are his wife. How then can I do such a wicked thing and sin against God?" (Gen 39:8–9) And when Potiphar's wife continued to pursue him, Joseph did not revisit the question. He remained firm in his decision, confident that he had been led to the best option, a decision that allowed him to retain his integrity as a careful thinker and as a member of God's family.

Not every decision you make requires the same amount of time and this very thoughtful approach. But if you are a Christian, those decisions that directly affect your integrity as a member of Jesus' household and impact your future life in a dramatic way deserve no less. This four-step process is one that challenges us to think through our decisions carefully. It calls on us to acknowledge all the details and circumstances that surround the decision. It requires us to carefully articulate the question we are trying to answer. It demands that we identify all the options we have and weigh the pros and cons of each. And most importantly, it calls us to think through the potential decisions in a way that honors our personal values grounded in the Bible.

My Aesthetic, Moral, and Personal Values

Behind the scenes of the process described above, our personal value system is at work shaping the response to the decisions we need to make. In reality, this system plays a much bigger role in our lives, shaping who we are and how we view the world. We will briefly discuss the nature of aesthetic and moral values before pursuing the larger and more critical discussion of personal values.

AESTHETIC VALUES

Aesthetic values may best be defined as your personal taste, evident in the music, the art, or the food you enjoy. The fact that your roommate loves country music while you detest it or the fact that you love sushi while your friend abhors it is evidence that people have differing aesthetic values. These preferences find their source both within the uniqueness of our creation and in the fostering hand of our cultural experience. Since these values are, in part, shaped by our cultural experience, people typically find that their personal tastes migrate under the influence of new people and new circumstances in life. For example, you may have refused to eat vegetables as a child but find that you now cannot get enough of them.

MORAL VALUES

By contrast, moral values are the part of our value system we use to make decisions about what is right or wrong, just or unjust in the world. When torn down to the foundation, a moral decision is principally built upon one of three foundations: reason, emotion, or authority. The Enlightenment's rationalism has strongly influenced modern thinkers to equate what is right with what is most logical. The person whose moral judgment is guided by reason may well see the death penalty as immoral since no one has adequately proved that the death penalty serves as an effective deterrent to crime. By contrast, a moral decision may be founded upon personal feelings or emotions. A couple may make the moral decision to have premarital sex based on the feelings of love they have for one another. Since the decision to have sex with one another feels right to them, they become confident that they are making the right decision. Thirdly, a moral decision may find its foundation in the authority of a respected book, person, or deity. For example, when a Christian student is tempted to plagiarize a paper from the Internet, he or she will step away from that act since it would be a violation of God's instructions given in his Word. Respect for this authority figure lies at the foundation of that moral choice. Thus moral values are those values used to make ethical choices and they are founded upon one of three foundations: reason, emotion, or authority.

PERSONAL VALUES

Our personal value system is influenced by our aesthetic values and moral values but has its own distinguishing characteristics. It is not just your personal taste in clothing and your perspective on the death penalty, but also the core beliefs you have about who you are, the world you live in, and the people that surround you in life. It is that part of us that shapes everything from how we vote in a presidential election, to when we read our Bibles, to how we deal with the homeless person who asks us for money on a busy street corner.

It can be more difficult to define your personal value system in the abstract. Perhaps the best ways to see it is in response to very practical situations you meet in life. Consider what you can learn about your personal value system by observing your reaction to the following statements:

> The Democratic candidate for governor is speaking on your campus next week.
>
> Your roommate has just revealed to you that her uncle is gay.
>
> Your brother has not gone to church for one year.
>
> You just found a purse with $ 1,000 cash inside it.
>
> Your friend is planning to sleep overnight with her boyfriend in the residence hall.
>
> You have been invited to spend this weekend at your friend's house but have learned that his mother is an alcoholic.
>
> Your boyfriend cheated on his final exam in chemistry.
>
> Several of your friends invite you to hand out leaflets opposing abortion at a medical clinic.

Watch Out For Intolerance

COLLEGE STUDENTS WILL, by design, encounter new ideas and interact with people who challenge their traditional point of view. In order for that experience to be a meaningful one, it is necessary for you to develop a tolerance that allows you to fully hear an alternate point of view before dismissing it out of hand. When you hear someone express a view that you have not traditionally owned, listen carefully. Make an effort to understand the arguments being made and the foundation on which those arguments have been built. While they make you uncomfortable, it is unwise to flee from those forms of interaction or isolate yourself from them. Tolerance is not the same as acceptance. You can be a tolerant listener, grow in your understanding of a position, and still leave the conversation without accepting the alternative point of view.

The reaction you had to each of these statements makes a statement about the content of your personal value system. As difficult as it can be to get a handle on that value system, well-educated people make a conscious effort to understand the personal value system that motivates their thoughts and actions in life. That is important for two reasons. First of all, it is important to have a sense of your personal value system so that you can understand and appreciate the thinking of those who do not agree with you. For example, your view of abortion may be radically different from the view held by the individuals with whom you work at your part-time job. Their arguments and their methods of arguing their point of view will make no sense to you unless you understand the personal value system that lies beneath their statements. You may be arguing your case from the foundation of the Bible's authority while the other person may see the Bible as just another book whose authority they do not respect. Perhaps they are using the foundation of reason, claiming that the fetus is not really a person who benefits from protection of the law until it is viable on its own. Suffice it to say that it is very easy for two people to simply talk past one another about a topic unless they clarify the foundation from which each of them is arguing their case.

Secondly, it is important to understand your personal value system so that you may be aware of the vulnerability associated with your own point of view. If you take a position in support of the death penalty and found it upon a logical argument, your argument will be most vulnerable if your logic is not sound. If you take a stand against abortion and base it on the authority of the Bible, your argument will be vulnerable if you have misunderstood the teaching of the Bible or if you have overestimated the expertise of your authority. It is important for careful thinkers to know and acknowledge where their particular position is most vulnerable. This does not prevent educated people from taking positions. But it does allow thoughtful people to take positions with an awareness that there is always a vulnerability to that position located in the foundation of their argument.

Rethinking My Personal Values

Now that you have had a chance to think about your personal value system, it is time to rethink that system under the influence of the Bible's teaching. Christians acknowledge the authority of the Bible in their lives and so seek to align their personal value system as closely as possible with guidance and direction offered in God's Word. One could argue that the entire Bible is designed to shape and edit the view you have of yourself, of your relationship to God, and of your relationship to others you meet in life. But one Bible passage in particular challenges us to rethink our personal value system. That passage is Micah 6:8.

In this book of the Bible, Micah criticizes those who claim to be believers but whose personal value system is far from what God intended it to be. In particular, he reproves the wealthy and the political power brokers who are using their wealth and power to exploit others. For example, in Chapter Two he says, "Woe to those who plan iniquity, to those who plot evil on their beds! At morning's light they carry it out because it is in their power to do it. They covet fields and seize them, and houses, and take them. They defraud a man of his home, a fellowman of his inheritance." (Micah 2:1–2) Micah criticizes the citizens of this state for seizing property that does not belong to them (2:2), for taking clothes off of people's backs (2:8), and for bringing physical harm to others in the process (3:2–3). Given these kinds of social injustice, it is no surprise to read page after page of criticism in the Book of Micah announcing God's displeasure with this behavior and the coming of divine judgment against those who practiced it. But by contrast to the lengthy criticisms found in the book, we find a positive verse that calls attention to itself by virtue of its brevity. Micah poses the critical question and then answers it with a striking trilogy: "And what does the LORD require of you? To act justly, to love mercy, and to walk humbly with your God." (Micah 6:8) Here in three brief phrases, Micah provides the outline for a personal value system. This is a clear call to rethink your personal value system and to see if the outline Micah describes is operative there.

TO ACT JUSTLY

The first charge Micah gives is to act justly. This, of course, implies that there is a standard against which our actions may be judged. In many situations in life, God has not given humans the authority to make up the rules for living or to change them when it suits them. Rather the Word of God is filled with volitional clauses that direct the actions and attitudes of humankind. In Deuteronomy 5, God articulates the Ten Commandments that offer a summary of what he means for human beings to act justly. This summary is enhanced throughout the rest of the Bible where God speaks about life and living. Since this blueprint that directs moral behavior comes directly from God himself, it cannot be improved. That is why God further states, "Do not add to what I command you and do not subtract from it, but keep the commands of the LORD your God." (Deut 4:2)

As we review those guidelines for just living, we find that some are widely accepted by society. For example, "you shall not murder" is a directive that controls daily life in most civilized societies. But there are other directives from God that seem to fly in the face of common sense and certainly in the face of common practice. Consider the directions of Jesus, "Love your enemies, do good to those who hate you, bless those who curse you, pray for those who mistreat you." (Luke 6:27–28) Whether the biblical directive is commonly held or contradicts common, societal practice, Micah challenges us to use them as a standard to measure whether or not we are acting justly.

Watch Out for Relativism

RELATIVISM IS A VERY powerful force in our current culture driven by an existential world view that encourages the value-free acceptance of nearly all ideas. While such relativism is certainly defendable in respect to aesthetic values, it runs into harsh opposition from the Bible when applied to moral issues. While relativism plays down the possibility of much objective truth, the Bible makes it clear that there is such a thing as objective truth, particularly in regard to moral issues. Relativism may claim that each individual has his or her own right to define truth as he or she sees it, asserting that what is morally true for one person is not necessarily true for everyone. The Bible honors the fact that while aesthetic taste is relative, moral truth is not. Watch out for the form of relativism that removes the authority of God's Word from the stage.

TO LOVE MERCY

Secondly, Micah challenges his readers to check their personal value system and see if it celebrates and encourages the merciful treatment of others, "to love mercy." The Hebrew term that stands behind the English translation, "mercy," is somewhat more broad and powerful than this translation suggests. There is no single English word that fully communicates the idea. We come as close as we can with the phrase, "a loving-kindness that endures." People can act justly for a variety of reasons. People can act justly because they feel they will get something out of it if they do. Others may act justly because they feel you should just be good for goodness sake. But the Bible challenges its adherents to live a life characterized by an enduring, loving-kindness enacted in thanks for the greater mercy that has been shown to them. "This is how God showed his love among us: He sent his one and only Son into the world that we might live through him. This is love: not that we loved God, but that he loved us and sent his Son as an atoning sacrifice for our sins." (1 John 4:9–10) This Gospel message has so changed the life of believers that they are capable of loving even their enemies. "We love because he first loved us." (1 John 4:19)

TO WALK HUMBLY WITH YOUR GOD

Finally, Micah challenges us "to walk humbly with your God." Considering all that God has done for the believer and all that believers are able to do through the power of God, they could easily become filled with an inappropriate pride. But the Lord cautions that this pride is out of place in the life of a Christian. In fact, the Apostle Paul warns that the person who is feeling a prideful over-confidence is the person standing at the brink of failure. "So if you think you are standing firm, be careful that you don't fall!" (1 Cor 10:12) By contrast, Paul holds up the example of Jesus. "Your attitude should be the same as that of Christ Jesus: Who, being in very nature God, did not consider equality with God something to be grasped, but made himself nothing, taking the very nature of a servant being made in human likeness. And being found in appearance as a man, he humbled himself and became obedient to death— even death on a cross!" (Phil 2:5–8)

Our personal value system lies at the very core of who we are. It impacts the way we make our decisions. It impacts the way we live our life in relationship to God and the way we treat others around us. Well-educated people know something about their personal value system and edit it as necessary. Micah challenges those honored by God's forgiveness to walk justly, to love mercy, and to walk humbly with their God.

Exercises for Success

It Is Decision Time

In this chapter, you encountered a decision-making process that could be used when making an important decision in your life. Now it is your turn to practice with that process by addressing a decision you are facing at the moment. Either sit down at your computer or take paper and pencil in hand and work through the following steps:

Step One: Clarify the circumstances and the question you need to answer.

Step Two: Clarify your options.

Step Three: Identify the pros and cons of each option.

Step Four: Decide and proceed with confidence.

At the conclusion of this process, you will have positioned yourself to make a decision. But what is more important, the experience will help you determine what portions of the process you will edit to fit your needs.

Identifying My Personal Values

To learn more about your personal values, place a check mark next to each of the following statements that you feel strongly about. Then go back and pick out the top eight and list them in the order of importance to you.

I want to be very well educated.

I want to bring someone to know Christ.

I want to be a community leader.

I want to make a lot of money.

I want to have a healthy spiritual life.

I want to enjoy good relationships.

I want to have as much personal freedom as I can find.

I want to be happy.

I want to make other people happy.

I want to enjoy my work more than my leisure time.

I want to be known as a person of integrity.

I want to be known for my creativity.

I want to be known for my athleticism.

I want to eliminate racial prejudice from the world.

I want to become famous.

I want to be married and have a family.

I want to become involved in politics.

I want my children to grow up as Christians.

I want there to be a cure for cancer.

I want to be known for my good looks.

I want to know my Bible better than my peers.

I want to be a leader in my church.

I want to live a healthy lifestyle.

I want to feed hungry children.

I want to enjoy my leisure time more than my work.

Personal Values and a Moral Dilemma

Susan came from a small town where her widowed father was a Christian minister. He raised her very strictly and it was only with great reluctance that he allowed her to come to the state university. He feared that the big city and secular professors in college would corrupt her morals. After the initial college orientation, his final words to her were a warning, "If I ever find out that you have been fooling around with boys or using alcohol or drugs, I'll cut you off from all financial support and never let you enter our home again."

Susan had always obeyed her father and intended to do so while at college. Her professors did challenge her value system and at times seemed to make fun of the Christian views she expressed. Nevertheless, she honored her father's request and stayed away from drugs and alcohol. But in November, she began dating Larry, a student in her history class. Eventually Larry invited her to parties where alcohol flowed freely. He said to her, "I know that you don't want to have anything to drink. I respect that decision, just come and have fun with me and my friends." At first, she refused the drinks offered to her at the party, but eventually her friend Alison persuaded her that "one drink wouldn't hurt." Consuming alcohol was new for Susan. It made her feel free and liberated. Finally, she felt that she was doing something that she wanted to do.

Susan began to attend parties more regularly and kept experimenting with more and more alcohol. One night when she had become very drunk, Larry convinced her to have sexual relations with him. Susan hardly remembered what had happened but the physical evidence told her that she had gone to a place she had never intended to go. Susan felt guilty and devastated. She wanted to talk to Larry about what had happened but he refused to speak to her about it. In the end, Larry told her that he did not want to see her any more. Alison saw how devastated Susan was and felt like she needed to get out and meet new people. She told Susan that the best way to get over this loss in her life was to find someone new. Alison was dating Jim and his fraternity was having a party that night. Susan agreed to go. Once there, Susan began to drink more heavily than she ever had before. She drank so much that she became very, very sleepy. Susan went to a back bedroom in the house to lie down and passed out in the bed. While lying on her back in an unconscious state, she choked to death on her own vomit.

List the characters in this story and rank them from the person you see as most responsible for Susan's death to the one least responsible for Susan's death. Compare your conclusions with those of others. Where do you agree and where do you disagree? How did your personal value system impact the way you organized your list?

Micah 6:8 and My Personal Values

Earlier in this chapter we saw how Micah 6:8 challenges us to demonstrate three qualities in our system of personal value system. Below is a list of statements to which you may apply your personal value system. Select three of the statements that are of greatest interest to you. Pretend that a friend of yours has made the statement. Write your response to them and demonstrate through your response that your value system lives up to the one outlined in Micah 6:8. Demonstrate that you act justly, love mercy, and walk humbly with your God.

War is a necessary evil.

Abortion is an appropriate method of contraception.

We must support our political leaders no matter what.

No church leader should be a practicing homosexual.

Honesty is always the best policy.

People who do not work for a living should not be given public financial support.

Cheating is only wrong if you get caught.

Love will always find a way.

Treat others as you would like to be treated yourself.

Spiritual Reflection Journal

Read the story of Abram in Genesis 12:10–20. Write about your reaction to the decision that Abram made in regards to Sarai and the method he used to make the decision. Do you feel the decision was an honorable one? What was missing from the decision-making process reported by the author in this story? What meaningful application do you find for your own life in this story?

Time in Prayer

In your personal time in prayer or in connection with others in your class, pray for the following people and needs.

* For the person you know who is in the midst of making a difficult decision

* For your church and government leaders making difficult decisions at this time

* For your parents and family members in the midst of critical decisions they are making

* That God would help you to carefully think through your value system in light of Micah 6:8

* That God would give you the strength to live out your personal values in the midst of the challenges you face

On the Net

The Internet can be a helpful resource for you as you look for ideas to make yourself a more happy and successful student. Visit the College Success page offered by Thomson Wadsworth for web links that will help you grow further on this topic. Go to *www.success.wadsworth.com* and click on Resource Web Links. For even more on the topic of values and the college student visit *www.collegevalues.org/articles.cfm*.

Seeking and Maintaining Healthy Relationships

Dear friends, since God so loved us,
we also ought to love one another.

1 John 4:11

- What kinds of relationships will I have in college?
- How do those relationships impact my pursuit of success?
- How will diversity enhance my education?
- How can I keep my relationships healthy?
- How can I manage conflict in my relationships?

ROM THE BEGINNING, God designed human beings to be connected to one another in close, meaningful relationships (Gen 2:18). Those relationships are not merely tangential to our happiness and satisfaction, they are fundamental to our well being. In a perfect world, we would always feel happy and satisfied with our relationships. But in a world that has been ruined by sin, we find ourselves depending upon and managing relationships that are far from perfect. We need to turn no further in our Bible than the pages of Genesis to find such troubled relationships: a husband turns on his wife (Gen 3:12), a brother's jealous rage leads him to commit the first murder (Gen 4), a young woman is sexually assaulted (Gen 34), and a brother is sold as a slave (Gen 37). Consequently, the deep need we have for meaningful relationships lives in constant tension with the potential harm that those same relationships may bring into our lives. This chapter is about managing the relationships that live in that tension.

We will begin with an overview of the various types of people that impact you as a college student: old and new friends, romantic partners, spouses, parents, roommates, and faculty. Among those relationships, you will be interacting with people who are different from you, so we will also explore the nature and importance of diversity on a college campus. And because relationships can be helpful or harmful to your pursuit of success, we will examine the qualities of healthy relationships and offer advice on managing the conflict that is bound to surface within those relationships. One thing is clear, the relationships you have as a college student will impact both your chances for success and your well being. As you work to improve your relationships, we pray that the love of God might guide you in the process so that we might truly love one another in the same way that he has loved us.

Different Types of Relationships

Most people are surprised when they stop to count all the different kinds of personal relationships that impact their lives. If you take the time to make such a list, you too will find yourself connected to many different people and supported in many different relationships during your time in college. Consider the following list as a starting point for your own thinking.

- Parents
- Siblings
- Spouse
- Friends

- Roommates
- Romantic partners
- Stepparents
- Faculty
- Children
- Grandparents

The relationships that you enjoyed before going to college will likely experience some change if for no other reason than that you yourself will be changing as a result of your advanced education. You will become a better thinker, you will become more informed about the world, and your personal views about life may be edited. As you bring the "new you" to your old relationships, be patient with your parents, siblings, friends, and others who may need time to adjust to the person you have become. Good relationships go through those kinds of adjustments and become stronger through them. When the road gets a bit rocky, try employing the conflict management suggestions offered later in this chapter.

NEW FRIENDSHIPS AND OLD FRIENDSHIPS

From the moment you stepped onto the campus, you were surrounded by a sea of new faces. Remember those first orientation sessions and classes? Some of you will celebrate the opportunities to meet new people, while others may feel uncomfortable with the thought of making new friends. In either case, we hope that you have been getting away from the computer and spending time in the student union, at athletic events, and at parties. Coming to college is an exciting time in your life, and one of the powerful commodities you will take with you when you leave is those new friendships. Seize the opportunity. Now is the time in your life to meet people with different interests and backgrounds. Make a point of breaking out of the old crowd and getting to know someone who is from a different country or of a different race. You will grow in ways that you cannot imagine.

But not everyone finds it easy to meet new people. If you are one who has difficulty making new friends, consider the following suggestions. Make yourself available. If you have been in the habit of sitting in your room with the door closed, others may assume you want to be left alone. Open your door and leave your room behind for those places on campus where the students go to have fun. It is also helpful to participate in activities beyond the classroom. Your school likely has a variety of clubs, teams, and organizations that allow people of similar interests to get together. Joining such a team, club, or organization will not only foster your mutual interests but be a conduit for finding new friends.

Then there is the question of what to do with your friends back at home. We all like to stay in contact with our old friends and the technology of today allows us to do that with minimal cost. Most college students have access to email and messaging that allow immediate access to old friends in other cities and states. This is an excellent way to maintain those relationships, but beware of spending too much time in chat rooms and in messaging to one another. This can become an obstacle that prevents you from interacting with new people on campus. As you stay in contact with your old friends, make sure you reach out to the people in your campus community.

Finally, not every relationship you have had in the past will make the transition with you to college life. Honor the fact that while you have changed, others may not have changed or they may have changed in ways that are not compatible with the way you have changed. This means some relationships will never be what they were before. Some old friendships will survive the challenge of distance and change. But expect that some of your past relationships will best be retired to happy memories as you move forward with your life.

Are Your Friends Helping You Succeed?

How are your friends influencing you? Not everyone will be as committed or concerned about your success as you are. If your friends interrupt your study time, encourage you to skip class, or keep you up all night, you need to stand up for your best interests. Your friends may not be aware of the impact they are having on you. Speak to them. If they do not listen, take action and do what you need to do in order to be successful.

ROMANCE IN COLLEGE

College can also be a time when romance blooms in your life. Romantic relationships are important because they fulfill our need for companionship and intimacy. Both are natural and very important needs that may be filled in a variety of ways. This requires us to make decisions in our romantic relationship about the level of intimacy we will pursue and where we will draw the line. Poor decision making in this arena can result in low self-esteem, feelings of guilt, a broken relationship, pregnancy, or even a sexually transmitted disease. That is why God has provided us with directions and limitations when exploring sexual intimacy with others. In his Word, he challenges us to flee from sexual immorality, for he has chosen our bodies to be his temple (1 Corinthians 6:19–20).

As you consider the level of intimacy in your romantic relationships and where you choose to demonstrate that intimacy, consider God's message to you in passages like the following: Hebrews 13:4, 1 Corinthians 13:1–13, and 1 Corinthians 6:12–20. After you read these passages, discuss them with your partner, your Christian friends, or your minister. Through your reading and these conversations, the Holy Spirit will lead you to clarity on appropriate ways to express your intimacy with a romantic partner and what kinds of intimacy are best left for a later time. One thing is clear. The time to make a decision about the level of intimacy in your romantic relationships is before you find yourself physically aroused by your partner in a setting where temptation is harder to resist.

Another decision that needs to be weighed very carefully is the one to limit your dating to just one person. Common wisdom recommends that it is wise to date many different people during this time of your life. Through these dating experiences, you will come to know what you find most and least desirable in a romantic relationship. Before you become exclusive, allow yourself the time and experience of dating an array of people.

COLLEGE AND THE MARRIED STUDENT

Being married while you are attending college has its own unique rewards, but also presents some unique challenges. Your spouse can be an invaluable source of support and encouragement. Keep your spouse involved in your campus life by including him or her in campus activities. Attend guest lectures, drama productions, or sporting events as a couple. Invite classmates to your home for dinner. And if your university allows people to audit classes, ask your spouse to join one of your classes for fun.

If you have children while you are attending college, you will need to be strategic when planning your study time. Your children certainly deserve and need good quality time with you. But that does not mean giving them attention whenever and wherever they demand it. Some parents choose to do all their homework after their children are asleep. This is an option, but not always the most productive one. One alternative to consider is waking up earlier in the morning before your family wakes up and spend 30 to 60 minutes studying. If you are attending classes on campus during the day, be strategic with your schedule. Time scheduled between class sessions may be time that you can spend in the library on research projects or doing homework. If not the library, find a place on campus that is quiet and free from distractions.

Spending time with your family is necessary for your relationship and enjoyable for all involved, but some parents feel guilty if they study during times that used to be strictly family time. Honor the fact that you are in a new situation that is temporary, requiring everyone to make adjustments for a time. Find a balance between time spent with children and study time. If you do study at home in the evening, and it is very likely you will need to do so, establish some boundaries. When you are in your office or at the kitchen table with books in front of you, let everyone know that this is study time and interruptions should be kept to a minimum. Be sure to let your children know that they have time with you prior to their bedtime when you will be playing with them. Your children can adapt to that kind of schedule and you will be modeling excellent studying habits and time management behaviors.

PARENTS

The transition from adolescence to young adulthood typically brings a change in your relationship with your parents. Young adults who go to college often experience greater freedom in their time and more responsibility for their decisions. You are changing and growing as an independent person. While most parents want to see their children grow to become responsible adults capable of being on their own, it may be difficult for your parents to see this change in you. Be patient with them. Talk with them and get their perspective on the changes they see in you. God calls for us to honor our parents for the unique contribution they make to our lives (Exod 20:12). It will be easier to do that at some times rather than others; but love, patience, and honest communication will help everyone make the necessary adjustments.

As you learn more about life, grow, and change, remember that your parents have walked that same road you are now walking. They have the advantage of experience and so can offer you a wealth of advice and direction. Make a point to stay in contact with them, seek their advice, and let them know that you love them. They may well be missing you more than you realize.

Unfortunately, not everyone has an ideal relationship with their parents. If your relationship with a parent or parents is strained, seek support from other adults who have a concern for you. It could be grandparents, an aunt or uncle, a stepparent, or other adults on campus like a counselor or advisor. But do not dismiss your parents. Do what you can to stay in contact and pray for the strength and guidance necessary to mend that broken relationship.

LIVING WITH ROOMMATES

If you live on campus, you will probably have one or more roommates. Perhaps you were able to choose your roommate or the university may have placed you with someone you had not met before. Regardless of your situation, new students who live on campus will at some point have a conflict with their roommate. Later in this chapter we will discuss conflict management, as using good conflict strategies is essential when living with a roommate. But even before a conflict arises, you can be proactive in addressing potential problems before they occur. First of all, give your perspective a quick check. Many students have an overly romanticized picture that their roommate will be their best friend and confidant. This could happen, but it puts a tremendous amount of pressure on everyone involved in the roommate relationship.

First and foremost, your roommate is your living partner for a relatively short time. A friendship may or may not develop between you. But even before a friendship can develop, basic living guidelines will need to be discussed, adopted, and honored. Will we share the right to use personal items we have brought to campus? How will we share responsibility for cleaning the room? When will we have quiet study time in the room? And when will we turn out the lights and go to bed? Those topics are best discussed before they become issues of discontent. If that happens, you can have an excellent relationship with your roommate, even if you are not best friends. Since you will be managing a living arrangement with this person or persons, focus on the keys to successful living and let the friendship develop as it will. If you and your roommate are simply unable to negotiate basic living arrangements, it is perfectly acceptable to change roommates at the appropriate time designated by your residence director. A comfortable and peaceful living environment is vital to your success.

FACULTY CONNECTIONS

The professionals who have been given the greatest responsibility for your intellectual growth are the faculty members who teach your classes. College teachers are different from other teachers you have had both in their professional life and in the way they present their classes. They will have advanced academic degrees in specialties like history, business, or biology. Not only do they teach, but many spend time writing books and articles as well as speaking publicly on their area of expertise. Most college faculty members also spend time advising students and serving on committees that are vital to the function of the university.

By their very nature, the classes they conduct ask more of you. The faculty will assign more reading over less time and give you exams on that reading even if they have not discussed that material in class. They expect you to bear the responsibility for keeping up with the class requirements. As such, they may not remind you to read assignments or pester you about the due dates for research papers. They are less likely to check up on either your class attendance or note taking. Because they have advanced their thinking skills to a high degree through their own advanced education, they will be less tolerant of simple answers to complex questions. And they will be interested in maturing your thinking, as they engage you in conversations that require you to express and defend your own views.

The differences between college teachers and other teachers you have had may lead you to conclude that they assign too much work or are treating you unfairly. In time, you will come to appreciate them for the professional work they do. And as you make the adjustment to this new teaching style, be sure to give your college teachers the respect and patience they deserve. Jesus may serve as something of a model for us here. When he was a young man, he traveled to the Temple and sat among the teachers. Jesus first listened to those teachers and asked questions (Luke 2:46) before criticizing some of their conclusions later on in his life. This is a model worth considering and emulating.

You can be sure that as you are thinking about your college teachers, they are also forming opinions about you. That makes it critical to show your instructors that you are a serious student who has a passion to succeed. You can send that message their direction in a variety of ways. Consider the following in that light:

- Attend class and be on time. You cannot make an impression if you are not present. Students who regularly attend class not only benefit from the consistent learning, but also show they are serious about their studies. Similarly, we know of no faculty who are favorably impressed with late students. If you are consistently late for class, apologize to the instructor and make arrangements to be on time in the future.
- Know the syllabus. If you have a question regarding attendance policies, grading, scheduling, or other course expectations, always check the syllabus first before questioning the instructor.
- Sit near the front of the classroom. You will find it easier to listen to the lecture and involve yourself in class discussions.
- Participate in class. Most instructors appreciate students who contribute thoughtful questions and comments during class. If you find this difficult, try developing several questions from the assigned readings so you can ask them during appropriate moments. You can also contribute by incorporating current events into the discussion or relating your own relevant past experiences. If you disagree with something said during class, do not be afraid to say so. However, be ready to

defend your position. Faculty are there to help you become a better thinker and participating in class discussions is one way of doing that.
- See your instructors during office hours. Generally, instructors indicate on the class syllabus when they are open for student appointments. Call for an appointment and use those times to discuss assignments and exams or get feedback on papers.

Living with Difference and Celebrating Diversity

The world we live in is a mosaic of people all uniquely created to be who they are by the hand of God. The study of those differences and the construction of a society that benefits from that diversity lies at the heart of the university experience. As you travel about the campus, you will meet faculty, staff, and students who are both visibly and invisibly different from one another. The campus community is intentionally designed this way. When we live and work around people who are just like us, we learn less than when living and working with people who are different from us. This diverse community challenges us to see the world and its issues through various perspectives as we confront new ideas, people, and cultural practices.

Take a walk through the hallways and down the sidewalks of your school and pay attention to the differences of those you meet. Your walk may bring you into contact with people of a different gender, race, age, religious affiliation, or political ideology. You may meet someone with a disability, from a different culture, or who has a different marital status from yours. These are just a few of the differences that exist on a university campus. This diversity is designed to enhance your learning experience. But that diversity can produce discomfort, tension, and even fear. When we are confronted with people who are different from us, we may retreat to old stereotypes.

STEREOTYPES

Stereotyping is a way of thinking about other people who are different from you. We have a tendency to place people in categories and assign certain traits and qualities to all the people in the category. Some experts argue that stereotypes serve as "mental maps."[1] These maps might contain reliable information based on first-hand experience. However, that is rarely the case. Most

---

[1] Gregory Sawin, "How Stereotypes Influence Opinions about Individuals," in *Understanding and Managing Diversity: Readings, Cases, and Exercises*, ed. C. Harvey & M. J. Allard (Reading, MA: Addison Wesley Longman, 1995).

likely, our stereotypes are assumed to be correct but are the result of very little first-hand experience with that group of people. As a result, our beliefs about different people are subject to error. These beliefs can range from the mundane to the serious. For example, if your mental map of African-American women says they are all great cooks, that belief will not cause too great an impact on your behavior towards African-American women. However, if your mental map says African-American women are spiteful and untrustworthy, that will indeed impact your behavior. You might even refrain from interacting with African-American women based on this inappropriate generalization. When stereotypes become negative, rigid, and irrational, they will likely lead to prejudice.[2]

PREJUDICE

Whereas stereotypes have the potential for negative outcomes, prejudicial thinking, by definition, is negative. Prejudice is a negative feeling, attitude, or generalization about a group of people that leads someone to prejudge an individual based on these inaccurate beliefs and stereotypes. The stereotype about African-American women being spiteful and untrustworthy creates the prejudgment that your African-American history teacher will be unfair when she grades your paper and tests. Your stereotype of an entire group has resulted in prejudicial thinking and expectations about your history teacher. Entering a class with such a prejudiced view is bound to negatively influence your experience in that class and your interaction with that teacher.

YOU AND DIVERSITY

We often fear the unknown. Have you been reluctant to seek help from a professor because you felt uncomfortable with his or her religious affiliation or cultural background? Has your relationship with your roommate been strained because you felt uncomfortable with her or his disability or body weight? Our discomfort with people who are different from us has the potential to create barriers that block our association with others. If that has happened to you, try the following:

- See your level of comfort with others as a habit and realize that habits can be changed. You were not born with prejudicial attitudes.
- Try to become aware of times you make assumptions about people based on external characteristics like age, skin color, gender, or disabilities.

---

[2] Norma Carr-Ruffino, *Managing Diversity* (Boston, MA: Pearson, 2002).

- Read about different cultures. Knowledge is a powerful opponent to prejudice.
- Read about the psychological and sociological effects of stereotypes, prejudice, and discrimination.
- Begin changing that habit by stepping out of your comfort zone and intentionally building relationships with people who are different from you. You can join a study group or campus organization. You can sit near someone in your class and strike up a casual conversation.
- Before you explore the differences, see the common ground that all humans share. We all need to eat, sleep, love, be loved, and find hope in life. Seek common ground with personal preferences like music, sports, hobbies, or art. These similarities can increase your comfort with those who are different from you in other ways.

Fear and prejudice not only hurt the targets; they hurt you too. Open yourself to God's glorious and diverse creation. Let your curiosity lead you to appreciate the unique experiences and insights others have to offer.

Maintaining Healthy Relationships

The relationships we have with faculty, family, friends, and mates need care and attention. You can reflect on the quality of your relationships in many different ways. If you search the aisles of your local bookstore, you will find shelves of books dedicated to the study of healthy relationships. So what is offered in this section is only a starting point for reflecting on our key relationships. Here we will explore the general qualities of a healthy relationship and speak about strategies for managing conflict that develops within a relationship.

THE QUALITIES OF HEALTHY RELATIONSHIPS

All relationships vary in the level of their health. The best personal relationships are built on qualities like the following:

- Mutual trust
- Mutual respect
- Effective communication
- Kindness
- Patience
- Forgiveness
- Mutual support
- Shared interests
- Similar values

Do your personal relationships embody most of these qualities? Reflect on the relationships that are important to you personally and to your success in college to see if they exhibit such healthy qualities.

MANAGING CONFLICT IN RELATIONSHIPS

Even the healthiest relationships experience conflict. The inspired author of Proverbs implies that when he says, "The kisses of an enemy may be profuse, but faithful are the wounds of a friend." (Prov 27:6) The wounds from our friends are a product of relational conflict. You and your roommate may have had words over the time the lights get turned out at night. You and your parents may have quarreled over your choice of major. Perhaps you and your spouse disagreed about household duties. Are you afraid of conflict? You might think that having an argument will hurt the relationship or that it is a signal that the relationship itself is bad. You may even fear conflict because you think it might expose some undesirable qualities like pettiness or a need to control.

Having an argument does not automatically hurt the relationship, nor does it mean the relationship is bad. Conflict is an inevitable part of any relationship. It is a product of our being different from one another and not always seeing the world in the same way. The goal then is not to avoid conflict, but to maintain a healthy relationship even in the midst of conflict.

The first step in managing a conflict involves understanding the very nature of the conflict you are facing. The clash may center on either the *content of your conversation* or the *nature of the relationship* itself. For example, let us say that you and your significant other are arguing about the amount of time you spend together. If that conflict centers in the content, it may literally be a disagreement about the number of days and hours you spend together each week. On the other hand, if the conflict is generated by the nature of your relationship, then you may be disagreeing about who is really committed to the relationship or who is not. Successful conflict management begins with addressing the true causes of the conflict. Does it lie in the content of the conversation or in the nature of the relationship?

The second step in managing a conflict means looking carefully at the communication habits being employed by the participants. "Reckless words pierce like a sword, but the tongue of the wise brings healing." (Prov 12:18) Maybe you never thought that your method of handling a conflict can greatly influence the health of the relationship, but it can. Some habits are helpful and facilitate effective communication behaviors. Some habits are harmful to the process of conflict management. These obstruct effective communication behaviors.

Poor communication habits obstruct the open and honest sharing that people can have in a relationship. Instead of communicating directly, people who engage in the following behaviors often do not get to the real issue and so prolong the relational tension. Over time, the relationship can suffer great harm if these become the primary tools of managing conflict.[3]

Avoiding This is the unwise avoiding of a conflict. It could be either a physical or mental retreat from the scene or topic, like walking out of the room or ignoring the other person while watching TV. Time apart may be necessary to collect ourselves before managing a conflict but prolonged avoidance will only lead to more harm. It is important to note that we are not offering that advice to you if you are in a relationship in which you are being physically or verbally threatened. In such a case, physical separation from your partner is an absolute necessity to avoid further harm.

Blaming Conflict in a relationship almost always has more than one contributor. When we blame our partner, we make accusations and place all the responsibility for the conflict on the other person.

Uncontrolled Anger It is not wrong to be angry at someone since anger can stem from righteous motives. Remember that God describes himself as being angry at times. However, anger is a vice when it springs from sinful motives or when that anger results in the physical or emotional harm of another. James says, "Everyone should be quick to listen, slow to speak, and slow to become angry." (James 1:19)

Dumping Some people do not confront the issues as they arise. Instead they keep long lists of past grievances. When they become involved in a personal conflict, they may not focus on the most recent problem but dump all the stored up grievances on their partner.

Hitting below the Belt We are all more sensitive to some issues than others. And the closer we are to someone, the more we know what pushes their buttons. Someone who hits below the belt is not trying to manage the current conflict,

---

[3] Ronald B. Adler and Neil Towne, *Looking Out, Looking In*, 10th ed. (Belmont, CA: Wadsworth, 2003).

but is using their personal knowledge of their partner's sensitive spots to lash out and harm them.

Withholding Sometimes people hope to be victorious in a conflict by withdrawing their love, affection, or civility from their partner. They may give others the "silent treatment" in hopes that this will so hurt their partner that he or she will give in.

Inappropriate Joking Humor can be very helpful in diffusing a tense moment. However, inappropriate humor is a form of avoiding that blocks the open exchange of thoughts and feelings. When people joke inappropriately, they may also be sending the message that they do not take the conflict seriously.

Did you see yourself in any of the descriptions above? All of us from time to time engage in obstructing communication habits. What is important is that you recognize your habit and try to replace your obstructing behavior with communication that facilitates an open and honest exchange. Instead of relying on poor communication habits, try to use the following when you are having a conflict.

Engage in the Conflict Although you may need a "cooling off" period during a conflict, most issues will not get better with age. Confront the issues sooner rather than later.

Use "I" Messages An "I" message expresses your personal feelings without accusing the other person. For example saying, "You never let me make my own decisions," will probably provoke the other person to defend him or herself. Instead, an "I" message would sound like this, "I feel like I need to make my own decision about my major."

Stay Focused Focus on the issues within the present conflict, as opposed to bringing up past grievances. Stay focused by seeking clarification from your partner. Are you really listening to what your partner is saying? Is your partner hearing what you are saying? From time to time it is helpful to tell your partner what you are hearing him or her say. "If I am hearing you correctly, you are saying that we need to spend more time together." It is critical not to talk past one another. Be sure to ask questions in order to understand the other person's perspective.

Apologize If you have intentionally or unintentionally harmed someone, say you are sorry. Remember that you only need to apologize for your actions, not your feelings. Say that you are sorry for slamming the door when you left the room, but do not apologize for being upset. Sincere apologies show you are taking responsibility for your part of the problem and usually help diffuse some of the tension that may exist.

Be Truthful Although the truth may hurt, it deserves to be heard. You may be afraid of hurting someone else by telling the truth. You can still be sensitive to the other person's feelings by stating the truth with kindness. Speak the truth, but always do it in love (Ephesians 4:15).

Finding healthy ways to deal with relationship problems is important. The next time you are involved in a conflict, reflect on whether the conflict centers on the content of the conversation or is about the relationship itself. Then look carefully at the habits you typically use to manage a conflict. Are there obstructing behaviors you need to eliminate? Are there facilitating behaviors you need to foster? For some, it is hard to concentrate on anything else when relational problems arise. If you find that relationship conflict is seriously affecting your well being or day to day functioning, you might want to seek advice from a counselor or pastor.

Finally, remember that the love of God in our lives gives us the ability to treat even those who have sought to harm us with love and respect. After David had been identified by Samuel as the next king of ancient Israel, King Saul aggressively sought to end the life of this royal rival. But again and again, David spared Saul's life (1 Sam 24 and 26). The power of David to forgive and respect even a man who had attempted to kill him is a power that lives within every Christian. Jesus himself challenges us to love even those who seek to harm us. "Love your enemies and pray for those who persecute you." (Matt 5:44) And this same Jesus models that love on the cross, forgiving even those who were encouraging his execution (Luke 23:34). Because he shows the way and empowers Christians, they are able to love in this way too. "We love because he first loved us." (1 John 4:19)

College life is full of relationships. Everyone needs to feel connected to other people. You have had the opportunity in this chapter to reflect on the relationships in your life and on the quality of those relationships. If you find that your key relationships have weak spots, strengthen them. If you have discovered that there is a severe shortage of people with whom you have healthy relationships, then it is time to pursue new relationships that will provide the support you need.

Exercises for Success

Examine Your Critical Relationships

In order to be successful, you will need to be connected to a number of persons with whom you share a healthy relationship. This exercise allows you to put several of your close relationships to the test and see if they are dominated by the qualities of healthy relationships. Pick three relationships that you would like to evaluate. Write the name of each of those people behind each statement below if it accurately describes your relationship with them.

I enjoy spending time with her/him.

I trust him/her with personal information.

I can turn to him/her during a difficult time.

He/she respects me and my needs.

I can talk easily and openly with him/her.

He or she is kind to me.

We do not hold grudges.

We bolster each other's self-worth.

We share similar interests and values.

As you reflect on your responses, answer the following questions. Are my relationships filled with healthy qualities? What quality that is important to you is not being met in any of the relationships you have evaluated? If one of your important relationships has few or none of the qualities listed, can it be nurtured to greater health?

How to Say "I Love You" without Having Sex

We can express our love for one another in ways that do not violate God's direction. Ask your partner to join you on this exercise. Think creatively about all the ways you can express love without engaging in sexual intimacy that God has forbidden. For example, you can make hot chocolate on a cold night, send a funny note or card, cook your partner's favorite meal, or take a drive through the country. Join with the other members of your class to create an even longer list. See if you can find one hundred ways to say "I love you" without having sex.

Interview Your Instructors

Getting to know your instructors is well worth the effort. Pick out one or two instructors that you would like to get to know and arrange for an informal interview. They could be potential advisors or mentors or people that simply seem interesting to you. Here are some possible questions:

1. Where did you go to college? Why?
2. What was the most significant event in your first year of college?
3. What advice would you give to first-year students?
4. When did you decide to become a college teacher?
5. How can students be successful in your class?
6. What are your research interests?
7. What are your outside interests or hobbies?

My Favorite Kind of Professor

College teachers are different from other teachers you have had, but that does not mean they are all the same. If you were to visit a number of classes being taught on your campus, you would find faculty with a variety of personalities and presentation styles. Since not everyone likes the same kind of teacher, this exercise will help you find the qualities that are important to you. It will create a picture of your favorite teacher.

Pick a favorite teacher from the present or recent past. Assess that instructor according to the criteria below. Put an "x" on the continuum to indicate the relative strength or weakness of that teacher related to each teaching quality. The last two lines are blank so that you can add important qualities we may have missed.

Knows the subject well

Weak _____ Strong

Keeps my attention

Weak _____ Strong

Is organized

Weak _____ Strong

Stops and starts class on time

Weak _____ Strong

Is approachable

Weak _____ Strong

Has a sense of humor

Weak _____ Strong

Grades fairly

Weak _____ Strong

Is available for meetings

Weak _____ Strong

Weak _____ Strong

Weak _____ Strong

Using the information from the list, answer the following questions.

1. What qualities does this teacher have that helped you learn more easily?
2. Since you may have the option of taking a college class from more than one instructor, what three qualities will be most important to you in making that choice?

Expand the Diversity in Your Relationships

Membership in a wide array of relationships will help you grow as a person. Review the following list. Write down the names of at least five people whom you know in each category.

Someone . . .

. . . of a different gender. _____

. . . from a different cultural background. _____

. . . from a different ethnic group. _____

. . . who has a different political ideology. _____

. . . who is ten years older than you. _____

. . . of a different socioeconomic status. _____

. . . from a different religious background. _____

. . . who has a disability. _____

Now think about the results of this exercise. Where was it easiest for you to list names? Where was it more difficult or impossible for you to come up with just one name? As you think about the latter question, what is it that keeps you from engaging in relationships with people in those categories? Where would you like to see changes occur in your habits to improve the diversity in your relationships? Write a two-page paper exploring the answers to these questions.

Spiritual Reflection Journal

Love lies at the foundation of all our relationships. Read 1 Corinthians 13 where Paul provides a definition of love from God's perspective. Write about ways in which you will be able to put this definition to work in the relationships in your life.

Time in Prayer

In your personal time in prayer, consider praying for the following people and needs:

* For family and friends

* For wisdom to handle conflicts effectively

* For the courage to confront your stereotypes and prejudice

* To remain pure in the face of temptation

* For opportunities to develop meaningful relationships with people who are different from you

* For helpful relationships with faculty members

* To use your relationships with others to win them for Christ

On the Net

The Internet can be a helpful resource for you as you look for ideas to make yourself a more happy and successful student. Visit the College Success page offered by Thomson Wadsworth for web links that will help you grow further on this topic. Go to *www.success.wadsworth.com* and click on Resource Web Links.

Check out the following sites that promote and encourage respect for diversity.

www.splcenter.org
www.tolerance.org
www.diversityweb.org

Maintaining the Temple: Physical and Mental Wellness

Do you not know that your body is a temple of the Holy Spirit . . . ? Therefore honor God with your body.

1 Corinthians 6:19–20

- What can I do when I am unable to fall sleep?
- How can I eat in order to sustain my energy level and alertness?
- How often should I exercise and what forms of exercise are beneficial?
- What can I do when stress overwhelms me?
- What can I do when the world crashes down around me?

*W*E HAVE BEEN CAREFULLY designed by the divine hand so that there is an intimate link between our ability to think and the health of our body. Mind and body are so closely linked that neither will survive for very long without the life-giving support of the other. When both mind and body are healthy, they produce a wonderful symphony of actions and attitudes. But if the health of either deteriorates, the health of its partner is also compromised. This book has paid a great deal of attention to developing your mind as a college student. It is now time to give the body its due. The Apostle Paul calls upon the family of God to take special care of those bodies we have been given. For while we may grasp the wonderful promises of God with our mind, it is the body that Paul calls the "temple of the Holy Spirit," a place worthy of respect, care, and attention. If we fail to maintain this temple, then we will face both physical and mental consequences of that inattention. Our bodies will break down and our ability to grow as thinkers will be compromised.

Consequently, the role of this chapter is to check in on the physical and mental health habits that have a powerful effect on your success as a student. If you have been living on food that comes from vending machines, sleeping poorly, and living under too much stress, now is the time to commit to a course correction. Getting physically and mentally healthy is too important to put off for another day. Now is the time to develop healthy habits that not only will propel you to greater success as a college student but also will enhance the quality of your future life. The Lord was so passionate about your body that he sent his Son to redeem it from death by dying on a cross. And even now, he has sent the Holy Spirit to reside within it. One way we can give him the proper thanks is by taking care of this mobile temple. To that end, this chapter will lead you to think about both your physical and mental health habits, discussing topics like sleep, diet, exercise, alcohol, stress, worry, suicide, and responding to personal tragedy.

Physical Health Habits

SLEEP

Good physical health starts with careful consideration of our sleep habits. In order for our bodies to function at their peak, we need a sustained period of deep sleep. Such sleep can easily elude us when we are sleeping in a new and unfamiliar place, when we attempt to sleep at the wrong time of the day, or when nagging events from the day keep us from relaxing. Here we will explore sleep and the college student, investigating how much sleep we need, when to sleep, and what to do when we have difficulty sleeping.

How Much Sleep Do I Need? While the amount of sleep that any one individual needs varies greatly from one person to the next, the average person requires eight hours of sleep every night to fully recharge.[1] When college students have compared their own sleep habits to that standard, many have found they are getting one to two hours less sleep per night than their bodies may require. But perhaps the best way to determine if you are getting enough sleep is to check for the physical and emotional symptoms that are associated with too little sleep. These symptoms include the following:

Inability to concentrate	Poor emotional control
Falling asleep during classes	Headaches
General feeling of exhaustion	Impaired memory

While these symptoms may have other causes, one or more may combine to indicate you are getting too little sleep.

Another way to measure whether or not your current sleep habits are giving you enough down time is to note the way you wake up. If you are waking up on your own without an alarm clock and if you are feeling alert within a short time after coming to in the morning, you are likely getting enough sleep. However, if you require an alarm to rouse you from sleep or if you are feeling groggy well into the morning, these are signs that you are getting less sleep than your body requires.[2]

When Is It Best to Sleep? As you consider how much you sleep, it is also critical for you to give thought to when you sleep. Our bodies appear to respond to a certain circadian rhythm that seeks to align our sleep with the hours of darkness and the time when we are awake with daylight hours. If you have traveled quickly across the globe or even between the coasts of our United States, you may have experienced jet lag. This jet lag is the confusion that results as our bodies work to adjust our sleep and wakeful time to the new daylight and dark cycles of our destination. We can force our bodies to stay

---

[1] Michael Breus, "How Much Sleep Do You Really Need," n.p. [cited 30 August 2004]. Online: *http://my.webmd.com/content/article/62/71838.htm.*

[2] Ibid.

awake late into the night and sleep during the day, but this often results in less than satisfactory results. If you are feeling the need to sleep more effectively, check out the time during the day when you sleep and remember that the more consistent your bedtime and rising time the more restful your sleep patterns are likely to be. Sleeping in on the two days when you have a later class may not be as helpful as keeping your rising time consistent.

This, of course, also leads to the question about taking a nap during the daylight hours. There is some debate on the value of such naps, with advantages and disadvantages cited for each perspective. Begin by considering the relationship of a nap to your time management plan. Is the time you are napping giving you a greater benefit than if you had employed that time in some other way? From the physiological perspective, a couple of things seem certain. It is unwise to sleep during the daylight hours as a substitute for sleeping during the nighttime hours. This daytime sleep has less restorative power than nighttime sleep. Secondly, if you are going to take a nap, be sure that it does not last too long (20 minutes is often recommended). A nap that takes you into the deepest sleep modes will cause you to awaken groggy rather than feeling refreshed and may make it difficult for you to get to sleep that night.

What Can I Do when I Cannot Sleep? The inability to fall asleep at night can be caused by either physical or mental discomfort. For example, if you have things on your mind that are causing you stress, adrenaline will be produced that jolts you into a greater state of alertness rather than into the relaxed state you require for sleeping. Alternatively, if you are in the habit of using some form of stimulant (like coffee or a soft drink with caffeine in it), that may be the chemical culprit that is keeping you awake.

If you are having difficulty falling sleep for any reason, then it is time to take some form of action. Consider changing your lifestyle in one of the following ways. Since we are all creatures of habit, it is wise to reserve your bed for sleeping rather than other daily activities like studying for exams, which may cause you stress. Then when you climb into bed, your body will unconsciously associate this environment with relaxation and sleep rather than with an activity that demands alertness and action. If you are in the habit of napping during the day, try to either shorten or eliminate those naps and do your sleeping at night. And as your day comes to a close, plan the hour before going to bed carefully. Give yourself time to disengage from the daily activities that are part of your work life. Instead, read for pleasure, watch television, exercise, or take a warm shower as a way of creating a transition between your work life and your sleep time. If you are in the habit of using some form of caffeine or other stimulant during the day, restrict the use of that beverage to the morning or noon hour so that your body has a chance to eliminate that chemical stimulant before bedtime. If your brain clicks on at just the time you are trying to shut down for the night, keep a pad of paper and pencil near your bed so that you can write down the thoughts that circle through your mind again and again. By doing so, you can give yourself permission to set them aside for the night and take them up again in the morning rather than rehearsing them over and over again at night. In this regard, you may also find it helpful to distract your mind from those matters by refocusing your attention using the relaxation techniques described later in this chapter.

DIET

Going to college is hard work. As our bodies require rest and sleep to function at their peak, so they also need appropriate fuel. God designed us with this need and has provided nutritional resources for us to use in this world. As the provider, he has invited us to pray for those daily needs in the Lord's Prayer, "Give us today our daily bread" (Matt 6:11), and he has promised to provide the raw materials for our nourishment (Ps 136:25). Here we will explore how the use of this food contributes to our success as a college student.

What Should I Eat? God has permitted us to find nourishment from both the plant and animal kingdoms (Gen 1:29 and 9:3). In this way, he has provided us with the critical vitamins, minerals, fiber, protein, fat, and carbohydrates that maintain and strengthen our muscles and bones, give us energy, aid digestion, and create immunity from disease. Specific diet plans that emphasize one type of food over another come and go. But as a starting point, it is safe to assume the value of the basic food pyramid that you learned about when you were in grade school.

At the base of the pyramid is the grain group. Foods in the grain group include bread, cereal, rice, and pasta. The recommended six to eleven servings per day provide us with B vitamins and some iron. But even more importantly, whole grains (rather than white flour products) provide us with the complex carbohydrates that are the primary energy source for the body. If you are feeling a lack of energy, check your diet for the presence of these foods before looking for a candy bar or soft drink that can offer a quick burst of energy but fail to sustain our energy for the day.

Together with the grain group we need a healthy portion of vegetables and fruit in our diet. The vegetable group provides us with vitamins, minerals, and carbohydrates as well as plenty of fiber that helps us digest the rest of our food more efficiently. Three to five servings are recommended per day. In concert with the vegetable group is the fruit group. Two to four servings of fruit each day make an important contribution of vitamins, carbohydrates, and fiber to our diet.

Further up on the food pyramid are the dairy and the meat, bean, egg, and nut groups of foods. Since these portions of the food pyramid reside above the first three groups we have discussed, the portions of our diet from these two groups will be somewhat smaller, two to three servings for each of the two groups. Nevertheless, they have an important contribution to make of their own. Foods identified with the dairy group include milk, yogurt, and cheese, providing us with the calcium and protein we need. By contrast, servings from the meat, beans, eggs, and nut group provide iron, zinc, and protein.

Finally, at the top of the pyramid are the fats, oils, and sweets groups. While the items from this group have a pleasant taste and can give us a feeling of satisfaction, they actually provide the least overall benefit to us. So while the simple sugars in a big chocolate chip cookie can give us an alertness boost for our afternoon class, too many cookies will leave us feeling full but starved for the critical nutrients that allow our body to function at its peak. The key to a healthy diet is variety, balance, and moderation. When we consume a balance of items from these food groups on a daily basis, we are providing our bodies with the fuel needed to accomplish our daily tasks. For more information on the food pyramid, visit the National Agricultural Library (*www.nal.usda.gov/fnic/index.html*) and the Center for Nutrition Policy and Promotion (*www.usda.gov/cnpp/pyramid.html*).

What Are the Danger Signs of Unhealthy Eating? Because we live in a world ruined by sin, even food can bring us harm when it is misused. Check your lifestyle for any of these signs that you may be eating in an unhealthy way:

Excessive weight gain

Substituting soft drinks for water

Relying on vending machines and fast food for your meals

Excessive weight loss

Not eating as a way of gaining a feeling of control in life

Eating excessively as a form of comfort

Designing a diet from the top of the food pyramid down rather than from the bottom up

Eating Disorders

*A*S NEW COLLEGE STUDENTS go through the stress of adjusting to college life, it is possible that a form of eating disorder may become evident. Each one is treatable, but if left untreated can cause significant emotional and physical harm.

Anorexia nervosa is the unnatural fear of becoming fat that is not diminished with weight loss. Those suffering from this disorder have a distorted self-image that does not improve even in the face of continued self-starvation.

Bulimia nervosa is a disorder that is an inappropriate method for dealing with stress. Those suffering from this disorder overeat to compensate for their feelings of stress but then are overwhelmed with a concern for gaining weight. After eating, the person struggling with this disorder will purge that food from their system either through forced vomiting or through the use of laxatives.

If you or someone close to you suffers from an eating disorder like those above, you can learn more about the disorder and how to help by visiting the counseling offices on your campus or visiting one of the following sites:

National Association of Anorexia Nervosa and Associated Disorders *www.anad.org*

Anorexia Nervosa and Related Eating Disorders, Inc. *www.anred.com*

National Mental Health Association *www.nhma.org*

Eating Disorders and Prevention *www.closetoyou.org/eatingdisorder*

EXERCISE

As first-year college students get busy with the demanding academic and social life of college, it is easy to give exercise a back seat to other activities. But a strong exercise plan is just as critical to maintaining your physical health as healthy eating and sleeping. If you are already involved in a weekly exercise regimen, you are on the right track and may find ways to improve it in the following paragraphs. If you are not currently involved in such an exercise program, now is a good time to start and make it as much of a weekly habit as going to class or brushing your teeth. If you have had trouble staying motivated for such exercise, consider making a pact with a friend to keep your exercise sessions more regular and meaningful. However, one word of caution is called for here. If you are over 35 and have not exercised regularly for several years or if you have a physical condition like high blood pressure, heart trouble, arthritis, excessive weight, or other such physical ailments, please seek the advice of a medical professional before starting an exercise program.

What Kind of Exercise Is Right for Me? A complete exercise program will consist of activities that address four different components of our physical health: cardiorespiratory endurance, muscle strength, muscle endurance, and flexibility. The ability to sustain a physical activity over an extended period of time is directly related to the effectiveness of our lungs in providing oxygen to the bloodstream and the effectiveness of our heart and circulatory system in delivering that blood to our muscles. Cardiorespiratory exercise is designed to improve our endurance by improving those systems. Development of our muscle groups is important too. Muscle strength is the ability of our muscles to contract and sustain a force for a brief period of time. By contrast, muscle endurance is the ability to use a muscle or a group of muscles for a sustained period of time. Check your exercise program for activities that address both. Finally, flexibility is the ability to move our joints and our muscles easily through the full range of motion. This has been given increasing attention in the design of exercise programs and deserves a place in our workout schedule as well.

Each exercise session should begin and close with a 5- to 10-minute warm up and cool down period no matter what type or types of exercise are included in the session. Within your weekly routine, consider following a regimen that resembles this model. Start with three 20-minute sessions during the week in which you focus on aerobic exercises. These exercises are designed to address the health of your heart and lungs. Examples of aerobic exercise include walking, jogging, biking, swimming, cross-country skiing, dancing, handball, volleyball, basketball, cycling, and rollerblading. In order for those activities to be effective, they must be done so as to elevate your respiration and heart rate. The target zone for your heart rate can be defined using the following formula. Subtract your age from 220 and multiply the result by .60. Subtract your age again from 220 and multiply the result by .75. The two resulting numbers represent the target zone for your heart rate during the aerobic exercise sessions. For example if you are age 20, your minimum target rate would be 120 ($220 - 20 = 200 \times .60 = 120$) and your maximum target rate would be 150 ($220 - 20 = 200 \times .75 = 150$).

If you are engaging in aerobic exercise, you are also addressing strength and endurance of the muscle groups you are using. You can further address muscle development by weight lifting, calisthenics, push-ups, sit-ups, and pull-ups. In addition to your aerobic exercise sessions, consider adding two to three 20-minute sessions per week targeted at muscle strength and endurance.

Finally, include a time of daily stretching (10–12 minutes) to elongate muscles and create greater flexibility in the joints. These stretching exercises can be included in the cool down at the end of your workout.

What About Exercise and Weight Loss? Many people who begin an exercise program also intend for that program to help them lose unwanted weight. The exercise program outline above will do just that so long as you do not increase your caloric intake when beginning such a program. If you expend more energy than you take in, you will burn up stored fat reserves. Consider the following: A medium-sized college student who wants to burn off five pounds of fat needs to walk 150 miles! That may be too discouraging to contemplate. But if you set up a program that would challenge you to walk $2\frac{1}{2}$ miles per day for 60 days, you would have achieved your goal in two months. Exercise goals are great. Set them and design a plan of action to achieve them. But remember that goals must be realistic if they are going to be accomplished.

Fighting the Freshman Fifteen

*A*S FIRST-YEAR STUDENTS experience all the changes that college has to offer as well as the changes that are occurring in their own body chemistry, it is not unusual for students to gain weight, the so-called "freshman fifteen." The addition of this weight can lower one's self-esteem and make students feel less energized for the work ahead. If you find yourself gaining weight, intervene with changes in diet and exercise that keep you physically fit and mentally alert.

ALCOHOL AND DRUG USE

The college experience and experimentation with alcohol are closely linked in American culture. The Core Institute at Southern Illinois University closely tracks and studies the pattern of alcohol use on the college campuses of America. In a recent survey given to 54,000 undergraduates from 131 different colleges, 74% of those students reported that they had consumed alcohol within the last 30 days and of those students 84% did so in violation of the laws governing alcohol use in their state.[3] One thing is clear. As a college student, you

---

[3] "American Campuses: 2001 Statistics on Alcohol and Other Drug Use," n.p. [cited 30 August 2004]. Online: *http://www.siu.edu/departments/coreinst/public_html/recent.html*.

will be confronted with the invitation to use alcohol and to misuse prescription and non-prescription drugs. The time to make the decision on whether or not you accept that invitation is long before it comes, certainly before you take your first drink. From the moment you begin to consume alcohol, your ability to make an effective decision will have been impaired. As you make that early decision, there are a number of important matters to consider from the teachings of the Bible, the laws of your state, the student conduct code at your school, and what we know about the impact of alcohol and drug use on college success.

What Should I Consider when Making My Decision? The first place to begin is in reading Bible passages that take up the matter of chemical use, passages like Prov 20:1, 23:29–35, and Eph 5:18. Those passages speak directly to the misuse of alcohol but also find application in the way we use other drugs. It is also critical to consider the Bible passages that speak about the sturdy Christian character and the witness we bring to others about Jesus. In reading passages like these, some churches have come to the conclusion that it would be wrong for a Christian to ever consume an alcoholic beverage. If that is the position of your church, it deserves to be honored. Other Christians have read the passages and come to the conclusion that the occasional use of alcohol is not a sin but that the Bible clearly forbids the loss of control that comes with becoming drunk. And certainly all have concluded that it would be a sin to intentionally violate the laws and rules of authorities God has placed over us (Rom 13:1–7). This includes the violation of laws that restrict the use of alcohol and drugs.

Consequently, it is important for you to know the state laws that govern your campus and the penalties associated with violating them. In most states, if you have not reached the age of 21, it is illegal for you to purchase or to consume an alcoholic beverage. Furthermore, since the misuse of alcohol has very negative implications for college success, colleges and universities have their own alcohol policies articulated in places like the student conduct code that may further limit the use of alcohol even beyond the state's legislation. Given the importance of this topic, violation of state laws or the student conduct code typically have very strong penalties associated with them. Be informed about the law and its consequences before you drink.

As a college student who is passionate about success, you also need to be aware of the ways that alcohol can impact your plans to graduate with high grades from college. The same Core Institute study noted at the beginning of this section asked students to report on the consequences that attended their use of alcohol as a college student. Among the things they reported were poor test performance, getting into more fights and arguments, becoming physically ill, missing classes, and memory loss. The study clearly indicates that the more alcohol that a college student uses the less effective they are as a college student, a pattern that leads to lower grades and less overall success. As you consider your views of God's instruction about alcohol and drug use, the state and college regulations that govern their use, and the potential impact on your grades, you will be empowered to design a habit that keeps you in a healthy place, a place that honors God's temple.

Alcohol and Blood Alcohol Content

THE INTRODUCTION OF ALCOHOL into our bodies has an effect both upon our mood and our physical systems. Since two individuals of different sizes will respond differently to the introduction of the same amount of alcohol, the best way to know the impact of alcohol is through the percentage of blood alcohol content (BAC). From .025 to .050 BAC, a person will begin to feel animated and energized. From .050 to .080 BAC, that same person will begin to feel increasingly depressed emotionally and begin to demonstrate impairment in coordination and thinking. Above .080, the depression will continue and coordination and thinking will be significantly impaired. Above .20 BAC, the consumer of alcohol will face the risk of memory loss and blackouts. The body will also begin to react with spontaneous vomiting in an effort to rid the system of the harmful chemical. If you find someone who has blacked out from the use of alcohol, it is critical that you lay that person on his or her side, not the back. Do all you can to keep his or her airway clear and get medical help immediately.

What Are the Warning Signs? If you have become involved in the use of alcohol and are exhibiting any of the following warning signs, it is critical for you to seek help immediately.

You drink just because your friends think you should.

You drink to avoid feeling bad.

You drink to cope with life.

You have tried to stop using alcohol but could not.

You believe that your use of alcohol has no ability to harm you.

You regularly consume more than five drinks at one sitting.

You have experienced blackouts during your drinking time when you cannot recall what happened.

For help or more information, please contact a campus counselor or one of the following:

> Alcoholics Anonymous *www.alcoholics-anonymous.org*
> National Institute for Drug Abuse *www.nida.nih.gov.*

Mental Health Habits

A part of caring for your body also includes the strategic way you manage your stress, deal with worry and discouragement, address suicidal tendencies, and respond to personal tragedies in your life. This portion of the chapter will speak to each of these topics so that you may be thinking of ways to keep yourself mentally healthy.

STRESS

Since new challenges cause us stress, stress and starting college go hand in hand. Feeling stress for shorter periods of time in lower doses is a natural part of being human and in fact can stimulate and improve your academic performance. During these periods of stress you may note your breathing and heart rate increases, your muscles may begin to tighten, and you may experience "butterflies" in your stomach. None of these symptoms is inherently harmful in the short run. But this good form of stress can quickly degenerate into a bad form of stress that lasts for much longer periods of time and comes on with increased ferocity. This negative form of stress can cause us to lose sleep, become more irritable, be plagued by headaches, and have a variety of stomach complications including nausea, diarrhea, and even ulcers. This type of stress actually works against your success and well being as a college student and so needs to be addressed.

Life Change Events Miller and Rahe have explored the relationship between significant events in life (called life change events) and the risk of serious health problems. Their study has found that certain events are more harmful than others. For example, the death of a parent or the loss of a job are much more harmful than buying a car or leaving for college. However, even minor events that are less threatening by themselves can combine to create potential health problems. To determine if you are experiencing life change events that may compromise your health, see the study by Miller and Rahe entitled "Life Changes Scaling for the 1990s."[4]

---

[4] M. A. Miller and R. H. Rahe, "Life Changes Scaling for the 1990s," *Journal of Psychosomatic Research*, Sept. 1977, Vol. 43, pp. 279–92.

If the level of stress you are feeling at any one time is so significant that it is interfering with your ability to sleep or live life the way you would like to live it, then it is time to intervene. Masking the symptoms of stress through the use of tobacco products, use of alcohol, or via excessive sleep are not solutions. But by combining physical, mental, and spiritual interventions, you will be able to find ways to help you put stress in its place. Once again, the techniques described below are not meant to be a substitute for the professional counseling you may require.

Physical Interventions When we are experiencing heightened levels of stress, we respond physically by increasing our breathing rate and tightening our muscles. We are preparing ourselves physically to either flee or fight the perceived enemy before us. Thus one way that we can reduce our level of stress is to reverse that process by doing things that will slow our breathing and relax the tension from our muscles. Exercise is a wonderful way in which to turn our tension into an activity that is helpful for us. By going for a long walk, playing a game of basketball, or dancing with a friend, our body will have put that muscle tension to good use and send our body the signal to release the endorphins that will lead to greater feelings of happiness and contentment. Couple that form of exercise with a massage and you are on the road to significant stress reduction.

But going for a run or getting a massage may not be the answer if you are feeling high levels of stress during an exam or are lying in bed trying to sleep at night. In those cases, you can try an alternative form of physical intervention. Close your eyes or focus softly on something in the room. Observe your breathing rate and make a conscious effort to breathe more slowly and more deeply using the full volume of your abdomen. Then begin to progressively tighten muscle groups in your body and release that muscular pressure in the following way. Start with your feet. Curl your toes toward your heels and hold the muscle pressure to the count of five. Then slowly but steadily release that pressure over the next 20–30 seconds until you have completely relaxed the tension you introduced into that muscle group. Then move up to your calves and repeat the same procedure, tightening your muscles as much as possible for five seconds and then slowly releasing that tension. Continue up your body through every muscle group. You will feel a significant reduction in stress as you send the message to your body that it is all right to go into a more relaxed mode.

Psychological Interventions In connection with the physical interventions described above, adjust your psychological focus. Pause to consider what is causing your stress to surge. Then ask yourself what you can control and what you cannot control about the situation. For example, if your boyfriend or girlfriend back home has not responded to your most recent letter or phone calls, your stress level may rise because you are wondering why he or she seems less interested in your relationship. What do you control in this situation? You certainly cannot control the feelings or actions of your partner. Attempting to do so will only cause you to become more frustrated and stressed. What you can control is your own reaction to this perceived lack of interest on your friend's part. You can phone your friend and articulate your concerns about the relationship. That is empowering because it will allow you to clarify the reasons for his or her lack of communication. If your partner is no longer interested in pursuing a close relationship with you, you do not have the power to change them but you do have the power to identify and date another person and so meet the relationship needs you have. In the same way, you cannot control the fact that your grandfather has been diagnosed with cancer. But you can control your reaction to the news by seeking the support of others, reading your Bible, and praying for the medical team that is caring for him. It may sound too simple to be valuable. But one of the best places to begin when you are feeling stressed is to identify what you control and what you do not control about a situation. Then limit your thinking and actions to those things you can control.

Stress can be debilitating when it becomes something that we manage constantly. When a particularly stressful event occurs in our lives, we tend to narrow our focus to that event, ignoring all the other places of greater peace where we might focus our attention. We all deserve a break and there are any number of ways that we can refocus our attention on something else for a time. One way to distract yourself is via leisure activities like listening to music, exercising, playing a musical instrument, or enjoying a favorite hobby. Laughter is also wonderful medicine that can be amplified by enjoying a comedy or just spending time with a friend who has the ability to make us laugh.

And if you are alone and feel like you need to take a break, why not make it a thought vacation? Close your eyes or focus softly on something in the room and create an image of the thing that is causing you stress. Now remove that image from the stage and instead take a mini-vacation to one of your favorite physical settings. Whether it is standing at the base of the Rocky Mountains or idling on a sunny beach in Florida, go there mentally and get into the moment. Smell the smells you remember, feel the temperature, and recall the sounds of that place. A thought vacation may not be as good as being there, but it can recreate the feelings of contentment and peace when we vividly recall that favorite vacation spot.

Spiritual Interventions   Because we are sinful people living in a sin-damaged world, we may worry about our own relationship with God or feel that God is unable to help us in the days that lie ahead. There is no pain like the pain we have when we feel unforgiven. God does not want us to live in that guilty place and so he has sent various messages of comfort and assurance in his Word that are designed to address our spiritual concerns and our anxiety. As we live out our life, we can become very aware of our own failings. The knowledge that we have violated God's law leads to feelings of guilt and unworthiness before the holy God. Although God detests the sin that so infects our actions and thoughts, he does not want us to live with feelings of guilt or unworthiness. Read Luke 15:11–32. In this parable of the Lost Son, a young person drifted away from his father's home and lived a life that was in complete violation of all his father would want. When he had ruined his life, he returned to his father's home expecting nothing more than to become a hired-worker for his father. But as this young person came into sight, his father began a celebration. For the young person whom the father thought he had lost was found again. If you have wandered away from your Heavenly Father, he is anxiously waiting at home for your return to him.

Even people who have a personal relationship with Jesus and know they are forgiven can still struggle with the challenge of living in a sin-ruined world. Jesus himself said, "In this world, you will have trouble." However, he quickly added the next two sentences. "But take heart! I have overcome the world." (John 16:33) Because of who Jesus is and his power, he can share that victory over the sinful world with us. In Matthew 6:25–34, we find the discourse on worry that may be the most powerful sermon ever given on the topic. For people who are prone to worry about the essentials of life over which they have little control, Jesus challenges us to think about the way God takes care of birds and flowers, assuring us that he will do even more in caring for our needs.

In the end, we are empowered to do two things when confronted by a challenge in life that threatens our sense of well being. First of all, we can change our perspective. When confronted by a problem that seems too large to handle, we often focus on our own inabilities rather than God's presence and power. The psalmist offers a fresh perspective. "God is our refuge and strength, an ever present help in trouble." (Ps 46:1; see also Ps 73:25–26 and Ps 121:1–2) Secondly, we can put into practice the powerful tool of prayer. The invitation from the Lord is clear. "Call upon me in the day of trouble; I will deliver you, and you will honor me." (Ps 50:15) Jesus invites weary and worn people to come to him and find such rest (Matt 11:28–30).

SUICIDE

Discouragement and depression that is left untreated can lead to thoughts of suicide and even attempts to commit suicide. Those who have a relationship with the Lord are not exempt from such thoughts or actions. Consider the story of Saul (1 Sam 31), Elijah (1 Kings 19:4), and Judas (Matt 27:5). While the Bible does record these suicidal thoughts and acts, it absolutely does not condone such actions as the answer. Nevertheless, Christian college students are not immune from the risk of suicide, so the more we know about it and how to prevent it the better off we will be. Satan does have a way of causing us to spiral down, losing hope in God's interest in us or his ability to help us despite the clear words of the Bible to the contrary.

If a person is going to make an attempt on their life, they typically give off early warning signs that they are thinking seriously about this drastic measure. Watch for one or more of these indications in yourself or others close to you:

Change in eating habits

Change in sleeping habits

Loss of interest in school, friends, or activities

Expressions of hopelessness

Talking about "ending it all" or "just wanting out of life"

A passion to engage in risky, life-threatening actions

Giving away personal possessions

The actions and attitudes listed above need to be taken seriously. Do not assume that the person is not serious when they speak about taking their own life or assume that they are just trying to get more attention. Engage your friend or family member by being open and confrontational about the topic. "Are you thinking about taking your own life?" "Do you intend to harm yourself today?" Listen to what the suicidal person is saying and do not leave them alone. Rather, assure them that they can come to a better place. Pray for them, pray with them, and accompany that person into the presence of a mental health professional who will know what to do next.

For more information on this important topic, speak to the mental health counselors on your campus or check out the following sites: National Mental Health Association *www.nmha.org*, the National Institute of Mental Health *www.nimh.nih.gov*, or the American Foundation for Suicide Prevention *www.asfp.org*.

RESPONDING TO PERSONAL TRAGEDY

Students who are in college are not immune from experiencing significant personal tragedies, including divorce in the family, significant medical problems, or the death of a loved one. When such personal tragedies occur, they strike the new college student with even greater ferocity since that person may be some distance from supportive family members and in a new place with a growing but limited support group. Personal tragedies are so invasive that they can completely disrupt a student's already busy schedule, causing them to miss classes and get behind on assignments, adding to the stress the event has caused. For all of these reasons, it is critical to prepare yourself as a college student for the way in which you will deal with personal tragedy should it come knocking at your college door.

The book of the Bible that takes this issue on more directly than any other is the Book of Job. It asks and attempts to answer the tough questions that everyone asks when they are devastated by such events. Job is a man who faced an incredible series of personal tragedies. In a short amount of time, this wealthy man experienced the loss of his personal wealth, his children, his health, and the support of his marriage partner. "If only my anguish could be weighed and all my misery be placed on the scales! It would surely outweigh the sand of the seas . . . ." (Job 6:2–3) Dazed by this series of events, Job tries to make sense of it all. He asks the very questions we ask when personal tragedy visits our lives. Have I committed some sin for which God is punishing me? Is God simply unaware of what has happened? Is my God so powerless that he knows but cannot act? Or is my God so uncaring that he knows but elects not to act? Through long, painstaking dialogue with a series of "friends," Job articulates and seeks answers to these questions. In the end it is clear that God is not seeking personal revenge on Job for a particular sin he committed, that God is aware of what is happening, that he has the power to intervene, and that he cares. But the one question that is not answered is the one that may be most vexing: why does Job have to suffer in the way he did?

The answer to this question eludes Job and the reader. As no mortal speaker has adequately dealt with this issue in the book, the Lord appears on behalf of himself in a storm. "Who is this that darkens my counsel with words without knowledge? Brace yourself like a man; I will question you, and you shall answer me." (Job 38:2–3) In the verses that follow, God asks Job one challenging question after another, questions that are impossible for any mortal to answer. In doing so, God brings Job to confess his own limitations. "Surely I spoke of things I did not understand, things too wonderful for me to know." (Job 42:3)

The answer to why Job suffers is not revealed to him and it may remain hidden from us in our tragedy. But as God quiets this question, he seeks to respond to the frustration of not receiving an answer by confirming his loving intervention in our life even in the midst of personal tragedies. In Romans 8:28, Paul tells that all things, even tragedies, will work out for our own personal benefit even if we do not know what that benefit will be. At minimum, these tragedies will carry us through a process that will deepen our faith in the Lord and strengthen our relationship with him. That is Paul's message in Romans 5:1–5 where he challenges us to rejoice in suffering, knowing that this suffering leads to greater perseverance, to a tested character, and to a deeper hope. We may not know why God has allowed a tragedy to come our way, but he does tell us that he will remain at our side during this difficult time and engineer life so that the challenge we face draws us closer to him.

Success as a college student is much more than just studying effectively and developing our intellect. It is also about managing our physical and mental health. Our body is the temple of the Holy Spirit and so deserves thoughtful attention. Consider all that you have read and take steps to improve your physical and mental health where it needs such attention. In so doing, we are involved in an act of worship using our body as the place of worship.

Exercises for Success

Create a Sleep Diary

For the next week, keep a record of how long you sleep each day of the week and at what times of the day you are sleeping. Compare the results of your sleep habits to the suggested habits in this chapter and write down any specific changes you plan to make.

Keep a Diet Diary

Since we are what we eat, it is helpful to think through your weekly eating habits. For the next week, keep a record of the times that you eat, the type of food you eat, and the amounts of each kind of food you eat. Compare your habits with the suggestions in this chapter and write down any specific changes you plan to make.

Design a Weekly Exercise Plan

With all the activities competing for your time as a college student, it would be easy to get less exercise than you need. Consider again the four types of fitness that are important: cardiorespiratory, muscle strength, muscle endurance, and flexibility. After reviewing your current habits, design an exercise program that you can fit into your weekly schedule and that will help you remain physically fit.

Alcohol and the Law

Consult the statutes that govern the use of alcohol in the state where you are attending school as well as the university conduct code. Write a summary of what you find that includes the penalties for violating those laws.

Design a Stress Management Plan

Identify the top five sources of significant stress in your life and when they cause the greatest disruption to your life during the week. Then, using the ideas from this chapter and those gained from *www.managingstress.com*, design a plan that will diminish the negative affects of stress in your life. Write a two-page report that details both the causes of your stress and the plan you will use to combat it.

Prevent the Suicide of a Friend

It is possible that you will meet someone during your college years that is deeply depressed and is showing signs that they may attempt to harm themselves. Visit one of the Web sites that discuss suicide and deepen your understanding of this important topic so that you will have the correct words to say and will be prepared to act in a way that is helpful. Prepare a two-page report that identifies one of the Web sites you visited and briefly summarize what you learned about this important topic.

Personal Tragedy Preparation List

Some families have constructed emergency shelters in their homes that are stocked with the basics for life, including food and water. You too can prepare for personal tragedies that will touch your life or the life of someone close to you by assembling a set of Bible passages that you find most comforting in times of trouble. Build or expand that spiritual "emergency kit" and share the passages most meaningful to you with your class.

Spiritual Reflection Journal

Read Job 1–2 and 42. Considering the experience of Job, write about a personal tragedy that you have experienced and compare your personal tragedy to that of Job. What questions does Job ask that you yourself have asked or are asking? What insights did Job gain from his experience in life that are helpful to you? What passages from Scripture are the most helpful to you when handling a personal tragedy?

Time in Prayer

In your personal time in prayer or in connection with others in your class, pray for the following people and needs.

- That I would honor my body as the temple of the Holy Spirit by caring for it
- That I would develop a sleep schedule that gives my body adequate rest

- That I would be more conscious and careful about the kind of food I eat

- That I might avoid the temptation to misuse alcohol as a college student

- That I discover and employ techniques to diminish the harmful stress in my life

- That I would prepare myself to handle personal tragedy well

- For the person in our school who today is thinking about harming himself or herself

- For the person in our school who needs to be assured that his or her sins are forgiven

On the Net

The Internet can be a helpful resource for you as you look for ideas to make yourself a more happy and successful student. Visit the College Success page offered by Thomson Wadsworth for web links that will help you grow further on this topic. Go to *www.success.wadsworth.com* and click on Resource Web Links. In particular, seek out further information on the following sites:

> *www.siu.edu/departments/coreinst/public_html*
> *www.bacchusgamma.org*
> *www.factsontap.org*
> *www.edu.org/hec*

Seeking Satisfaction in My Career

A person can do nothing better than to eat and drink and find satisfaction in their work. This too I see is from the hand of God, for without him who can eat or find enjoyment?

Ecclesiastes 2:24–25 (author's translation)

- What will the work world be like in my future?
- What can I do to discover, confirm, or change my vocational goal?
- How does my status as a Christian influence my career planning?
- What can I do now, as a college student, to prepare for the day I look for a professional position?

*G*OD CREATED HUMANS WITH both the capacity and the passion for work. On a bad day, work itself may seem inherently evil, but the Bible portrays work as part of God's perfect creation. Early in the book of Genesis, the inspired author describes a wonderful world without the presence of sin. In that perfect world, God gave Adam and Eve the responsibility of working in and caring for the Garden of Eden (Gen 2:15). But once that perfect world became contaminated by sin, even the work of caring for the Garden of Eden became a tiresome burden. The work day was no longer filled with pure joy and satisfaction but rather was marred by literal and metaphorical "thorns, thistles, and sweat." (Gen 3:17–20) Talk to any professional and they will tell you that some days they find their work unsatisfying, frustrating, and emotionally draining. Fortunately, not every work day is like that. As the writer of Ecclesiastes states, it is still possible for us to find satisfaction and enjoyment in our professional work when we pursue it in connection with his plan for us (Eccl 2:24–25).

From the start, let us acknowledge that the selection of a career path and major is both complex and time consuming. In many schools, students will not be given formal, academic credit for the time and energy invested in this process. Nevertheless, this is a critical part of your college life that deserves an appropriate amount of your time, attention, and energy. Toward that end, this chapter will guide you through the process of preparing for your career as a college student. That process will include time invested in learning more about the work world in your future. It will offer you suggestions on how to discover, confirm, or change your career plans. And it will suggest specific tasks you can pursue as a college student that will prepare you for the first step into your professional world. At each step along the way, the authors will offer suggestions on how a member of God's family may investigate and pursue these very important plans. In doing so, we honor the thesis presented to us by the author of Ecclesiastes. "A person can do nothing better than to eat and drink and find satisfaction in their work. This too I see is from the hand of God, for without him who can eat or find enjoyment?" (Eccl 2:24–25, author's translation)

Today you may be absolutely certain about the career you will pursue. Today you may be absolutely uncertain about the career you will pursue. Within the month, your entire perspective on your career may change. But one thing is for sure. You have come to college because you believe that it will help you prepare for your future employment. This common ground among all college students will help you find something useful in this chapter as you seek to find your vocational place in God's world.

The World of Work in Your Future

You may be returning to school after having spent time in the work world or your work experience may be limited to part-time jobs you have had during the summer. In either case, the work world you will enter and experience in the first ten years of your career will be different from the one you have experienced in the past. For that reason, it is important for you to learn as much as you can about the world of work in your future.

A good place to begin looking for the picture of that world is within the general forecast articles available from the Bureau of Labor Statistics (*www.bls.gov*). The current postings on this site discuss the work world from the present to 2010. Here you may read projections both about the general work environment and about specific career fields. For example, it is predicted that your future workplace and its employees will increasingly be influenced by a global rather than a local economy. Despite this increase in the playing field, the speed of all sectors in the work world will need to become faster and more efficient to remain competitive. Finding a job will increasingly depend upon personal introductions by members of the organization rather than through anonymous applications. And once positioned, the future employee can expect to work more frequently in a team where effective communication and problem-solving skills are strongly valued. Since the knowledge and skills required for a position will continue to evolve, all professionals will need to improve their knowledge and skills through continuing education (home-study courses, seminars, and conferences). One thing that seems to be guaranteed is change. In that regard, have you stopped to consider that the job you will hold in the future may not even exist at the moment? This a fact that favors college graduates who have learned to educate themselves and adapt to new challenges.

Apart from these more general descriptions of the work world, the Bureau of Labor Statistics also offers predictions on specific career fields. For example, they predict that jobs in the service-producing sector will be the jobs that see the greatest growth towards 2010 (up 19%). Business services, social services, engineering, and management positions will account for one of every two jobs in 2010. Education positions will grow at a faster than average rate and 80 percent of the occupations that grow in the next years will be related to information technology. Medical service providers will also be in demand as large numbers of people enter their senior years. Those are the predictions for the moment, but those predictions will likely be modified in the years ahead. Consider spending time now learning as much as you can about the future work world because it will make a difference in how you prepare yourself today.

Discovering, Confirming, and Changing Your Choice

The process of making a career choice is one that calls for discovery, confirmation, and change. While it is important to keep moving forward towards a final career choice, it is unwise to rush the process. The typical college student will experience and even re-experience all three stages of making a career decision en route to a final choice. This will take time, but the key is to invest that time of reflection wisely. Toward that end, this portion of the chapter will raise questions you will wish to consider as well as suggest tools and techniques you may use in answering them. What does your work personality look like? What personal values will influence your decision? How can you identify career options that lend themselves to someone with your personality and values? What individuals and tools can be resources for this investigation? Finally, how does your status as a Christian affect this planning process?

WHAT IS MY WORK PERSONALITY?

God has created each of us and shaped us through our experiences in life. As a result, we all have a unique personality we bring to the career search. The more we know about that personality, the easier it will be to pick careers that are commensurate with who we are. As a starting point, consider the following list of adjectives that may describe a person's personality. Where do you find yourself on this list?

Logical	Outgoing	Modest
Intellectual	Shy	Fiery
Cooperative	Energetic	Curious
Adventurous	Forceful	Emotional
Aggressive	Calm	

Dr. John Holland, a psychologist at Johns Hopkins University, has studied the people employed in various career fields and observed a connection between the types of careers people enjoyed and their personality. This led Holland to separate people into six general personality types: realistic, investigative, artistic, social, enterprising, and conventional. He further identified the careers that tended to attract people of one type rather than another. Using this research, an individual is able to measure their personality and then learn what careers attract people of their personality type.[1]

Realistic people are individuals who have a preference for careers in science or mechanical areas that require fine motor coordination and physical strength. They see themselves as practical people who prefer to invest themselves in tasks that produce concrete results. Realistic personalities are attracted to careers like agricultural engineer, electrical contractor, electronics technician, or computer graphics designer.

Investigative people like intellectual stimulation. They would rather work on an abstract project that requires thought and organizational skills rather than a project that requires them to work manually on a concrete task. These are the analytical, rational problem solvers. Investigative personalities are attracted to careers like urban planner, chemical engineer, flight engineer, quality control technician, computer programmer, physician, and college professor.

Artistic people also enjoy the abstract world but prefer the aesthetic to the scientific. They prefer to work independently and without a lot of structure on creative projects that give voice to their own self-expression. Artistic personalities are attracted to careers like architect, actor, interior decorator, journalist, sculptor, librarian, and public relations specialists.

Social people place a premium of importance on interpersonal relationships that allow them to express kindness, care, and understanding to others. They enjoy speaking with others one-to-one or in small groups with the goal of providing help and support. Social personalities are attracted to careers like nursing, teaching, social work, counselor, minister, travel agent, and convention planner.

Enterprising people are interested in people and carrying forward the mission of their organization. They are risk-taking and assertive, working as leaders directing and persuading others in their course of action. Enterprising personalities are attracted to careers like banker, health administrator, judge, lawyer, sales representative, and city manager.

Finally, conventional people are detail-oriented people who like to plan and organize. They are self-controlled and structured individuals who enjoy following clear guidelines in their work life. They finish what they start and value that quality in others. Conventional personalities are attracted to careers like accountant, data processor, hospital administrator, insurance administrator, office manager, auditor, and statistician.

It is clear from this small sample of John Holland's work that a career choice may be greatly influenced by our personality. As part of your career

---

[1] John L. Holland, *Self-Directed Search Manual* (Odessa, Fl.: Psychological Assessment Resources, 1994).

investigation process, you may elect to complete the John Holland Self-Directed Search online (*www.self-directed-search.com/index.html*).

WHAT ARE MY WORK VALUES?

In addition to our personality, our personal values can play a key role in the selection of a career. These values are related to your personality but deal more generally with your perspective on the work world. In order to get a clearer picture of your work values, consider how you would answer the following questions:

> Do you see your career as primarily a way to make money or primarily as a way of helping others?
>
> Is it important that your work be an extension of your Christianity?
>
> Are you willing to work weekends and holidays?
>
> Do you wish to travel extensively or remain close to home?
>
> Do you wish to dress up for work or dress down for work?
>
> Are you willing to take work home at night or not?
>
> Would you prefer fewer hours at a less satisfying task or more hours at a more satisfying task?
>
> How does work time relate to family time?
>
> What income and benefit package will give you the lifestyle you desire?
>
> How much vacation time do you need each year?

The answer to these and other questions like them will give you a perspective on the general work values you currently hold.

Since others can help us see ourselves for who we are, it is wise to make use of the services offered by the career center on your campus when investigating both your work personality and work values. There you will find professionals who will be anxious to help you in this process. They will provide you with instruments that allow you to investigate both your personality and your work values. These instruments may include the Keirsey Temperament Sorter, the Strong Campbell Interest Inventory (SCII), SIGI Plus, Focus II, and the John Holland inventory mentioned above. Conclusions drawn from one assessment tool alone are not as meaningful as conclusions drawn from several assessment tools. That is why your career counselor will likely suggest that you complete more than one form of vocational inventory. Then personal time spent with a career counselor can help you interpret the results of those inventories and build the bridge between where you are now and where you would like to be with your career planning.

The Call to Ministry

A S JESUS PREPARED TO send out 72 of his followers to announce the coming of his kingdom, he noted that the "harvest was plentiful but the workers were few." (Luke 10:2) Today there are still thousands and thousands of people who need to hear about Jesus and who need to grow their faith. Thus there remains a need for pastors, teachers, missionaries, and evangelists (Eph 4:11–13). Listen carefully for the Lord's voice. Perhaps he is calling you to such service.

HOW DO I PERSONALIZE MY CAREER CHOICE?

Once you have come to a better understanding of your work personality and work values, it is time to personalize your career choice. There are two approaches to personalizing your career choice, each with its own advantages and disadvantages. You can decide to pursue a specific career and then select a major that will lead to it or you can select a major first and then determine which career you will pursue later. In either case, it is important for first-year students to do some research.

If you have already selected a career toward which you are working, it would be wise for you to pause and broaden the scope of your search. The first-semester college students we have met can name about 50 specific occupations when they are asked to create a list. By contrast, *The Dictionary of Occupational Titles* published by the US Department of Labor lists some 20,000 occupations. That means many college students are making an initial career choice knowing less than 1% of the options available to them. A little research can open your eyes to occupations previously unknown to you but that may fit very well with your personality and work values. Since the average college student changes his or her major three times, you should not feel that this kind of change indicates any kind of weakness in you. It is a natural part of getting to know yourself and the work world better.

If you have selected a major but are uncertain about which career to pursue, it would be helpful for you to know how graduates from your school holding your major are currently employed. Your career center may have collected this type of data. If not, visit the site maintained by Dickinson College at *www.dickinson.edu/career/majorcareer/index.html*. This archive lists all of the major courses of study offered by the college as well as the occupations in which the graduates of their majors have found placement.

Once you have settled on a possible career or (even better) careers, it is time to investigate those occupations more completely. You will want to know answers to questions like the following.

What would I be doing on a weekly basis if I took this job?

What working conditions are associated with this job?

What education, training, or experience is necessary to enter this occupation?

What are the prospects of my finding a job like this when I graduate?

What income and benefits would I enjoy in this occupation?

The career center on your campus will be an important ally to you in answering these kinds of questions. Those professionals have access to a number of resources and will likely encourage you to consult with your academic advisor, attend job fairs, join the campus association or club associated with your major, and speak with recruiters. You may also wish to pursue the answers to these questions online. One of the most productive online sites you can visit for this information is the one posted by the US Department of Labor, Bureau of Labor and Statistics, *www.bls.gov/oco/home.htm*. Each year, they provide visitors to their site with an updated Occupational Outlook Handbook. Each of the questions above is answered for the occupations they have researched. In certain cases, you will find out that your career path will require a graduate school degree. If that is the case, consider visiting *www.gradschools.com* for a detailed listing of graduate schools that have an academic program tailored to meet your needs. For additional electronic sites that will support your career investigation, see the list provided later in this chapter in On the Net.

As you personalize your career choice, be careful that you do not fall into any of the following attitudes or behaviors that will make your search less productive:

Making your choice without knowing all the options available to you

Focusing on just one factor when making your decision (e.g. salary)

Ignoring the potential impact on your family life

Making a decision without speaking to someone who is working in that career

Rushing your decision and not allowing time for extended reflection

Limiting yourself to just one career option without an alternate plan

Taking a major because it is supposed to be "easy"

Believing that you will only have one career during your lifetime

Pursuing a career only because someone else thinks it's a good idea

Undecided or Underdecided

*I*N SOME WAYS, schools are designed for people who have already made a decision about their major. That can make it uncomfortable for students who are either undecided about their major or who have significant reservations about their current choice. If you are undecided or underdecided, realize that you have a great advantage over students "who know for sure" what they want to do. You can approach the career investigation phase of your college life in a less biased way, allowing you to see options that a decided student may miss. Your academic advisor, academic advising center, or career center can be a wonderful aid to you as you work towards clarity. Just keep moving forward. There is nothing wrong with being undecided as long as you are doing things that help you move forward toward a decision.

HOW DOES MY CHRISTIANITY AFFECT MY CAREER CHOICE?

A story from the book of Joshua reminds us of how perilous it is to make major decisions, like a career choice, without first consulting the Lord. As the Children of Israel entered the Promised Land, they were faced with a very significant decision. God had commanded them to take possession of all the major cities in the land and not negotiate any form of alliance with those residents of the land they might encounter. After Joshua and the Israelite army had taken possession of Jericho, Ai, and Bethel, the residents of Gibeon knew that they would be next. Consequently the Gibeonites sent a delegation to the Israelites to pursue a non-aggression pact with them. The Gibeonite delegation was carefully dressed in clothing that was worn and tattered, their equipment patched, and their food dry and moldy. They had traveled little more than one day to meet the Israelite leaders but it appeared to human eyes that they had been traveling for weeks. When the delegation reached the Israelites, they stated that they had come from a very distant country and wished to make a peace treaty with the Israelites. The Israelites initially hesitated. But upon inspection of the deceptive evidence, the Israelites cut a deal. Their leaders sampled the provisions of the Gibeonites but did not commit the matter to the Lord in prayer (Josh 9:14). As a result, they were taken in by the Gibeonite ruse and agreed to make a peace treaty. Within a short time, the Israelite army arrived at the city of Gibeon and then they realized their mistake. This city that was strategically located right in the middle of their new land would not be obtained for Israel because they had made an important decision without consulting the Lord.

As you are faced with a critical decision about your major and career choice, it is critical that you "sample the provisions," do all that you can to learn about the future work world, the projections for various careers, your own personality, and your work values. But Christians will also consult the Lord, asking for his direction and support during this time of decision making. The author of Proverbs states a general axiom that offers you a better plan than the one chosen by the Israelite leaders. "Commit to the LORD whatever you do, and your plans will succeed." (Prov 16:3)

The question of how to pray about such a matter will depend on how you read and understand the Bible when it speaks about God and your future. Has God already determined the specific career you will have in life or has he allowed you the freedom to make a free choice in this matter? Bible-believing Christians have looked at the evidence and come to both conclusions. On the one hand, the Bible gives very clear examples that illustrate God's selection of specific vocations for certain people. In the case of Jeremiah and even before his birth, the Lord predetermined that Jeremiah would be a prophet of God who would speak to the nations. (Jer 1:4) Based on texts like these, some Christians have presumed that God predetermines the vocation of all believers. If that is your belief, then you will wish to pray to the Lord so that he might reveal to you what he has planned your life to be.

By contrast, other Christians have been reluctant to take such Bible passages and generalize them to all believers. They believe that the Lord gives Christians the free will to select from any number of vocational paths although he knows the subsequent outcome of any choice they might make. If this is your belief, then you will want to pray for insight from the one who knows the advantages and disadvantages of your options so that he might lead you to the path that will be best for you. In either case, it is critical to avoid the error of the Israelites who were taken in by the Gibeonite deception when they sampled the provisions but failed to consult the Lord.

Furthermore, the process of selecting a career path and a future employer will also be impacted by the values that you have as a Christian. Clearly one of the advantages of graduating from college and pursuing a career is that it will produce an income for you and for your family. Unfortunately, the blessing of an income can turn into an obsession. As the author of Ecclesiastes looks for meaning in life, he considers whether or not meaning might be found in accumulating more and more wealth. His conclusion is clear. "Whoever loves money never has money enough; whoever loves wealth is never satisfied with his income. This too is meaningless." (Eccl 5:10) This same caution comes to us in the New Testament as well. Jesus tells the story of a wealthy man who became completely obsessed with his growing wealth. He was determined to build more and more storage barns for his grain and his goods, presuming that this would create a life of happiness and ease for him. But Jesus notes that in the midst of his celebration, he had failed to take into account his own spiritual health. The very night he was planning his earthly life of leisure, he died and his property became the property of another. "This is how it will be for anyone who stores up things for himself but is not rich toward God." (Luke 12:21) Christians will certainly take income into account as they select a vocation, but they will carefully guard against an obsession with financial matters that distorts reality.

The Bible also affirms the importance of time off from work and time in God's Word. Among the Ten Commandments, there is a clear directive to set aside time each week to rest physically and to spend time in worship and meditation on God's Word. "Remember the Sabbath day by keeping it holy. Six days you shall labor and do all your work, but the seventh day is a Sabbath to the LORD your God (Exod 20:8–10a). As you do your vocational planning, it is critical to ask if the career you are considering will allow you to have time both to rest physically and to grow spiritually during the week.

Finally, the Bible challenges us to see our career not merely as a means of generating income for our family, but also as a tool that glorifies God and advances the cause of his church on earth. This perspective is more and more difficult to maintain in a world that bombards us with the message that we are the center of life's stage. That is not the view encouraged in God's Word. When Jesus wished to summarize all of the law, he offered the following encouragement. First of all love the Lord with all your heart, soul, and mind. Secondly, love those with whom you share this world as you would love yourself (Matt 22:34–40). These words challenge us to think of our career in a way that the world does not. And that teaching challenges us to consider ways in which the career we select might glorify God and helps others.

Living College Life to Get an Interview

All the advice and direction that you have read above suggests that there are important things that you can be doing now as a college student to select a career. Once you have made that career choice, there are a number of other things you can do during your college years to position yourself for that first job interview. These include gaining personal experience in the career you have chosen, gathering the evidence that you will use to make your case, organizing your résumé, and preparing for a job interview.

GET PERSONAL EXPERIENCE

You can read about it, but there is nothing like being there. So it makes sense to use every opportunity to make personal contact with someone in the career you have selected, or even better, the very organization you hope will employ you when you graduate. This personal contact can take a number of forms. You can interview several people holding the career that is interesting to you. Find out what they find enjoyable and what they find less enjoyable about their work. One or more of those individuals whom you interview may also be willing to let you shadow them as they go about their work. This "job shadowing" may lead to a part-time job, a summer job, an internship, or volunteer opportunity that allows you to have more sustained contact with this career or organization. This personal experience will help you confirm your career choice as well as build a network of people who can help you in the future.

GATHER YOUR EVIDENCE AND SUPPORT TEAM

In almost all career fields, you will be competing with other applicants for the position you desire. That makes it critical for you to know what will make you look like a desirable hire and how you might begin collecting that evidence even as a first-year student in college. It is unwise to assume you will know the type of evidence your future employer is seeking without investigation. When you are interviewing people who hold the type of position you would like to have and when you are working part-time or volunteering at that organization, find out all you can about what qualities a desirable applicant brings to the application process. In this regard, each career and even each organization may have some unique qualities they find desirable. For example, is there a minimum college GPA that is required for application? What is the GPA of those who are subsequently granted interviews? Will my membership in a campus organization or my leadership of such an organization be looked upon favorably during the hiring process? What type of volunteer work will make my application stand out from others? The answer to these and other questions like them will help you identify the evidence that will help your cause.

Furthermore, as you work, intern, or volunteer in the career field that is interesting to you, you will be networking with individuals who may be of great assistance to you in getting your first career placement. When an employer posts an opening in their organization, they are likely to receive dozens if not hundreds of applications. One way that your application for that position can stand out in contrast to the other applicants is a personal recommendation from someone who is already working in the organization.

Even if you have worked at a lower-level position in that organization, personal knowledge of your work ethic, your honesty, and your intellect can give you an advantage that other applicants will not have. It is well worth the time and effort you spend in building a strong professional network.

PREPARE YOUR RÉSUMÉ AND COVER LETTER

Typically, your prospective employer will ask to see your résumé as part of the application process. A résumé is a summary of your qualifications and is intended to convince your prospective employer you are worthy of an interview. It is your first opportunity to sell yourself, so you will want to make it as effective and convincing as it can be. A typical recruiter will spend only eight seconds scanning your résumé before making a decision on whether or not to interview you, so you will want your prospective employer to see accessible and convincing evidence within those eight seconds.

The format of the résumé will depend to some degree on the type of career path you chose. In order to determine the general format for the résumé used by applicants in your career field, visit with your academic advisor or the career center. Generally, a résumé will be one page in length, providing the reader with a summary of your qualifications under several standard headings. At the very top of the page you will place your full name and contact information, including current address, phone number, and email address.

Beneath this contact information the reader will expect to encounter several standard categories that summarize your desires, experience, and strengths. The first will be OBJECTIVE. Under this heading, you will identify the specific position that you wish to have within the organization. Keep the language simple and clear, using terminology that is unique to the organization with whom you are seeking employment.

EDUCATION will be the next category. Provide the reader of your résumé with the names of all the schools you have attended since graduating from high school beginning with your most recent graduation. Identify the institution(s) from which you have graduated, the degree you have received, your areas of major and minor concentration, any academic honors you received, and your GPA so long as it is greater than 3.00 on a four-point scale.

In the third category on the résumé, you will summarize relevant EMPLOYMENT HISTORY. Again beginning with your most recent employment, identify the jobs you have had that would impact your ability to do the job you are seeking. Provide your reader with the name of the organization or company, your title (if applicable), and a summary of the responsibilities you had in that position. Do all you can to showcase the skills your future employer would find desirable and in particular those that demonstrate the level of responsibility you carried.

The fourth category of your résumé will present the ACTIVITIES in which you have participated that were not directly connected to past employment. Once again, you will want to provide your reader with the names of the organizations, the positions you held in those organizations, as well as any relevant accomplishments associated with the organizations that suggest your desirability as an employee.

Under the fifth category, INTERESTS, you will want to provide your prospective employer with any unique hobbies or passions you enjoy. Here you might communicate your interest in building your own airplane, in reading mystery novels, in acting within a local theater troupe, or in driving a stock car. This information will not play a larger role than your educational experience or related work experience in convincing your reader to give you an interview, but the unique interests you have may cause your name to stand out on the list of prospective candidates in ways that are difficult to predict.

The last item on the résumé will be about REFERENCES. References are those people who have volunteered to either write letters of recommendation on your behalf or who are willing to give an oral summary of your value as potential employee. Select two to four people whom you believe will give you the strongest recommendation and always seek their permission before offering their names as potential references. If your future employer would like to contact these references, they will let you know. So rather than consuming page space with a list of potential references and their contact information, simply put a note on your résumé stating that references are "available upon request."

Every résumé that you send out to a potential employer should have its own unique cover letter. This is a business letter that briefly introduces the résumé to the one about to read it. Because it is the first evidence judged by your employer, be sure that it gives a very strong first impression. Use a business format for the letter that clearly addresses a specific person within the organization. In this regard, you may need to make an initial phone call to the organization to find out to whom this letter would be addressed. The cover letter will be no longer than one page in length. It will briefly introduce you, explain why you are the right person for the intended position, and identify how you may be reached for further information or an interview.

Given the important impression that the résumé and cover letter give, be sure to have others read and check your manuscript for typographical and grammatical errors. You do not want an error in spelling, grammar, punctuation, or spacing to give the impression that you are careless and less than thoughtful in your work. Since larger employers have also taken up the habit of using computer technology to scan hundreds of résumés and sort them for their value, speak with your career center about selecting words for your résumé that will be persuasive not only to the human eye but also that will be detected by the electronic eye. The presentation of your résumé may seem too remote for consideration at the moment when research papers and lab reports are demanding your time and attention. But now is the time to begin. Create a file entitled "professional résumé," and begin to enter evidence under each of the categories. This file will be a reminder to you of things you can currently do to enhance your employability and function as a repository for evidence that might otherwise be forgotten.

GET READY FOR THE INTERVIEW

If your résumé is persuasive, it will eventually lead to one or more interviews with the organization. The interview process will highlight your oral communication skills, your general presentation, and your ability to think on your feet. In that light, it is desirable for you to practice oral presentation as often as you can as a college student so that you can refine your poise and delivery. When offered an interview, be sure that you show up on time and dressed in a professional way. Be polite and be prepared to sell yourself in response to the questions you will be asked. Do not let over-attention to modesty prevent you from providing a convincing summary of why you are the right person for the job.

Your career center can again help you prepare for the process of the interview, even arranging mock interviews that allow you to practice sitting in the interview chair. That center may also provide you with a list of questions that interviewers typically ask so that you can practice responding to them. The following are examples of the questions you may be asked:

> What do you see as your greatest strength?
>
> What do you see as your greatest weakness?
>
> Describe a time when you were criticized at work and how you responded.
>
> What is the most important thing you have learned about yourself?
>
> What three things are most important to you about this job?
>
> What are your long-term career aspirations?
>
> Why should I hire you for this position?

The process of coming to clarity on your career choice can be both complex and time consuming. But the strategic investment of time and energy as directed in this chapter will pay off in the long run for you. And as you think, also take time to pray so that the Lord may guide you to a career where you may find satisfaction.

Exercises for Success

Developing a Mission Statement

Effective career planning requires a vision of where you would like to be at the close of your career planning. Franklin Covey has helped thousands of people come to greater clarity on this topic through workshops and published material. Visit *www.franklincovey.com/missionbuilder/index.html* where you will be led through an exercise that helps you produce your own personal mission statement.

Exploring Your Career Personality and Values

Visit the career center on your campus and find out which tools you might use to explore your career personality and values. You may find them pointing you to the Keirsey Temperament Sorter, the Strong Campbell Interest Inventory (SCII), SIGI Plus, or Focus II. Many students have also used the John Holland Self-Directed Search to learn more about their vocational personality and values. This inventory is available online at *www.self-directed-search.com/index.html*. It takes about 15 minutes to complete and will result in a 8–16 page personalized report that not only summarizes your personality and values but also provides a list of occupations that most closely match your interests. There is a fee charged for this service.

Vocational Interview

Pick three careers in which you have an interest. Identify people who currently are employed in each of those careers and interview them for at least fifteen minutes. Find out all you can about what they do every day at work, what they like most about their work week, and what they like the least. Condense the product of your interviews into a two-page summary report.

Career Evaluation

Pick one of the careers that you are most closely drawn to at this time and complete the following evaluation form. Behind each statement place a "+" if it is true of you, a "–" if it is not true about you, and a "?" if you are not sure. Write any thoughts you have about that statement in the box at the right.

Statement	+ – ?	Additional Thoughts
My personality and values are in harmony with my choice.		
I have visited the career center to learn more about myself.		
I know what the entry-level requirements are for this career.		
I can afford the time and money necessary to prepare for this career.		
I have personally visited with someone who works in this career.		
I know both the advantages and disadvantages of this career.		
My teachers, friends, and relatives think I would be happy in this career.		
My weaknesses will not be a problem in this career.		
I am aware of the salary and benefits offered in this career.		
I know the future outlook for this career.		
I have spent personal time working or volunteering in this career area.		

Writing Your Résumé

Visit your career center to learn all you can about the type of résumé applicants use for the career that is of greatest interest to you. Prepare a blank copy of that résumé with its major headings and then fill in as much information as you can at the moment. Be sure to keep this initial résumé in a file folder so that you can add to it throughout your time in college.

Spiritual Reflection Journal

Work has been part of the life of human beings since the Garden of Eden. It is through such work that we are able to purchase the basics of life like food, clothing, and shelter. But the money from work can also be used for "luxury" items that can appear to be necessities. Read the words of Jesus in Matthew 6:19–24. In your own words, explain what that portion of Scripture means to you as you think about your future career.

Time in Prayer

In your personal time in prayer or in connection with others in your class, pray for the following people and needs:

* For the Lord's guidance during your time of career investigation

* That he might lead you to clarity about the career you will pursue

* That he might encourage the person(s) in your class who is struggling with this decision

* That the Lord would lead you to full-time church work if that is his will for you

* That the Lord would encourage those called to mission fields

On the Net

The Internet can be a helpful resource for you as you look for ideas to make yourself a more happy and successful student. Visit the College Success page offered by Thomson Wadsworth for web links that will help you grow further on this topic. Go to *www.success.wadsworth.com* and click on Resource Web Links.

www.bls.gov	*www.rileyguide.com*
www.monster.com	*www.careerswsj.com*
www.ajb.dni.us	*www.jobweb.com*
www.careerpath.com	*www.salary.com*
www.internships.com	*www.jobhuntersbible.com*
www.dbm.com/jobguide	*http://keirsey.com*

Index